CISTERCIAN STUDIES SERIES: NUMBER TWELVE

RULE AND LIFE

CISTERCIAN STUDIES SERIES

CISTERCIAN STUDIES SERIES: NUMBER TWELVE

Rule and Life

An Interdisciplinary Symposium

edited by

M. Basil Pennington ocso

To the wonderful Community at Barre, with thanks & prayerful best wishes, Basil Pennington

CISTERCIAN PUBLICATIONS

Spencer, Massachusetts

1971

Cistercian Studies Series ISBN 0-87907-800-6
This Volume ISBN 0-87907-812-X

Library of Congress Catalog Card Number: 79-148204

Ecclesiastical permission to publish this book was received from Bernard
Flanagan, Bishop of Worcester, November 13, 1970.

Printed in the Republic of Ireland by
Cahill & Co. Limited, Parkgate Printing Works, Dublin 8

IN PUBLISHING THIS VOLUME

THE EDITORS OF

CISTERCIAN PUBLICATIONS

WOULD LIKE TO PAY TRIBUTE TO THE MEMORY OF

A PARTICIPANT OF THE SYMPOSIUM

GEORGE SUPRY ocso

WHO WAS KILLED IN A TRAGIC AUTO ACCIDENT

WITH TWO OF HIS CONFRERES

CYRIL CORNISH ocso

HENRY MALONEY ocso

NOVEMBER 23, 1970

R. I. P.

CONTENTS

PREFACE

ON MAY 5, 1970, THIRTY-THREE SCHOLARS, monks and nuns, religious and laymen, from twelve nations and four continents, gathered at the Abbey of Our Lady of the Holy Spirit, near Atlanta, Georgia, for what was to prove to be a very challenging experience, an effort at genuine interdisciplinary collaboration, not only on a speculative level but in responding to a practical question that had immediate relevance to the lives of thousands.

The group was an interesting one including many international figures. There was Jean Leclercq OSB, professor on the faculty of religious psychology at the Pontifical University of the Gregoriana in Rome, a man who has lectured across all the continents in not less than fifty different nations, who has over six hundred items in his multi-lingual bibliography and has almost singlehanded carried through the monumental work of preparing the critical edition of the extensive writings of Bernard of Clairvaux. Mother Kathryn Sullivan, a Religious of the Sacred Heart of Jesus and research professor of Sacred Scripture at Manhattanville College, New York, had just recently returned from a round-the-world tour and would leave for another extensive lecturing tour in Europe when the Symposium was over. Dom Vincent Martin OSB, who earned his doctorate in sociology from Harvard University, has held responsible positions in such varied places as Belgium and China, California and Jerusalem, a life experience which not only deepened his sociological insight but has enriched his dynamic personality. By contrast there was the quiet Benedictine scholar, Adalbert de Vogüé, a monk of Pierre-qui-vire, who has an unrivaled international reputation for his studies on the Rule of St Benedict, although he has rarely left his monastery save to lecture at the Benedictine International College at Rome. Chrysogonus Waddell OCSO is only now beginning to publish the fruit of his years of manuscript research on the Continent but he is already well known both in Europe and America as a liturgist and musicologist. From Canada came another liturgist and monastic scholar, Armand Veilleux OCSO, whose study on the liturgical life of the first cenobites has won an award from the Canadian government. And there were others: Ambrose Watham OSB, architect of the *Covenant of Peace*, the new life charter of the Benedictine Federation of the Americas; Claude Peifer OSB, a Scripture scholar who has published a comprehensive study of monastic spirituality; and Sr Michael Connor OCSO, an American who now holds a responsible position in Canada and who has been exploring historical antecedents for woman's emerging role in ecclesiastical government.

This second Cistercian Studies Symposium sought to build on the studies and conclusions which emerged from the first Symposium. The previous meeting had sought to discern more fully the spirit and aims of the Founders of the Order of Cîteaux.[1] In its concluding statement it asserted that the Founders "came to Cîteaux to live the Gospel according to the Rule of St Benedict."[2] This second Symposium sought to discern the full implications of this assertion, not only historically, for the first Cistercians, but practically, for today's Cistercians in this hour of renewal.

In this it differed consciously from the first Symposium which was largely historical, although the latter did not fail to draw out of history some practical pastoral considerations. This second meeting sought to harness the forces of many different disciplines and while not neglecting the data coming from historical research, its face was set resolutely toward the future. The behavioral sciences were well represented: pastoral theology, psychology, sociology, and had a very significant impact on the discussions and conclusions of

1. The papers and conclusions emanating from this meeting have been published in M. Basil Pennington, ed., *The Cistercian Spirit: A Symposium,* Cistercian Studies Series, no. 3 (Spencer, Mass.: Cistercian Publications, 1970).

2. *Ibid.,* p. 267.

the Symposium. It was a lived theological experience in the best
sense of these words.

In renewing their religious life the Church has called upon all
religious to bring the principles of the Gospel and the spirit and aim
of their Founders into confrontation with the exigencies of the
present times and modern scientific studies and findings. The
Symposium sought to do this and the present volume shares the
fruit of this experience with all who would take and read. From
this point of view the papers and reports presented here have value
and relevancy for all religious concerned with renewal, not only
those committed to the rule of St Benedict. This experiment in an
interdisciplinary dialogue opens up new avenues of approach for
all. Also many of the principles developed here in relation to the
particular concern of the Symposium are of universal application.

However, the value of these papers is not limited to their practical
service to the renewal of religious life. Historians of monasticism
and students of Cistercianism will find here many valuable insights,
sociologists will find some interesting new applications of their
principles and liturgists will find hitherto unpublished data on
twelfth-century liturgical development. For Scripture students the
comparative appraisal of early Scriptural studies will be of great
interest. For all in education concerned with the development of
interdisciplinary relations the experience of this Symposium will be
significant.

It is with the hope and indeed with the firm conviction that it will
prove a service to many that we present this volume, expressing
our sincere gratitude to the many scholars and all the other
collaborators, too many certainly to name, who have made its
publication possible.[3]

M. Basil Pennington ocso

---

3. I cannot, however, fail to make special mention of the assistance given to
me by Fr Tarcisius Conner ocso, one of thesecretaries of the Symposium, in
preparing the brief reports of the discussions, and Fr Bernard Johnson ocso,
who assisted me in innumerable ways.

INTRODUCTION

DURING THIS PAST WEEK I received in the mail some literature, including posters and buttons, from a group of ecologists and their supporters who are deeply concerned with our environment, the need of balancing man and his environment. We know today that there is very widespread concern in regard to this question, especially on the university campuses. And it is daily becoming more widespread.

However, this is not something wholly new. We have always been conscious that man's environment has to be adapted to favor the full development of human life. And men through the centuries have striven, in the past in more primitive ways, today more scientifically, to accomplish this.

The greater the fragility of the life to be preserved and fostered the greater the importance there is in preparing and adapting the environment. An example of this, of course, is the child in the incubator; everything is carefully controlled because there is present such a fragile life.

I think this pertains to the role of the Rule. It is to control the balance, to create a favorable environment for a special kind of life. And the greater the fragility of that life, the more strength there has to be in this environmental control. Perhaps today we have to admit that in many cases the monastic life, the Cistercian life, is not so strong as we might like to think it is, as we might like it to be. And thus perhaps we have now a greater need than in other times, some other times in any case, of environmental control so that we can grow strong and then live in what would be the more ideal situation.

This is something of what I have tried to say in my paper when I said:

> Certainly the Rule is for the monk, not the monk for the Rule. The Rule is there to protect the personal charism of the individual. The candidate coming to the monastic life studies the Rule and examines how it is lived in this monastery, to see if he can identify with it, if his way is to be found within. If so, he enters into life under it, and it protects and preserves, in face of the community, his right to live according to his own personal call. The same is true on the level of the Order. The Rule and the Charter of Charity and complementary secondary legislation mark out the way of life of the Cistercian community as such. If a monastic community can identify with this way, it can find a place within the Cistercian federation. At the same time these documents protect and preserve in the face of the Church the freedom of the monasteries and the federation to live according to their shared charism.[1]

This is somewhat how I see the Rule, as fostering and protecting and creating a climate in which we can live our particular charism.

I have just been reading an interesting chapter in Father Gleason's book *Contemporary Spirituality*, Chapter Twenty-one: The Crisis of Christianity: A Sociological Perspective, by Thomas O'Dea.[2] Some of the thoughts that he brings forward in his chapter can be applied quite aptly to our question.

He points out, and I think we would all readily acknowledge this, that we are in a period of crisis. I think Christianity though has always been in crisis in a certain sense. The time of crisis is a time of separation, when things that have been going along together are coming apart, and it is necessary to consider new relations and

1. See below, pp. 16f.
2. R. W. Gleason, *Contemporary Spirituality* (New York: Macmillan, 1968), pp. 299–315.

changes and to make new decisions and choices. The lived experience of the life under the Rule which we have had has, in the face of all the cultural, sociological and psychological changes that are taking place in our world today, to meet a completely new situation in many respects. We cannot continue to do just as we were doing because that would involve the greatest change and would be the least human way to meet the crisis. We need, first of all, to accept that it is a time of crisis and decision. And then with new creative and creating response seek to bring our life today into confluence with the stable norm of the Rule. The response is to be one of renewal, not *creatio ex nihilo*. It is to be a life that is still identified with the Rule, to be Cistercian life in continuity with our Founders.

Now the Rule sought to answer the problem of giving a transcendent life a stable, human, social expression. The great virtue of institutions or institutes is to provide stable points of reference, to establish the forms which will facilitate an on-going human and Christian way of life and acting. Great charismatic persons and movements can, while the motion of the Spirit is strong, stand on their own and move forward. But the average man needs a favorable environment, needs supporting elements in order to be true in day-to-day life to a charismatic call. The inspiration and the ideal must be brought within the operational scope of the ordinary and everyday performance of men. So the Rule of St Benedict sought to institutionalize a great charismatic insight and movement, one which I believe was not so much the charism or insight of a particular man but of a whole movement, the monastic movement of the preceding centuries—a special strain of it maybe, a special current—but a living tradition. Perhaps the genius of the author of the Rule is that of an organizer, a practical person who could put things together in a way that would make them quite viable for an ordinary man.

Now institutionalization brings a certain stability to the ordinary day-by-day following of the charismatic movement by bringing to the support of the central thematic demand many secondary motivations which harness the whole of the life movement of the person.[3] There are few men who have such a strong insight and such commitment to it that their whole life can be drawn up into a single response. And so in the structuring of the life according to this response for the ordinary man there is harnessed a whole collection of motivations, which obviously should be interrelated and in service of the primary one. Thus one of the questions we have to ask the Rule, I think, is, are the motives that have been mobilized in service of the primary charismatic movement, are these secondary or supporting motivations still really moving today? Do they really motivate? Are they really helpful toward the principal or central movement? Are they perhaps made too much of or have they been made too much of and obscured the central movement? Are there perhaps different emphases to be placed today; are some of the secondary motivations emphasized in the Rule perhaps to be more de-emphasized, and others which are not so emphasized in the Rule to be more emphasized? For example, perhaps the Rule emphasizes more vertical response than horizontal relationships, and perhaps today we should be emphasizing more the horizontal.

Another role which the Rule has in institutionalizing a charismatic form of life is that it seeks to objectify the expression of the values involved, the response to these values, the response to God, so that they can be lived together in a common and social way. And yet when this is done there is the danger that this objectification will get too far away from the subjective experience so that the individual will not readily identify with it. This objectification, this objective expression of the values involved, is conceived so as to mold, form, and strengthen those who are following in this way. But if it is too far away from the individual and not sufficiently related to him, it can lead to some kind of external performance, conformity, and acceptance without having a real vital influence in his life and entering into the vitality of his charismatic response. And so the question that is to be asked here is whether the objectification of revealed and human values in the Rule of St Benedict is

3. *Ibid.*, pp. 302–304.

too far away from our present life context so that they cannot be readily related to it and cannot be identified with our living out of this charismatic life. It is the problem of objectification leading to alienation.[4]

Another area is the question of delimitation.[5] The Rule in service of the ordinary man and in service of the community tries to mark out a way of attaining to values, to a goal, a way that can be brought into relation with the prosaic daily life of the ordinary person. And again the danger is that one will be satisfied with living the Rules, living the norms, this again leading to externalization rather than growth and development of response to the essential charismatic movement which is at the heart of the matter. Therefore the specifics of the Rule have to be questioned in this way: Do they really help to attain to the full living of this charismatic movement?

Now these questions, obviously, cannot be answered in a global way. Rather the Rule has to be studied with great care and these different elements have to be examined individually and individual responses given to them. But before they can be judged there has to be a norm which can be the basis for the judgment or guide to the judgment. So it is necessary first to see what really is the life for which the environment is being created, what is the charismatic insight that is being institutionalized, what are the values that are being objectified, what is the charismatic thrust that is to be delimitated and socially regulated.

I would venture to set forth what is my own conviction or vision or insight as to what is the answer to the question and say that for me it is expressed quite well in St Benedict's question which the novice master is supposed to ask of everyone who comes: "Does he truly seek God?"[6] Truly seek God—seek God in himself directly, personally, intimately and truly. By "truly" I would understand him to mean with intensity and totalness. This is the basic element there; a man who is athirst, who is striving, organizing, and

4. See *ibid.*, pp. 304–306.   5. *Ibid.*, pp. 307–308.
6. RB 58:7.

orienting his whole life to seeking an immediate direct experience of God.

I have tried to express this elsewhere with the help of an article by Dom Pierre Miquel, the Abbot of Ligugé:

(He) singles out three characteristics of the Rule which mark the climate within which a life lived according to the Rule should unfold. They are life-qualities that respond perfectly to the aspirations of our times: realism, a sense of the sacred, urgency. For realism (and I might add, the traditional Cistercian simplicity) is just another term for authenticity. Man's present-day thirst for the sacred is eminently evident. As he attains to an undreamed of command of the natural and the material, he must needs reach beyond; as he goes to the moon, he has to read Genesis. The Rule of St Benedict invites the disciple and shows him the way to experience imminent transcendence even now, even in man's most humble tools, while promising him the full attainment of it. And finally, what could better respond to the demands of the "now" generation than a rule of life that presses on with urgency to the attainment of this promise?

Would it be an oversimplification to say that it is these three elements—an urgent response to the real with all its transcendent meaning, all its divineness—that form the inner logic of the Cistercian way of life that must be concretely lived in the way that today's reality demands? Is that not another way to say that we are pilgrims hurrying on, that this is an eschatological life that demands the freedom of celibacy, poverty, separation from the world, and the directness of orientation that comes from evangelical obedience?[7]

When we see clearly what is this basic norm, this life that we are creating an environment for, the charismatic insight that is being institutionalized by the Rule, the central value that is being objectified, the thrust that we are setting up a social life to support and order, then in order to be really faithful to the Rule we can see what adaptation is called for in its doctrine and provisions so that it does truly lead to the creation of the desired and needed environment, that it does create the proper structures and forms that stabilize and

---

7. See below, pp 18f.

B

support this form of life, that its values are communicatively and formatively expressed for our times, that its norms truly embody and serve the basic, final, and central charismatic thrust.

In a symposium like this we certainly do not want to take refuge in purely essentialist discussions and neglect the existential analysis of the real happening we are living through. Father Bernard Besret in his commentary on *Perfectae caritatis*, not all of which I agree with by any means, in a number of places makes the distinction between what he calls the essential ideal, the theological insight, the philosophical expression, and the actual historical living out of this.[8] And he goes back into different periods and shows where the distinction was really present. I think we have to keep sight of that, there has to be the ideal as a goal and an aim, but then there is also the historical reality, the historical reality of today, and tomorrow too, which are on the way to that but have not yet attained the ideal and the goal. However, if we do not keep the ideal and the goal in view then the "on the way" will be the "on the way" to where? Both are important; we want to stay very much in the whole context of the question and not merely discuss goals and ideals.

This is why we have, at the recommendation of the last Symposium, entered into an interdisciplinary approach. And that is why we have the particular topics which we will consider during this Symposium.

With Father Adalbert de Vogüé's help we will try to examine more deeply the theological foundations of the idea of living according to a rule and study the tensions that exist between having the stabilized authority of the Rule and a living, evolving life and authority in the community. Father Vincent Martin will bring to this question the contributions of a sociologist who sees it in its full sociological dimensions. Father Jean Leclercq will give us some of the historical theologian's insights into how the question was seen and worked out in the past. But the Rule itself is normative and has

---

8. Bernard Besret, "La Vie monastique," *Vatican II: L'Adaptation et le rénovation de la vie religieuse*, Unam Sanctam, no. 62 (Paris: Cerf, 1967), pp. 268ff.

its meaning only in relation with the Gospel. We said at the last Symposium in our conclusion that it is "a practical interpretation of the Gospels."[9] And so with the help of Mother Kathryn we will explore some of the implications of this perspective of the Rule in relation to evangelical living. And then Father Chrysogonus Waddell will take up one of the particular areas, one of the more important ones, the liturgy, and help us to share the experience, an exemplary one, of the early Cistercian Fathers from which we hope to learn much that will guide us today. With the help of Father Claude Peifer we will try to approach the rather challenging problem of how to see that this is handed on.

That is more or less the work of this Symposium.

It occurs to me that this is somewhat a project of discernment. And thinking of it this way, I turn to perhaps the man who has most fully written on and used the processes of Christian discernment to great success, St Ignatius Loyola. He based his teaching on discernment on the Gospels and on the monastic Fathers, so what he has to say belongs in a special way to monks. In any case we can profit from the use of it.

For him discernment was primarily being able to hear and respond to the Word of God here and now. I think that is primarily what we are about. The Word of God as it is spoken through the Scriptures, the Rule, our own daily life, the witness each one of us can give, the witness of our times, and the sciences which the various experts will share with us.

Ignatius had four key concepts in his development of discernment. The first one was *parecer*, which to him meant an opinion, an initial opinion which is formed from observing appearances. This concept was used by him in a very generic way. This initial opinion or impression could be anything from a very subjective self-deceiving idea to something that was perfectly true, evident and manifest from the reality of the situation. It refers to the position the person has when he starts out. I dare say all of us have opinions

9. M. Basil Pennington, ed., *The Cistercian Spirit: A Symposium*, CS 3 (Spencer, Mass.: Cistercian Publications, 1970), p. 269.

of what life according to the Rule should be. Some of them are undoubtedly very objective, true, and solid, but undoubtedly in all of
us too there are some elements of subjective self-deception. So we
start from there.

The second concept of Ignatius was *mirar*. For him this meant a
prayerful and deep reflection, in the light of a norm or norms, upon
all the evidence in the situation to be discerned, including one's own
inner feelings. Prayerful, not so much to obtain through prayer the
answers, but rather through prayer to attain to that full liberty of
spirit so that one would be truly open to the real answers, and to the
light of the spirit coming through the different channels through
which it does come:

> Prayer is absolutely essential for authentic discernment, whether
> individual or communal, in order that each man can arrive at
> true spiritual liberty. . . . It is important to note, however, that
> the light sought and given in this prayer is not some kind of
> revelation of the *content* of the decision to be made. . . . Rather,
> the content of the decision is to be reached through prayerful
> reflection upon all the evidence available from every source
> helping to discover the word of God in the actual situation. . . .
> Ignatius himself warned of the necessity of distinguishing an
> authentic divine visitation from its consequent "afterglow,"
> when one's own ideas and opinions, which are not immediately
> from God, come to the foreground of consciousness.[10]

In other words, we are not looking for answers in prayer so much
as openness to the Spirit.

There must be deep reflection in the light of the norm or norms
(this is where the charism comes in) on all the evidence that the
situation is offering. Father Futrell says on this:

> In order to arrive at the content of the decision reached at the
> end of the process of discernment, it is necessary to read the
> signs of the times and to amass all the necessary knowledge
> and information for prayerful reflection upon the existential
> word of God. In cases of communal discernment, then, this

10. John C. Futrell, "Ignatian Discernment," *Studies in the Spirituality of
Jesuits* 2 (1970): 60.

evidence must be sought from all relevant sources: experts who are Jesuits [in our case Cistercians] and those who are not, research into the causes and the nature of the problems faced, attention to all the concrete circumstances of persons, place, and time. The experts do not free the Jesuits [Cistercians] from the responsibility to discern in the light of the "scope of our vocation," [and this is the norm] but they do help to provide the needed content for discernment.[11]

So we see somewhat what we are trying to do, especially in the discussions: to use the input from our experts who will help us to be objective as well as to give us the data to work with while we in the light of our vocation try to discern what is truly the role of the Rule. He goes on to say: "If this dialogue is to be successful and not actually to lead to polarization and disunion, all the interlocutors must have achieved spiritual liberty and openness to the Spirit through prayer...."[12] This is one of the reasons why the Symposium was geared to a slower pace so that there was more time for personal reflection and prayer so that all could be more open in seeking and searching. Father Futrell goes on to spell out more concretely the meaning of this openness:

> In the concrete this means that all must really listen to one another's proposals as each man himself intends them, and that all must make the sincere effort to understand one another's feelings and attitudes. A man's attitude would demand the correction only if it turned out actually to be based upon improper motivation or upon inadequate knowledge or insufficient prayerful reflection.[13]

The third element for St Ignatius in discernment is *sentir*. This is for him a love-knowledge. I was struck at how much his ideas here related with the ideas of William of St Thierry on love-knowledge as he develops them in his *Exposition on the Song of Songs*.[14] This

---

11. *Ibid.*, pp. 61–62. Brackets added.   12. *Ibid.*   13. *Ibid.*

14. William of St Thierry, *Exposition on the Song of Songs*, trans. Columba Hart, *The Works of William of St Thierry*, vol. 2, CF 6 (Spencer, Mass.: Cistercian Publications, 1969), no. 57, and note 18 there with its parallel references.

is a knowledge which is more complete than a knowledge which is possessed by intellectual concepts alone. And yet it is something much more solid than the fluctuations of feelings and emotions. It is here where the lived experience of the shared Cistercian charism orientates our whole outlook and comes to our aid, comes to the aid of our intellectual quest to give us further light and certitude. Father Futrell expresses this idea of the role of our charism when he says:

> It is the result of a radical existential attitude, a shaping of the spirit, a "bent of being," a profound dynamic orientation of the person . . . this radical existential attitude expresses the structure of a man's personal identity formed through his basic personal commitment.[15]

It is this total life orientation which we have as Cistercians that so colors our whole response to things that can guide us and give us a certain sureness in our search. In the case of the communal search such as we are engaging in here:

> It supposes the commitment of all the members . . . to consecrate all their lives and energies to achieve the end of the whole body. Unless this profound communion—*unio animarum*—exists as the common norm for all discernment, true communal discernment is simply impossible.[16]

This is a very important element in this kind of discernment that comes to play here. It is important too, I think, because unless we have this kind of basic and total life commitment we certainly will not be caught up and really live and find true value in the responses we come forward with. And then we certainly will never be able to hand them on to others.

The fourth element for Ignatius in his process of discernment is *juzgar*. It is judgment, decision, the coming to the conclusion, so to speak. Ignatius at this point places a great importance on the fact of this needing to be confirmed by the Lord. For him this confirma-

---

15. Futrell, *loc. cit.*, p. 56.   16. *Ibid.*, p. 58.

tion comes from an experience of deep inner peace within the spirit of the individual or of all the members in a community. It is sensing the compatibility and the responsiveness of this conclusion to the total life movement which we have and share. Of course it does not mean that all the answers are tied up nice and neat and everybody is feeling very comfortable and happy, but it means that there is a deep experience that things have come together and touched the reality. I think we experienced this at the last Symposium. Father points out:

> This peace leads to a profound joy "at the bottom of the heart" that can co-exist with feelings of real repugnance "at the top of the head." It is the experience of the Spirit described by St Paul: "But the Spirit produces love, joy, peace, patience, kindness, goodness, faithfulness, humility, and self-control."[17]

It can be a Paschal experience in that when one is saying "yes" he experiences that he is with Christ in Gethsemani. And yet it brings forward this deep, basic joy and the responsiveness of Easter, a profound peace and a power to act and suffer with joy that bears testimony that through this death the Spirit has brought forth new life.

However, for Ignatius this confirmation was not ultimate. It is open to further revision if additional information comes or new situations arise. The ultimate confirmation is given only by God's active love in history. As Father again well expresses it:

> This contentment is only penultimate confirmation, since in accord with the dynamic mental structure of Ignatius whose teacher was always living experience, decisions are always subject to reform through renewed discernment if experience shows this to be necessary. Ultimate confirmation is given by God's active love in history.[18]

As Christ would say: "By their fruits you will know them;"[19]— may we not be false prophets.

---

17. *Ibid.*, p. 64.   18. *Ibid.*, p. 65.   19. Mt 7:20.

If the results of the renewal within our Order, in our life in response to the Rule does actually produce men and women finding true human and Christian fulfillment in the way of life traced out by the Rule, then we will know that we have truly received a mandate to renew Cistercian life and have fulfilled that mandate. In the end all we can do is to do our best as best we see it under the light of the Holy Spirit today and leave the results to him. As Father Futrell expresses it quite well:

The _response_ here and now is the important thing, and interior confirmation can occur because the decision reached is a truly free response to what is discerned as the word of God here and now. In this sense it is true to say that on the deepest level one has found and is doing "the will of God": the actual living of love. When it appears later on through experience that some necessary evidence has been inadvertently overlooked or unavailable, the necessary modification of decision is made in peace, and in trust that from the very "mistake" the Father will work a transforming good, a Paschal creation of "new life."[20]

M. Basil Pennington ocso

St Joseph's Abbey,
Spencer, Massachusetts

20. Furtell, _loc. cit._, p. 65.

RULE AND LIFE

THE ROLE OF THE RULE IN CISTERCIAN LIFE

THE SYMPOSIUM, "Towards Discerning the Spirit and Aims of the Founders of the Order of Cîteaux,"[1] was not only able to present with a certain sureness and clarity the fundamental elements of the Cistercian charism but to give a very real witness to its present-day relevance and vitality. Yet at the same time the studies and discussions of the meeting made all painfully aware of how much yet needs to be done in the area of Cistercian studies: documentary research, reflective analysis, theological synthesis, interdisciplinary enrichment.[2]

In the course of the meeting many very real questions and problems did come to the surface, but perhaps none with as much acuteness as that of the role of the Benedictine Rule[3] in Cistercian life. The Special General Chapter of the Order of Cistercians of the Strict Observance which took place in Rome shortly after the

1. The papers from this Symposium and the conclusions have been published in a book entitled, *The Cistercian Spirit: A Symposium* (Spencer, Mass.: Cistercian Publications, 1970). (Hereafter referred to as CS 3.) A synopsis of the proceedings and discussions can be found in M. B. Pennington, "Towards Discerning the Spirit and Aims of the Founders of the Order of Cîteaux," *Studia Monastica* 11 (1969): 405–420. (Hereafter referred to as SM.)

2. In relation to this see the excellent article of A. Veilleux, "The Technical Requirements of Fidelity," *Cistercian Studies* 4 (1969): 286–298.

3. I do not wish to enter here into the very complicated question of the origins of the Rule. Suffice it to say if I do speak of the Rule of St Benedict (hereafter cited as RB) I do not intend to affirm that the question of the authorship is a closed question.

I

Symposium[4] also found itself confronted with this same question. And while it did make a provisional statement in relation to it in its *Declaration on Cistercian Life*,[5] its decisions none the less included a mandate for a study of the matter.[6] This question however is not exclusively nor primarily a question for scholars or legislators. The Symposium included many who were not scholars, yet the concern was shared by all. And the General Chapter approached it much more from the view of pastoral concern rather than from jurisdictional provision. In the end it is a question that concerns every monk and nun who has made profession "according to the Rule of St Benedict." In this time of renewal when there is a good healthy quest for authenticity[7] questioning so many things long taken for granted and when so many familiar structures and observances are slipping away, many are quite frankly asking themselves just what their profession of a life "according to the Rule" actually imports. Have the changes been such, or is there the danger that the changes might be such that one can no longer authentically profess to live "according to the Rule"? As the General Chapter bluntly put it, do we need to change our profession formula? And in all this where does fidelity to our Founders lie? In a word, what is the role of the Rule in Cistercian life yesterday and today?[8]

The 1969 Symposium

As we have already mentioned, when the monks and nuns, scholars and superiors sat down together in February of 1969 to

---

4. March 11–29, 1969.   5. See Appendix 1, pp. 213–214.

6. See below, p. 15.

7. Authenticity has a different meaning today than it had in the time of the Cistercian Founders. For us it usually means genuine and meaningful. In the twelfth century something was considered authentic because it was authoritative, it conformed with the original. The Cistercian Founders certainly sought authenticity in both senses. See C. Waddell, "The Origin and Early Evolution of the Cistercian Antiphonary," CS 3, pp. 195–196.

8. Concern about the Rule also arises from the directives for renewal given by the Second Vatican Council: "Nevertheless everyone should keep in mind that the hope for renewal lies more in the faithful observance of the rules and constitutions than in multiplying laws."—*Perfectae caritatis*, no. 4.

seek greater insight into and clearer expression of the spirit and aims of the Founders of the Cistercian Order, they became very painfully aware of how much basic scholarly work has yet to be done in establishing texts and analyzing them before any conclusions can stand on solid scientific foundations. Indeed the vast lacunae may make this a permanent impossibility. As long as the texts are not approached in a truly scholarly fashion there is the danger that one might impose modern conceptions on our monastic forebears in order to find an immediate relevance. And thus, instead of growing in openness and insight through dialogue with the tradition, time could be simply wasted corroborating current habitual ways of thinking. There is, without doubt, a great need to move ahead expeditiously in the preparation of critical texts, especially of our fundamental documents, and of subjecting them to serious study.

Yet renewal cannot be suspended until all this important work is accomplished. We must employ to the full what we have at the moment while wholeheartedly encouraging scholars to go on with their work. To affirm that we do not have enough at hand now on which to base a truly meaningful monastic life in the Cistercian tradition would be to condemn ourselves to a meaningless existence as Cistercians. One of the great dangers of our times is the malaise of the problematic. This throws everything into question, so that it becomes impossible to commit oneself to anything. The result: men, unfulfilled, uncommitted, fall by the wayside. The Symposium therefore, placing confidence in a shared charism, and using as fully as possible the resources available, concluded with an affirmation or Statement[9] which it developed under eight

---

9. The concluding Statement of the Symposium is as follows: The Order of Cîteaux, as an historical event, was the result of the movement of the Holy Spirit in and through men, the monks from Molesme who came to Cîteaux to live the Gospel according to the Rule of St Benedict. As time went on, they gave expression to their way of life in different writings and documents such as the Charter of Charity—the fruit of their lived experience, which was fostered, in a special way, by the union of their monasteries.

In developing this way of life, when they made specific choices their ultimate aim was a response to Christ in love. Accordingly, for the nuns and

headings.[10] I shall try to bring out here some ideas flowing from the 1969 Symposium which are relevant to our present topic and which set the question more into relief.

An Authentic Response to the Gospels

As Christian men there is no doubt that the most basic aspiration of the Founders of Cîteaux was to live the Gospel message. At Molesme they had such an experience of Christ and the meaning of his call that they became men of courageous ardor, ready to face and overcome not only verbal opposition but even physical persecution, in order to live their monastic response to the full. As they discussed the matter among themselves fidelity to their vision and ideal crystalized around a more integral and pure observance of the Rule which they had professed.[11] Finally this fidelity left them no other course but to separate from their brethren and begin anew in circumstances that demanded the utmost courage.[12] While we do

---

monks who, like them, follow Christ in this way, certain elements accidental to the other forms of the Christian life become essential to this specifically Cistercian form of the Christian life, and certain values, common to Christians as a whole, are given special emphasis (e.g., prayer and penance).—CS 3, pp. 267–268.

10. The headings are: renewal, the experience of God, charity, community, the Church, the Rule of St Benedict, poverty and solitude. See CS 3, pp., 268–270.

11. "These men, while still living in Molesme and inspired by divine grace often spoke, complained and lamented among themselves over the transgression of the Rule of St Benedict the Father of Monks."—*Exordium Parvum* (Hereafter cited as EP), c. 3, ed. J.–B. Van Damme (Westmalle:Typis Ordinis, 1959), p. 7; trans. R. Larkin, in L. Lekai, *The White Monks* (Okauchee, Wis.: Cistercian Fathers, 1953), p. 253. "Thereupon the Abbot and his brethren, mindful of their vows, unanimously decided to establish and keep the Rule of St Benedict in that place."—EP, c. 14, Van Damme, p. 13; Larkin, p. 262.

12. This is hinted at in EP, c. 7: "So he (Robert) returned with some of the monks who did not find the desert to their liking."—Van Damme, p. 9; Larkin, p. 257 and also in c. 15: "Nevertheless, almost all of those who saw or heard of the unusual and almost unprecedented rigor of their manner of life, instead of approaching them, tried anxiously to avoid and forget them." —Van Damme, p. 14; Larkin, p. 264.

not have as complete a report of the events at Molesme as we have for the affairs at St Mary's of York,[13] Thurston of York assures us that the latter were but a repetition of what occurred at the former.[14] The reformers' aim is clearly stated: "We must undertake with all our strength to observe by God's grace the true and age-old service of our blessed Father Benedict, or rather, the more ancient Gospel of Christ, which precedes all vows and rules."[15]

Two questions seem to emerge here. How precisely did the Founders[16] see the Rule as related to the Gospels? What response to the Rule did their quest for authenticity[17] demand of them? As can be readily seen, the response to the second will in some measure depend on the response to the first.

The participants of the Symposium struggled over these questions and while there was in the end a fair unanimity in regard to the response to the first question, reading over the papers and studying

13. Thurston of York, Archbishop, in a letter to William of Corbeil, Archbishop of Canterbury, gives a very full, first hand, blow by blow account of the events that led up to the founding of Fountains by a group of monks from St Mary's under the leadership of the Prior, Richard: PL 182:697–704. An English translation with introduction, M. B. Pennington, "Three Early Documents," *Cistercian Studies* 4 (1969): 145–158. There is a later edition with interpolations which seeks to justify further the ideals of the Cistercian reform, which by contrast only serves to strengthen and highlight the authenticity of the original text. See C. Bethell, "The Foundation of Fountains Abbey and the State of Saint Mary's of York, in 1132," *Journal of Ecclesiastical History* 17 (1966): 11–27. L. G. D. Baker, in a recent article, "The Genesis of English Cistercian Chronicles: The Foundation History of Fountains Abbey I," *Analecta Cisterciensia* 25 (1969): 14–41, has called into question the authenticity of the Letter of Thurston (p. 17) and promises a future article in which he will attempt to justify his conclusions (p. 15).

14. "We ought to recall what happened in the affair of the Molesmes monks which is quite similar." Letter, no. 22, *loc. cit.* p. 157.

15. *Ibid.*, no. 5, p. 150. These words are attributed to Richard by Thurston.

16. While it is fairly evident who are the Founders of the New Monastery, later called Cîteaux, it is not so clear as to who exactly are the Founders of the Order of Cîteaux. See M. B. Pennington, "Towards Discerning the Spirit and Aims of the Founders of the Order of Cîteaux," CS 3, pp. 2, 15–16.

17. Authenticity is taken here in both of its senses. See above, note 7.

the transcription of the discussions[18] one does not find so solid a basis for the conclusion as one would like. The clearest testimonies are the affirmations of Thurston of York.[19] One would like to see a comprehensive study of all the extant writings of the Cistercian Fathers, as well as the documents we have, to see to what extent they would bear out this affirmation.

An apt formulation of this relation was not so easy to come by. The Statement of the Symposium as it was initially proposed to the assembly by the Conclusions Committee[20] spoke of the Founders "who came to Cîteaux to live the Gospel specified for them by the Rule of St Benedict . . . ." This was contested and many other formulations were proposed: ". . . to live the Rule as the lived interpretation of the Gospel . . . to live the Gospel as interpreted by the Rule . . . as reflected in the Rule . . . to live the Rule which incarnates the Gospel spirit . . . to live according to the Rule in the spirit of the Gospels . . . to live the Rule as the practical means to live the Gospel message . . . to live the Gospel in the way of the Rule of St Benedict . . . to live the Gospel mediated through the Rule . . . to live the Gospel by living the Holy Rule more exactly . . . to live the Gospel according to the Rule, according to the way of life expressed in the Rule, according to the purity of the Rule . . . to live the Rule as their particular answer to the evangelical message, as their

18. The transcription of the discussions is available on tape in most of the American Abbeys of the Cistercian Order. A synopsis of them can be found in SM (see above, note 1).

19. In addition to the statement given above in the text, Thurston quotes Richard as saying: "So, venerable Father (speaking to the Abbot of St Mary's), if you will allow, we will hasten back to the purity of the Gospel, to evangelical perfection and peace."—l. c., no. 5, p. 151. "We think of the monks of Savigny and Clairvaux who recently came to us. The Gospel so clearly shone out in them that it must be said that it would be more useful to imitate them than to recite it. When indeed their holy life is seen, it is as if the Gospel is relived in them. . . . Happy, indeed, are men such as these whose clothing, food and whole way of life savors of the Gospel."—*Ibid.*, no. 6.

20. The Conclusions Committee was made up of Abbot Edward McCorkell, chairman, Abbot Anthony Chassagne, theology, Father (now Abbot) Michael Abdo, philosophy, Father Raphael Simon, psychology, and Sister Gertrude Ballew.

particular form of the evangelical life . . . ."[21] In the end the Statement spoke of "the monks from Molesme who came to Cîteaux to live the Gospel according to the Rule of St Benedict."[22] And the development stated: "The early Cistercians strove to live the Gospel. Their fidelity to the Rule was simply an expression of this, for they saw the Rule as a practical interpretation of the Gospel."[23]

We will see later that the Special General Chapter also struggled with this question of formulation and in the end adopted a very slight but significant modification.[24]

It is true that the prevalent climate in the Church at that time gave the Founders little or no choice in regard to referring their reform to the Rule of St Benedict. All monks in the West were expected to live according to this Rule. And the growing canonical emphasis demanded more and more that such a reform be based on a recognized document such as the Rule. However, in regard to our question I do not think that in itself this is a particularly significant fact. There was a most ample freedom in regard to what this relevance would mean in practice, in how one would interpret the Rule. St Peter Damian and his Camaldolese brethren could comfortably profess it and even the Carthusians could refer to it.[25] What is significant is that the Cistercians did interpret it in a particular way, made specific options, related to the Rule in a special way and established the General Chapter[26] and the visitation

---

21. These quotations are taken from the taped transcription of the discussion which followed upon Abbot Edward's presentation of "Towards Conclusions: A Pre-position paper," CS3, pp. 254–262. This discussion is briefly summarized in CS 3, pp. 263–266.

22. See above, note 9.   23. CS 3, p. 269.   24. See below, p. 14.

25. See L. Lekai, "Motives and Ideals of the Eleventh-Century Monastic Renewal," CS 3, p. 44; A. Veilleux, "The Interpretation of a Monastic Rule," CS 3, p. 53.

26. "In the General Chapter, the abbots shall consult upon matters that appertain to the salvation of souls, and shall ordain what is to be corrected, or what carried out in observance of the Rule and the institutions of the Order. . . . If any abbot be less zealous about the rule than he ought . . . he shall be charitably reprimanded in the General Chapter. . . ."—Charter of Charity (Hereafter cited as CC), c. 6, ed. J.-B. Van Damme, *op. cit.,* pp. 17–18; trans. D. Murphy, in Lekai, pp. 270–271.

system[27] to see that all the communities were faithful to this interpretation.

What would be significant would be to see what effect the requirement to have an authentic document (here taken in the medieval sense of authoritative) had upon the Cistercian Founders' course of action and choice of options because of their own desire and, we might say, charism to seek authenticity (here taken in our present-day sense). If historical circumstances were such that their authentic desire to live the evangelical life in a monastic way could be fulfilled only by professing the Rule of St Benedict, would it be only an historical accident that their authenticity was confronted with this Rule? And given other circumstances and times where they would have been free, would they possibly have chosen or written another Rule? Or was it a part of the inner workings of grace, of their charism, that they saw that the authentic monastic following of the Gospel which they sought was indeed identifiable with the principles and values laid down in the Rule of St Benedict? This is perhaps a question which will never be answered with certitude. It does throw us into the realm of possibilities which must always remain uncertain. However, here again a comprehensive study of the extant writings of the Fathers, along with the documents that have come down to us, might give us some more solid basis for affirming that their adherence to the Rule came from a conviction of its relevancy to their aims rather than merely from a quest to be authentic which would say: "We have professed the Rule, therefore to be authentic we have to live it to the letter." A careful comparison of the values and principles constantly enunciated by the Fathers in their sermons and writings with the values and principles found in the Rule would give evidence of such an inner consistency.

27. "If he (the visiting abbot, in this case the abbot of Cîteaux) shall perceive that any of the precepts of the Rule or the institutions of the Order are violated in the monastery he is visiting, let him, with the advice and in the presence of the abbot, charitably endeavor to correct the brethren. But if the abbot of the monastery be not present, he shall nevertheless correct what he finds amiss."— CC, Van Damme, c. 4, p. 17; Murphy, c. 3, p. 269.

I do not think it can be denied that according to the documents authenticity did give immediate motivation to their renewed response to the Rule. We have the statements of the *Exordium Parvum*[28] and the Letter of Thurston of York,[29] as well as the early Epistle of St Stephen on Hymns.[30] Perhaps the strongest expression we have witnessing to the fact that the Founders' authenticity felt it had to express itself by responding to an authentic document is the statement of William of Malmesbury which he places in the mouth of St Stephen: ". . . more recently through St Benedict a Rule comes to us from God by which nature is called back to reason. If there is anything in it whose reason I am not able to understand, I think none the less it is to be accepted on authority."[31] Undoubtedly this statement reflects attitudes prevalent at the time, but I think we can question whether St Stephen ever actually made such a statement.

That the appeal to authoritative texts and documents was a growing phenomenon in the twelfth-century Church and in the evolution of the early Cistercians seems to be evident. That there are some very early examples of it as in the Epistle of St Stephen[32] and in the whole approach to the chant texts also seems to be established.[33] But this in itself does not seem to postulate that these

28. ". . . to fulfill their vows through the observance of the holy Rule."— EP, c. 3, Van Damme, p. 7; Larkin, p. 253. "Thereupon the Abbot and his brethren, mindful of their vows, unanimously decided to establish and keep the Rule of St Benedict in that place. They rejected what was contrary to the Rule. . . ."—c. 14, Van Damme, p. 13; Larkin, p. 26.

29. ". . . let it never seem to be impossible to hold fast to the Rule of St Benedict . . . let us render at least our way of life and profession conformable to our Rule. . . ." no. 7 (quotation of Richard of Fountains), Pennington, *loc. cit.*, p. 152. "He (Prior Richard) wrote that they ought to conform to what the Rule permitted in speech, clothes and food." no. 9; *ibid.*

30. *De observatione hymnorum,* ed. C. Waddell, CS 3, p. 206; trans. M. B. Pennington: ". . . our blessed Father and Master Benedict in his Rule, which we have decreed must be observed in this place with great care, prescribes. . . ." —"Three Early Documents," p. 145.

31. *Gesta Regum Anglorum,* ed. W. Stubbs (London, 1889), 2:318 (trans. mine).

32. See above, note 30.

33. See Waddell, CS 3, pp. 195–196.

C

men were dominated solely or even primarily by this motive in their adherence to the observances of the Rule rather than opting for them because they saw an inner coherence between these observances and the authentic monastic response to the Gospel to which their grace and charism was calling them.

If (and note, I say here, *if*) the inner driving force was authenticity and it was only due to an historical accident that their authenticity was confronted with the Rule of St Benedict, then fidelity to their spirit in a time such as ours when history no longer demands of all monks adherence to the Rule of St Benedict would not necessarily demand adherence to this Rule. This might at least be our conclusion *in abstracto*. But then do we not have to face the concrete? In actual fact Providence, the giver of charism and vocation, gave it in such circumstances; and the confrontation with the Rule necessarily profoundly informed the outlook, aims and spirit of these men. The Rule became so woven into the fabric of the Cistercian heritage that it could hardly be recognized as the same heritage if this golden thread were to be removed.

While I think it is necessary to conclude that profession according to the Rule is something the Cistercians cannot abandon and still be authentically Cistercians, yet the question remains, what is the authentic attitude for a Cistercian vis-à-vis the Rule? Simple reverence, such as the Rule itself directs towards the Rule of St Basil,[34] does not seem sufficient.[35] The essential principles and values, which in large measure flow quite directly from the Gospels, must be sincerely embraced and lived.

But this leaves us with yet two difficult questions.

What are the essential principles of the Rule and what are rather applications of these? To take a concrete example, the weekly psalter. This is stated categorically enough. Yet is it really a principle or the application of another principle?[36]

I think the response to this first question can be found only

34. RB 73:5.
35. SM, p. 413.
36. I would judge it to be yet an application of a more basic attitude toward monastic prayer which is the principle.

through careful study[37] and then serious reflection and dialogue. In the end I think it will be the charism alive in today's Cistercians which will finally discern what are indeed the essential principles and values that we must retain and live today in today's way.

The second question concerns the provisions and observances which flow from the essential principles and in many instances have been described in some detail in the Rule. These often entail the taking of certain options.[38] Can one authentically profess the Rule and be said to be living in the spirit of the Cistercian Founders, and at the same time be free to set aside these provisions and options? The early Cistercians did without doubt practice the Rule in the sense of embracing its many prescriptions and observances. Yet it is also clear that they formulated complementary customs and in some instances adapted the provisions of the Rule. What were the principles or criteria which guided them in this? I would suggest that the principles and criteria they were employing were not all that clear to them themselves, that they never sat down and explicitly defined them. Certainly they have nowhere bequeathed to us any explicit and clear statement. Their bequest was one of basic fidelity to the Rule as it was lived and experienced at the New Monastery.[39] In the last analysis I believe they depended, consciously or unconsciously, on their God-given charism. And in the end I believe that is what the Cistercians today must also do, in community chapters, in regional meetings, and above all in the General Chapter, which is an essential part of the Cistercian heritage and

37. I would like to draw attention here to the excellent article by R. Bonpain, "Les adaptations et la Règle de saint Benoît ou la double relativité de l'observance," *Collectanea Cisterciensia* 31 (1969); 247–264.

38. E.g., the role of the abbot, the way of appointing the prior, the community celebration of the *Opus Dei*.

39. "We Cistercians, the original founders of this community make known to our successors through this present writing by what canonical procedure, under what authority and by which persons as well as what time the community and their manner of living had its beginning. After the publication of this matter which has been written with sincere truthfulness may they love more tenaciously the place as well as the observance of the Holy Rule, which, with God's grace, we ourselves have somehow begun therein; and may they pray. . . ."—EP, Prol., Van Damme, p. 5; Larkin, p. 251.

was intended precisely to insure fidelity.[40] It should be primarily a charismatic assembly functioning with pastoral solicitude and love.[41]

In the course of the last Symposium one of the participants tried to pinpoint the question of the Cistercians' relation to the Rule by asking whether they did and should judge the tradition (monastic tradition) by the Rule or judge the Rule by the tradition. This is certainly a thought-provoking way to put it. Texts from the primitive documents and the writings of the Cistercian Fathers could be brought forth in favor of both sides. I would rather look at it another way. If I may express it in modern terms (which I am conscious are not the terms the Fathers would have used, but which I do think express the reality), I believe their approach was an existential one in which they entered, through the Rule, into dialogue with a wise old monk and through him with the monastic tradition.[42] The tradition was mediated to them through this Rule, with its options. The need is to discover what are the essential options, fidelity to which is necessary, if one is to live according to this Rule.

40. See above, note 26.

41. At the Symposium the question was insistently urged, and rightly so: if the interpretation of the Rule and what is essential was to be left to the charismatic leader, what was to be the criterion for judging the validity of his interpretation? Great and holy men have gone off. To some extent it is the Rule itself, but an extrinsic criterion is needed. In a general way it is the authority of the Church which blesses a way of life, an interpretation of the Rule. But the Church today is not apt to descend to details. This is why I have placed stress on the General Chapter. A particular charismatic abbot may well go astray. Given the abbot's role in the Cistercian community he might be able even to lead his community astray so that the discernment of the community chapter may not always be sufficient check. But even the most forceful and eloquent abbot is not apt to readily lead astray a large international chapter of similarly charismatic leaders. The example of the Special General Chapter gives us good reason for confidence that the Spirit will operate effectually through this institution which is itself an essential part of the Cistercian heritage. For the synopsis of the discussion on this point at the Symposium see SM, pp. 408–409.

42. There is an indication of this in c. 14 of EP: "And since they could not find either in the Rule or in the life of St Benedict that this teacher. . . ."— Van Damme, p. 13; Larkin, p. 262.

The Special General Chapter (1969)

As mentioned above, the Special General Chapter of the Cistercians of the Strict Observance which met shortly after the Symposium also faced the question of the relation of the Cistercians to the Rule.

With little hesitation (the vote was 73 to 3) the Chapter affirmed that the Rule of St Benedict and the Charter of Charity are the fundamental and primary legislation of the Order.[43] In the *Statute on Unity and Pluralism* which gives the guidelines which are to direct the life and development of the Order during this period of change and renewal it is stated categorically: "Faithful to the thought of their Founders, Cistercian monks live under a Rule and an Abbot."[44] And it goes on to make explicit reference to the Rule in a number of the guidelines.[45]

It was, however, in the discussion of the formulation of the provisional[46] *Declaration on Cistercian Life* that there arose the question of the relation of the Rule to the Gospel. The draft presented to the Chapter as the fruit of the discussion of a number of the commissions[47] read: "Following the first Fathers of our Order we find in the Holy Rule of St Benedict a practical interpretation

---

43. Declarations and Decisions of the General Chapter of 1969, no. 3.

44. See Appendix II, no. 1, p. 215.

45. No. 2: "The abbot, as spiritual father of his community, should try to discover the will of God. One important way of doing this is by listening to his brethren in the spirit of Chapter Three of the Rule." No. 3: "In our daily horarium we keep the balance between the *Opus Dei, Lectio Divina,* and Manual Work, as required by the Rule of St Benedict." See below, p. 216.

46. I speak of the *Declaration* as "provisional" for it was made clear in the course of the discussions that in the mind of the Chapter Fathers (at least some of them) this was not to be taken as a definitive statement but was rather to be reviewed by each successive session of the Special General Chapter.—*Compte rendu des Séances du Chapitre Général Special 1969* (Westmalle: Typis Ordinis, 1969), pp. 84ff.

47. "Commissions" is the term employed at the Cistercian General Chapter for the small group meetings of abbots that take place during the Chapter. The Chapter is usually divided into five "commissions" or six, based on the language to be used in the meetings: English, French, German, and Spanish. There are two groups for some languages.

of the Gospel."[48] A Father of the Chapter objected that the expression "an interpretation" was too weak. While he proposed an alternate formula: "We recognize in the Rule of St Benedict the way by which we are led toward God;" the Promoter proposed simply changing the "an" to "the." This was immediately objected to by those who felt this was too restrictive; the Rule is only one interpretation of the evangelical way as it unfolded in monastic tradition. A conciliatory monk sought to sidestep the issue by offering another text which did not immediately touch upon the relationship of Rule and Gospel: "In the Rule of St Benedict we can find the particular form of response to which we experience ourselves invited by God today." But it was urged that it was important to preserve the idea of the Rule as an interpretation of the Gospel. Another abbot, seeking to reconcile the first intervention, which basically sought to make the identification of the Cistercians with the Rule more strong, and that of the Promoter, proposed the text which was finally adopted: "Following the first Fathers of our Order we find in the Rule of St Benedict the practical interpretation of the Gospel for us."

This does indeed make the statement much stronger than the original proposal. Whether the Chapter Fathers will stand by this text as it is reviewed in succeeding renewal chapters remains to be seen. If they do there yet needs to be clarified exactly what in practice it means to say that the Rule is "the" interpretation. Perhaps we have here a situation analogous to that of the first Fathers where men guided by a charism which was not fully explicated, not even in their own minds, have made a significant decision—a decision which responds more fully to the spirit and ideals of the Cistercian Founders than anything study can yet establish.

However, the fact that the capitular Fathers were not wholly clear as to the relationship of the evolving Cistercian life to the Rule is evident in a practical decision that was made at another point in the Chapter. Up to the present the Cistercians of the Strict Observ-

---

48. For an account of this discussion see *Compte rendu*, pp. 82ff.

ance, unlike most other monks, have made profession to live simply "according to the Rule of St Benedict." Most other monastic Orders and Congregations require their men to include in their profession formulas some reference to their constitutions as modifying the observance of the Rule. In 1953 when the Cistercian laybrothers' ceremony of profession was adapted to bring it more in line with that of the monks, their very simple formula, "Father Abbot, I promise you obedience in all good unto death," was replaced by one identical to that of the monks except that it did add the phrase: "and the Constitutions of the Order," with the understanding that this modified many of the prescriptions of the Rule in their application to the laybrothers.[49] When the *Decree of Unification* of 1965[50] demolished the juridic structures which separated the monks and the laybrothers, the communities, under the leadership of the General Chapter, undertook to modify the life of both groups to bring about actual unification. The *Decree* called for essentially one form of profession for all.[51] And here is where the practical question arose. With all the adaptations and the pluralism introduced into the lives of Cistercian monks, can they still authentically simply profess the Rule of St Benedict without any modifying clause? Thus the special General Chapter voted 62 to 13 that the formula for solemn profession in the Order should be submitted to a new study, account being taken of the *Decree of Unification*.[52]

A personal question and responsibility

In these days questions such as we have been considering do not stay on the level of superiors and chapters. Very quickly, and very properly, they engage the simple monk. Each one has personally vowed to live according to the Rule of St Benedict. His profession is indeed "*in hoc loco*"—to live according to the Rule in this place, as it is lived in this place. Here very readily there come to mind the

49. *Compte rendu . . . 1953*, p. 15.

50. *Cum Monachorum*, Dec. 27, 1965; Prot. N. 16545/65 T. 34; published with English trans. in *Jurist* 27 (1967): 228–230.

51. See *ibid.*, no. 1, p. 228.

52. *Declarations and Decisions*, no. 70, *A Provisional Report . . .*, p. 13.

words of St Bernard: "So long as one is guided by the sound and legitimate customs of his house he is beyond any doubt, living according to the Rule. For the Rule admits of variations and local customs."[53] But at the same time we should not forget what Bernard goes on to say in the following paragraph: "Of course, it is a different matter for the Cistercians and for those who, like them, have promised an integral literal observance of the Rule rather than a life according to the Rule, since such is their interpretation of monastic profession."[54] The "place," the monastery within which the monk has made profession, is a Cistercian monastery, one committed to the Cistercian life and with the responsibility to the Church and to all God's people to renew and preserve the patrimony of Cîteaux which belongs to the Church. Each monastery is committed to the options of the federation and to its common heritage.

In these times of renewal and renewed authenticity each monk strives for the same dispositions of Robert and his companions at Molesme, of Richard and his companions at York. He makes his own the words of Richard: "We must undertake with all our strength to observe by God's grace the true and age-old service of our blessed Father Benedict, or rather, the more ancient Gospel of Christ, which preceded all vows and rules."[55] Yet in these times of co-responsibility it is not a question of going off to do this; each monk and nun seeks to collaborate to bring it about from within. Together, with their shared charism, they strive to discern how precisely this is to be done today.

Certainly the Rule is for the monk, not the monk for the Rule. The Rule is there to protect the personal charism of the individual. The candidate coming to the monastic life studies the Rule and examines how it is lived in this monastery, to see if he can identify

---

53. *De Praecepto et Dispensatione*, no. 48, in *S. Bernardi Opera* 3 (Rome: Editiones Cistercienses, 1963), p. 286; trans. C. Greenia, *Monastic Obligations and Abbatial Authority: St Bernard's Book on Precept and Dispensation*, in *The Works of Bernard of Clairvaux*, vol. 1, CF 1 (Spencer, Mass.: Cistercian Publications, 1970), p. 141.

54. *Ibid.*, no. 49.   55. See note 15.

with it, if his way is to be found within. If so he enters into life under it and it protects and preserves, in face of the community, his right to live according to his own personal call. The same is true on the level of the Order. The Rule with the Charter of Charity and complementary secondary legislation mark out the way of life of the Cistercian community as such. If a monastic community can identify with this way it can find a place within the Cistercian federation.[56] At the same time these documents protect and preserve in the face of the Church the freedom of the monasteries and the federation to live according to their shared charism.

Life Today

Today we Cistercians, like everyone else in the Church of which we are a part, are a pilgrim people searching for a clearer understanding of ourselves, searching for a surer hold on our own identity. We are seeking to see more clearly what unites us, the source of our unity; and what distinguishes us from others, our individuality. Obviously the latter is of less importance. Indeed we might find that there is nothing that distinguishes us from some others who share in the Benedictine tradition (those embracing the integral contemplative way) except the men and institutions through which our charism has been expressed and handed down to us. Without doubt the federal government of the Charter of Charity is an essential part of our Cistercian heritage.

Emphasis is to be placed, however, on the inner coherence that unites us that it might be the basis of an ever deeper and stronger bond of charity. The Rule of St Benedict definitely has its place in our identifying unity; we all have made profession to live together a life according to this Rule. We need very much to be able to say clearly what this profession means to us, what is its value.

It is truly a tremendous time to be alive. The greatness of the hour can hardly be exaggerated. In this decade the earth will

---

56. History shows us in the early days of the Order of Cîteaux how often this was the case when even whole congregations joined the Cistercian Order (e.g. Savigny, Obazine). All through its history the Order has had especially convents of nuns seeking a place within it.

welcome to its surface more men than in all the times past put
together. The call to fill out in these times what is wanting in the
passion of Christ opens out to us an unparalleled co-redemptive role.
We enter into the heritage of aeons of divine activity in creation, of
millennia of revelation, of centuries of Christian life. There is available to us as the fruit of an immense accumulation of human effort
a fuller understanding and the possibility of a fuller humanly
conscious activity in response to God. The universal consciousness
of the brotherhood of man, universal homonization, is reaching
toward an apex and invites us to embrace the values of self-tran-
scendence in outgoing love and concern for all men. Human life
offers today so patently such an infinite potential that it is no
wonder that the young find it so difficult to choose and commit
themselves irrevocably to one way of life. When they come to us
they rightly ask themselves and us (and to be honest, we ask ourselves, too) why choose a life according to the Rule of St Benedict—
does it have enough challenging, fulfilling meaning?

In a recent article,[57] Dom Pierre Miquel, the Abbot of Ligugé,
singles out three characteristics of the Rule which mark the climate
within which a life lived according to the Rule should unfold. They
are life-qualities that respond perfectly to the aspirations of our
times: realism, a sense of the sacred, urgency. For realism (and I
might add, the traditional Cistercian simplicity) is just another term
for authenticity. Man's present-day thirst for the sacred is eminently
evident. As he attains to an undreamed of command of the natural
and the material, he must needs reach beyond; as he goes to the
moon, he has to read Genesis. The Rule of St Benedict invites the
disciple and shows him the way to experience imminent transcendence even now, even in man's most humble tools, while promising
him the full attainment of it. And finally what could better respond
to the demands of the "now" generation than a Rule of life that
presses on with urgency to the attainment of this promise?

Would it be an oversimplification to say that it is these three

57. P. Miquel, "Trois caractères de la Règle de S. Benoît," *Collectanea
Cisterciensia* 31 (1969): 265–270.

elements—an urgent response to the real with all its transcendent meaning, all its divineness—that form the inner logic of the Cistercian way of life that must be concretely lived in the way that today's reality demands? Is that not another way to say we are pilgrims hurrying on, that this is an eschatological life that demands the freedom of celibacy, poverty, separation from the world and the directness of orientation that comes from evangelical obedience? Tradition calls to us, but we cannot link with it in the way we want without being in touch with today. Because we are today. And because this is a part of the genius of the spirit and charism of our Fathers. They linked tradition with their day and used the Rule of St Benedict to do it. If we are to continue to profess this Rule it should mean just this—we too, as our Fathers, experience a divine call, a charism from God, to use the values and principles, the options of the Rule of St Benedict to live a monastic response to the Gospels, living and creating today's monastic tradition.

M. Basil Pennington OCSO

St Joseph's Abbey,
Spencer, Massachusetts

DISCUSSION

The discussion which followed centered on charism and institution. It was pointed out that the two should not be seen in opposition to each other. Rather, the two are essentially related, and both are found in the Rule. The charism is made present and articulate through this tangible form, the Rule. One could not see monasticism unless it were exteriorized and thus institutionalized. It was admitted that there must be a dynamic and charismatic movement prior to exterior expression. But a posteriori the only way one can come to see this charism is by seeing it through the institution. One has to see through RB and perceive its basic thrust. Within the Rule itself, one must distinguish between the spirit, which is valid for all times, and the concrete situational provisions, which form the framework for the spirit. The charism or spirit always remains something greater than the framework within which it is found and it may, and often does call for adaptation of it.

RB is important for us as the objectification of the spirit which animated St Benedict. At the same time, though, the Rule is not only the expression of a lived experience. It was also intended to establish a way by which others could come to this lived experience. In this way the Rule not only expresses a spirit, it also creates an environmental framework or institution. However, if life within this institution becomes something routine, it can lead to alienation rather than to this lived experience. The institution is to foster and deepen charismatic living. If it does not do this it is not serving its purpose and is of little use. On the other hand, true charism can only be of profit to the institution.

SUB REGULA UEL ABBATE

A STUDY OF THE THEOLOGICAL SIGNIFICANCE OF THE
ANCIENT MONASTIC RULES

A T THIS MEETING, which has for its objective the study of the meaning of the rule for monks, I am supposed to handle the question from the theological point of view. I assume this role of theologian but not without some hesitancy because it is less familiar to me than the role of exegete or historian. I am, however, encouraged by the thought that theology does have a relationship both with exegesis and with history. Far from being beyond the confines of time, theology seems to be necessarily involved in historical time. What does theology mean, if not men of a certain epoch looking toward God and listening to God, not by ridding themselves beforehand of their historical condition, but rather in their very guise as men of this same epoch, with the resources and the limitations of this epoch, which make for a specific and irreplaceable manner of contemplating the unique Object and of hearing the unique Word?

Obliged as I am, even as a theologian, to place myself within time, it seems quite natural for me to place myself on the vantage ground which I know best, namely that of ancient monasticism and even more precisely, that of Latin cenobitism of the first centuries. I will then try to describe the attitude of St Benedict and the tradition to which he belongs vis-à-vis the monastic rule. Evidently, this attitude is more practical than theoretical, for we would search in vain for something akin to a *De praecepto* in a kind of literature which is so little speculative. The *Conferences* of Cassian, alone among other monastic writings, present a reflection on the role of religious law which might be applied in the particular case of the rules for monks, although he scarcely does this himself.

What, then, was the theological foundation and authority of these documents both for the authors and for the subjects of the ancient monastic rules? In other words, how did they conceive of their relationship with the Word of God? Then as now, it would be sufficient simply to read the Gospels and St Paul in order to be confronted with certain difficulties. Christ is our only master, his commandment of love is our only rule. The monastic rule, a code of very precise and even minute traditional observances, somehow brings to mind those "traditions of the ancients" against which Jesus addressed some severe words, reproaching his contemporaries for their preferring the traditions of men to the commandment of God.[1] More than this, it is difficult not to recall the opposition placed by St Paul between the slavery of the Law and the liberty of grace and of the Spirit.[2] In this perspective, subjection to a monastic rule could appear as a return to the regime of the Old Covenant.

This last difficulty could not escape the notice of an Augustine. He made a passing reference to it but one loaded with meaning, when he concluded his own Rule: the brothers of Hippo ought to observe this "with love, not as slaves under the Law, but as free men established under the rule of grace."[3] Even in our own day, in a beautiful article which analyzes the Jewish spirituality of the *Halakah,* Fr J. Goldstain shows no fear in setting up a parallel between this spirituality of the Law and that of the rule in Christian religious orders.[4] In fact, the two mentalities are closely allied. Using the fabric of the Scriptures they both try to weave a complexity of concrete obligations which encompasses the whole of life and would make of it a continual obedience to the divine will.

---

1. Mt 15:3; Mk 7:8.

2. Gal 3:13, 19–29; 4:1–11, 21–31; 5:1–6, etc.

3. Augustine, *Regula* 8:1. See L. Verheijen, *La Règle de saint Augustin,* vol. 1 (Paris, 1967), p. 437.

4. J. Goldstain, "La Halaka juive," *Vie Spirituelle,* no. 120 (1969): 385–399.

I will say briefly at the outset that the theological foundation of the ancient monastic rules seems to me to be twofold: on one side, they refer to the Gospels and to the tradition of the Apostles; on the other side, they emanate from men commanded by God to give laws to such and such a community.

THE DEFINITION OF CENOBITES FROM CASSIAN TO ST BENEDICT

These foundations will show themselves when we scrutinize the celebrated formula by which the Master and Benedict characterize cenobitism at the beginning of their respective rules: *primum (genus) coenobitarum, hoc est monasteriale, militans sub regula uel abbate.*[5] To be a cenobite means to serve under a rule and under an abbot. When these authors establish cenobitic life on those two principles of authority, a law and a superior, they develop in a very notable way the text of Cassian which they used as a source. In Chapter Four of his Eighteenth Conference, Cassian in fact defined cenobitism by only one principle, the authority of an "ancient" or a superior: *primum (genus) est coenobitarum, qui scilicet in congregatione pariter consistentes unius senioris judicio gubernantur.*[6] In this definition by Cassian, the "rule" is absent. The Master and Benedict have thus added this element to what their source had indicated. What is more, they have placed the rule, not in the second place, after the superior, but before him, which would suggest a primacy of value. Let it be noted that this is not an accidental arrangement. The couplet, rule-abbot, appears many times in the Rule of the Master and sometimes even in the Rule of Benedict. These passages present, for the most part and especially in the Master, the rule before the

---

5. RM 1:2; RB 1:2. See *La Règle du Maître,* ed. A. de Vogüé, SC 105–107, 3 vols. (Paris: Cerf, 1964); *Benedicti Regula,* ed. R. Hanslik, CSEL 75 (Vienna, 1960).

6. J. Cassian, *Conférences,* ed. E. Pichery, SC 42, 54, 64, 3 vols. (Paris: Cerf, 1955–1959), 18:4. (Hereafter cited as Conf.) See A. de Vogüé, *La Communauté et l'Abbé dans la Règle de saint Benoît* (Paris: Desclée De Brouwer, 1961), pp. 59–61. (Hereafter cited as *La Communauté.*)

abbot.[7] It is consequently a question of an attitude of mind: in the thought of the Master and Benedict, the law possesses a certain priority over the person.

The Simple Formula of Cassian in Tradition

This new definition of the Master and Benedict is all the more remarkable because the simple formula of Cassian was something of a classic in Latin monasticism. When Jerome and Sulpicius Severus wish to characterize briefly the cenobitic life, they contented themselves by mentioning only submission to superiors;[8] for them, as for Cassian, the cenobites lived simply *sub unius disciplina patris, sub abbatis imperio,*[9] without there being any question of *sub regula.*

A century after these initiators, at the same time as the Master and Benedict, the biographer of Fulgentius of Ruspe several times used the expression *sub regula.* It is, however, curious that instead of designating a law distinct from the authority of the abbot, as in the formula of the two rules we have mentioned, the *regula* for him is nothing else but the authority of the abbot himself: the two abbots, Fulgentius and Felix, agreed as well that the monks believed they were *sub unius regula constitutos,* under the authority of one superior.[10] Fulgentius himself left his monastery *ut deposito nomine abbatis sub regula uiueret in humilitate,* to cease being an abbot and to

---

7. RM 62:4: *praeceptum regulae uel abbatis;* 87:4: *regula in lectione expleta et omnia abbatis uerbis praedicta;* 90:5: *ex lectione regulae et dicto abbatis;* 92:8: *regulae obtemperans uel meis* (= *abbatis*) *actibus similis.* See also RM 89:8–12 (Rule, Scripture, abbot). The order is inverted, by reason of the context, in RM 90:67: *Ejus* (= *abbatis*) *uel regulae monitionibus.* The order rule-superior presents itself in RB 1:6–8 (= RM 1:6–8); 3:7–9; 23:1. The inverse order in RB 62:3–4; 65:16–17. In Benedict, the couplet is less clear than in the Master.

8. Jerome, Ep. 22:35: *prima apud eos confoederatio est oboedire maioribus,* etc.; Ep. 125:15: *uiuere in monasterio sub unius disciplina Patris consortioque multorum.* Sulpicius Severus, Dial. 1:10: *quibus summum ius est sub abbatis imperio uiuere.*

9. The same language is found in Faustus of Riez, Hom. 72; PLS 3:690: *sub ejus* (= *Honorati abbatis*) *disciplina Deo militare.* Cf. Denis, *Vita Pachomi,* 24: *sub ejus* (= *Pachomii abbatis*) *regula uiuere* (= G 23: *einai sun autô;* see H. van Cranenburgh, *La vie latine de saint Pachôme* [Brussels, 1969], pp. 138–139.)

10. Ferrand, *Vita Fulgentii,* 16; PL 65:125a.

live humbly under the authority of another.[11] Having to take up again his duty as superior, he once again aspired to abandon it: *cogitauit . . . quomodo . . . sub aliorum regimine constitutus ipse potius sub regula uiueret quam uiuendi regulam ceteris traderet,*[12] he thought of placing himself under the rule of other persons and to receive from them the rule of the traditional life, rather than having to impose this on others. Although the three passages of Ferrand do not give a general description of the cenobite's life as do the texts of Jerome and Sulpicius Severus cited above, nevertheless, that life does appear as being made up of submission to a superior and, what is more, this submission itself is designated by the expression *sub regula uiuere.*

At the end of the sixth century, the biographer of Benedict neither thought nor expressed himself in a different vein. When it is a question of the entry of two brothers into the monastery of Monte Cassino, Gregory writes quite simply that they put themselves under the direction (*regula*) of Benedict: *ejus se regulae in sancta conuersatione tradiderunt.*[13] If he wishes to characterize in one word the kind of life led by the monk Romanus at Subiaco, Gregory presents him as "living under the direction of the abbot Adeodatus": *sub Adeodati patris regula degebat.*[14] When there is question of evil monks who wander around outside their monastery, then Gregory writes that they "separate themselves from the direction of their abbot": *a proprii abbatis regula . . . abscedere.*[15] If it is a question of bringing them back to their duties, Gregory orders the authorities "to place every delinquent under the direction of the abbot": *sui abbatis sub regula . . . reddatur.*[16] For Gregory as for Ferrand, therefore,

---

11. *Ibid.,* 12; 128c.

12. *Ibid.,* 29; 132a. This time the personal authority is designated by *regimen,* while the *regula uiuendi* is a "rule of life" which the abbot is obliged to "transmit" (*traderet*). Between the two, *sub regula uiuere* designates submission to the norm of a traditional life, but only in so far as this is imposed by the superiors. It can be that *traderet* means simply "to impose, give" rather than to "transmit," *tradere* often being only a synonym for *dare.* (Cf. *Vita Fulgentii,* 15: *potestatem ei tradidit abbatis.*)

13. Gregory, Dial. 4:9.   14. *Ibid.,* 2:1.

15. Gregory, Ep. 1:42 = R 1:40 (first ref. to the Maurist ed. reproduced in Migne, PL 77; second ref. to ed. of Ewald-Hartmann, MGH, Ep. 1-2).

16. Gregory, *ibid.*

D

the word *regula* means nothing else than the authority of the superior. To live *sub regula* means to live under an abbot, he being the living rule of the monastery.[17]

This ensemble of texts agreeing as they do among themselves shows sufficiently that the definition of cenobites given by Cassian in Chapter Four of the Eighteenth Conference, expresses the common thought of the monks living in the time between the fourth and the sixth centuries. As a consequence it can be seen how much the thought of the Master and Benedict is original. In placing the rule at the side of the abbot,[18] and even before him, in their definition of cenobitism, these two legislators have introduced a new element and one of great interest.

The concept of the general rule in Cassian

However, not to exaggerate this novelty, it is important to consider not only Chapter Four of the Eighteenth Conference, the immediate source of the first chapter of our Rules, but also the following chapters of the same Conference. After giving the short definition in Chapter Four, Cassian then goes on to trace the history and portrait of the cenobites, the hermits and the sarabites.[19] The

17. In Gregory the *Regula* can also mean the general law to which all monks are subjected whether they are cenobites (Ep. 5:1 = Reg. 5:1: *monachica regula*), whether they are hermits (Dial. 2:12; 4:57: *monasterii nostri regula*) or finally, a written rule (Dial. 2:36).

18. It is not beyond the realms of doubt that the *regula* of RM 1:2 = RB 1:2 might not be a reality distinct from the abbatial authority, given the texts which we have just recorded. As in these texts, could not the *regula* of the Master and of Benedict be simply the authority of the abbot? We would then have an hendiadys: *regula uel abbate* which would be the equivalent of *regula abbatis*. However, the meaning usually given by the Master to *regula* would scarcely authorize such an interpretation. Discounting three passages where it is a question of a part of the Rule (RM 51:T; 53:65; 57:13), the almost sixty times that *regula* is used all have relationship to the RM in its entirety. Moreover, the couplet rule-abbot is familiar to the Master (above, note 7). It appears notably in the eighth degree of humility (below, note 26). It would seem then that the Master here is thinking of a written rule, such as his own Rule. He knew and he admitted that there existed other rules (RM 1:6 = RB 1:6; RM 92:7; see below, notes 48–49).

19. Cassian, Conf. 18:5–7.

cenobites, as we know, appeared at the time of the Apostles.[20] First in the order of time, their species is the continuation of the primitive Church of Jerusalem as it is described by St Luke in the Acts of the Apostles. They guard faithfully the "institutions of the Apostles." The "discipline" which they inculcated in their first disciples remains today that of the cenobites: *coenobitarum disciplina*.[21] In these phrases we see already the outline of a kind of cenobitic life and rule derived from the teaching of the Apostles.

This idea is affirmed and made more precise when Cassian sets about to describe the sarabites, for what is lacking to these is precisely the "discipline of the cenobites," the "traditions of the ancients" as well as the idea of submission to qualified superiors: abbot, cellarer, deans, ancients who are the authorized guardians of this discipline and these traditions.[22]

Although under a less striking formulation than the lapidary formula given in the Rule of the Master and the Rule of Benedict, we can nevertheless see very clearly how the couplet rule-superior emerges from the texts of Cassian. The *disciplina coenobiorum* of which there is no question in the definition given in Chapter Four, appears here, side by side with personal authority, as one of the constitutive elements of cenobitism.

From Tradition to the Written Rule

The Master and Benedict are then not as innovative as we might be led to believe when we consider only the immediate source of their definition. Nevertheless their originality appears again when we compare the *regula* of which they speak with what Cassian understands by the *coenobiorum disciplina*. According to the author of the Conference, this "discipline of the coenobia" consists in a corpus of doctrine, of rules, of usages and of observances which reach back to the Apostolic Age. Moreover, there is nothing to

20. On this theory, see our article "Monaschisme et Eglise dans la pensée de Cassien," *Théologie de la vie monastique* (Paris, 1961), pp. 213–240.

21. Cassian, Conf. 18:5: *coenobitarum disciplina; ea quae ab apostolis . . . meminerant instituta; ista . . . discipulorum . . . disciplina.*

22. *Ibid.,* 7: *coenobiorum disciplina (bis); seniorum . . . traditionibus.*

indicate that Cassian was thinking in terms of a written form of legislation; it is rather a question of an oral tradition, transmitted from generation to generation. Finally, this living tradition is conserved by the entire group of *coenobia*, at least in that ideal land of monasticism which is Egypt. It is both apostolic and "catholic."[23]

This concept of monastic tradition is evidently a very close copy of that ecclesiastical tradition to which Vincent of Lerins, a compatriot of Cassian, will give a formulation some ten years later in his celebrated canon.[24] It is important here to note, however, that Cassian has in mind a reality quite different from that of the Rule of the Master and the Rule of Benedict. The *disciplina coenobiorum* is a tradition going back to the Apostles, non-written, common to all monasteries. This is a far cry from the *regula* of our two authors which is a recent document, put down in writing, proper to only one monastery or to a rather restricted group of monasteries.[25] Thus we observe here that from Cassian to the Master and Benedict, there is a change of concept which will show itself again in a very salient way in the eighth degree of humility where our two authors will change the "common rule" of Cassian to the common rule *of the monastery.*[26]

So the expression *militans sub regula* of the Rule of the Master and the Rule of Benedict represents not only an addition to the formula of Chapter Four of the Eighteenth Conference but also a development of the thought expressed in Chapters Five to Seven of this same Conference. It is not enough, however, simply to establish or point out such a difference. Although the realities seen by Cassian

23. Cassian, *Institutions Cénobitiques*, J. C. Guy, SC 109 (Paris: Cerf, 1965), 1:1:2: *quidquid . . . catholice per omne corpus fraternitatis tenetur;* 1:2:3: *secundum catholicam regulam.* On the apostolic origin of Egyptian cenobitism, see 2:2–6. (Hereafter cited as Insti.)

24. Vincent of Lerins, *Commonitorium,* 1:2; PL 50:640: *Id teneamus quod ubique, quod semper, quod omnibus creditum est.*

25. The RM seems to have been written for several monasteries. See our article "La Règle du Maître et les Dialogues de saint Grégoire," RHE 61 (1966): 44–76. As regards the RB, written also for several communities, see the Introduction to our ed. (to appear in SC), Part I, c. I, no. 3.

26. RM 10:72 = RB 7:55. Cf. *La Communauté,* pp. 260–262.

on one side and on the other by the Master and Benedict are distinct, they are nevertheless connected and one derives from the other. Here, and above all in the eighth degree of humility, the passage from one to the other is a literary fact altogether real and one which in its own turn manifests a true continuity both institutional and doctrinal. The *regula* of the Master and of Benedict is indeed the continuation of this *disciplina coenobiorum* of which Cassian was thinking. The "rule" composed by these abbots of the sixth century for some monasteries in Italy have their roots in the ancient cenobitic tradition of which the author of the *Conferences* has made himself the spokesman. It is a product and a particular crystalization of this tradition.[27]

THE FIRST FOUNDATION OF THE RULES: TRADITION

We now have a first answer to the question which is before us, namely, the theological foundation and authority of our rules: the monastic rule is founded on tradition. It is not a question here only of a simple historical fact that can be verified, as we have seen, on the doctrinal, institutional and literary levels. The fact also has theological importance. The "tradition" of which there is question, in fact, unfolds itself from the teaching of Christ and of the Apostles. It is nothing other than the ecclesiastical tradition considered in the particular domain of asceticism and the common life. As Christian tradition taken in its entirety, it cannot be separated from the Gospels and the other apostolic writings where it receives its first expression, and in one sense, its definitive expression. In a more general sense, it forms a corpus or one whole with all of Scripture. It is a well-known fact that the monastic rules are replete with Scripture as well as with writings of the Fathers. Not without

---

27. Besides the use of Cassian in our two Rules in the chs. *De generibus monachorum* and *De humilitate,* we can also point out in RM 34:1–2, a ref. to the *instituta patrum,* that is to say to the Insti., 90:92; 91:48. The RB abounds in ref. to the Fathers, notably Augustine.

reason, the Master and Benedict assimilate their respective rules to
the "narrow way" preached by Jesus,[28] and to his Gospel.[29]

The Master and Benedict in relation to the Fathers

However, we cannot stress this scriptural and traditional character
of our two Rules and all others, without soon noting that the Master
and Benedict are not completely of the same mind in regard to
Scripture and tradition.[30] The Master gives to his work the aspect
of an inspired text, and likens it, in a certain degree, to Scripture
itself. As regards the writings of the Fathers, if he refers to them
with veneration, he does so in order to place his own directives in
continuity with their own. The Master does not see any break in
the continuity of these respective directives. He feels that he is on
the level of the Fathers and that there he wishes to be. On the
contrary, Benedict has the feeling that he is far beneath them. The
teachings of the holy Fathers are at the summit to which he lifts his
eyes only in shame and confusion. A similar abyss separates his
"small rule for beginners" from Holy Scripture. These two authors
then look with different eyes upon their respective works as well as
on the monks of their time to whom they addressed themselves.

The Role of the Law in Cassian

In presenting his Rule as a minimum, destined to serve as a brake
and a check-point on the slopes of decadence, as well as a base for
making the upward ascent again, something to which generous
individuals are invited, Benedict outlines a concept of the Rule
which is very much akin to the theories of Cassian on the role of
the Law in the religious society, either before Christ, or in the
Church, or within monasticism itself.[31] This thought of Cassian

---

28. RM pr 14; RB Prol. 48.

29. RM Ths 17 = RB Prol. 21.

30. About this question, see our edition of the RB, Introd. 1, 1, 2; Commentary, 1, 2, notes 209–217.

31. Cassian, Conf. 8:21–24: from the natural knowledge of good and evil to the Moasic law, a restraint to sin and a "teacher" leading to the Gospel; Conf. 21:2–7: the Mosaic law of the tithe continues to oblige imperfect

furnishes us with certain elements of an answer to the objection which we pointed out at the beginning of this study, namely, is not the monastic rule a revival of the Old Law? Certainly, if we might paraphrase Cassian, the rule plays a role analogous to the Law, but this role is completely auxiliary and pedagogical.[32] The Law did not present itself as an ideal or as an end and neither does the rule. Both only aim at lending assistance to sinful humanity and preparing it in its approach to perfection. The minimum imposed on all is only a point of departure for the effort proposed to those who are the more fervent. These latter will free themselves from the constraints of observances, not indeed by transgressing them, but by transcending them. To sum up, if the rule, both ecclesiastical and monastic, still has its place in Christianity, it is because there is still a great number of the faithful and of monks who remain subject to the imperfections of the Old Covenant. The role of the rule is to remedy this state of affairs. It is not a question of fixing the faithful and the monks in this state, but rather of preparing them and inciting them to go beyond and further, as true disciples of the Gospels.

From the Apostolic Rule to the Rules of Augustine, Basil and Pachomius

What has been said thus far makes certain differences appear between the attitude of the Master and that of Benedict vis-à-vis the Scriptural and patristic monuments of tradition and also certain analogies between Benedict and Cassian concerning the manner in

---

Christians who have not renounced all according to the Gospel; these, although Christians, are still under the yoke of the Law; on the contrary, perfect Christians who follow the evangelical counsel of renunciation which is total, free themselves from the Law by surpassing it; Conf. 21:29–30: the same theme but apropos to Lent; Insti. 2:5–6: after the spontaneous fervor experienced at the beginning, the modest canon of twelve psalms is decreed by the Fathers who foresee the lukewarmness of monasticism in the future; Insti. 3:1–2: the prayer of the Egyptian cenobites, solitary, continual and spontaneous, outweighs the communal, disconnected and obligatory prayer of the monks of other regions.

32. On this matter see the article "Monachisme et Eglise" (cited above, note 20), pp. 228–229, 239.

which they conceive the rule. Now we ought to return to the fundamental fact upon which we are reflecting, namely, the deep implantation of the monastic rules in tradition. This fact has been noted in the particular case of the Rule of the Master and the Rule of Benedict and it will not be pointless to illustrate this by means of other examples. The great ancestors of our legislators, Pachomius, Basil and Augustine, all three considered their monastic legislation, not as a "rule"—this term applies fully to Scripture alone—but rather as a modest collection of Scriptural precepts and commentaries on these.

"When Augustine became a priest," recounts his disciple Possidius, "he very soon founded a monastery in the dependencies of the Church and he began to live with the servants of God according to the mode and rule established by the holy Apostles." And the biographer quotes the celebrated passage from Chapter Four of the Acts of the Apostles concerning renunciation, the placing of goods in common and distribution to each one according as he had need.[33] The foundation at Hippo had no other law in the beginning than the "rule of the Apostles"; in other words, the writings of the New Testament. However, when Augustine leaves his community some years later to become a bishop,[34] he will sense the need to write some kind of directory which he designated only by the word *libellus* but which has received from posterity the name of *Regula Augustini*.[35] The phrases from the Acts which had served as a program at the time of the foundation will be found again in the first lines of this Rule and inspire the entire document. The latter appears as a commentary on this text of Scripture and on some others with the view of applying the teachings of the Apostles to

33. Possidius, *Vita Augustini*, 5: *uiuere coepit secundum modum et regulam sub sanctis apostolis constitutam.*

34. According to the hypothesis of L. Verheijen, *La Règle de saint Augustin,* 2:95–96; 115–116; 197–198.

35. Augustine, R 8:2, Verheijen, 1:437: *in hoc libello tanquem in speculo . . . inspicere.* The image of "mirror" calls to mind the Scriptures to which it is often applied. We find the formula *Explicit Regula Sci. Augustini Episcopi* in a very ancient ms. Paris Lat. 12634, f. 20.

the concrete life of the young community. Under different modalities, we can see here the same movement from the apostolic tradition to the monastic rule, from the general norm and one divinely inspired to the particular codification and this written by a superior of a monastery, as we observed before in comparing the texts of Cassian to those of the Master and Benedict. The "Rule of the Apostles" has given birth to the "Rule of Augustine."

When Basil, in his turn, wrote his Questions and Answers for the communities of Cappadocia, he never imagined himself as making a "rule," much less a "rule for monks." In his eyes, the only "rule" for Christians is the Scriptures, of which he has compiled a methodical compendium in his Moral Rules. In regard to the work Questions and Answers, to which Dom Gribomont has restored its original title of *Asceticon*,[36] it was only after him that it was called *Regula Basilii* in the West and *Orio* in the Greek tradition. In the preface, Basil points out clearly what he wishes to do: a priest, he will present only "divine teachings," the "manner of life according to the Gospels," the "law of the Lord" (Ps 1:2), his "word which will judge us on the last day" (Jn 12:48), the "words of the divinely inspired Scripture."[37] Then the work commences with a question on the order of the commandments of God. As in the case of Augustine, it is the elucidation of the sacred text which is the origin of the Rule of Basil.

In the case of Pachomius, the point which interests us is more difficult to establish since there are many obstacles which prevent us from ascertaining with certitude the thought of the Founder of the *coenobia*. When we read the translation of the Pachomian Rule by Jerome, we are struck by the fact that we find the word *regula* applied to two objects: the "rule of the Scriptures"[38] and the "rules

36. J. Gribomont, "Obéissance et Evangile selon saint Basile le Grand," *Vie Spirituelle,* Suppl. 21 (1952): 192–215, especially pp. 196–197.

37. See the Prol. *Humanum genus;* PL 103:487–488. Fragments of the Greek text are in PG 31:1080ab and 900b–901a. The last expression here cited is missing in the Latin which would represent the primitive redaction, according to Gribomont, *Histoire du texte des Ascétiques de s. Basile* (Louvain, 1953), p. 239.

38. Pachomius, *Praecepta et Instituta* (Hereafter cited as PI), Pref. in A. Boon, *Pachomiana Latina* (Louvain, 1932), 53:13; also, PI 10; Boon, 56:8.

of the monastery."[39] It happens at times that the two realities are linked together: an article condemns en bloc "what has been done against the rule of the Scriptures and the discipline of the monastery."[40] Taking into consideration only these Latin formulas, it appears legitimate to establish a relationship between the *regula scripturarum* and the *regulae monasterii:* the latter derive from the former and draw their name therefrom. However, in those places where the Latin translation can be controlled by the Coptic fragments, the latter hardly admit of such inductions.[41] It remains that the Pachomian Rule goes back undoubtedly to the Scriptures as the supreme norm, above all in its second and third collections.[42] As regards the ensemble of Pachomian literature, the veneration of the sacred text is very apparent there and so important is it that a recent commentator could entitle one of the sections of his study: "Scripture, the rule of the Pachomian Monk."[43] As a consequence we

---

39. PI 17; Boon 58:7; *Praecepta et Judicia* (Hereafter cited as PJ) 8, 12, 15; Boon 67:1, 68:10, 69:11. Cf. Orsiese, Bk. 26; Boon 127:19. We find also *conuersationis eorum . . . regulas* and *Patris nostri regulas* in Theodore, Ep.; Boon 105:20, 106:11.

40. PI 10: *quidquid contra regulam scripturarum est et monasterii disciplinam.* Cf. PJ 8: *praecepta maiorum et regulas monasterii quae Dei praecepto constitutae sunt,* but here the "precept of God" could be the command made to Pachomius to establish the cenobia to which the titles of *Praecepta* (Hereafter cited as Praec.) and of PI speak. See also PI 18; Boon 61:5–6: *sequatur praecepta maiorum et legem Dei,* where, however, the *maiores* could be "the saints" (= the Scriptures?), as it would appear from the Pref. of the collection (Boon 53:5) according to the Coptic text (CSCO 160:80, line 4).

41. The Coptic phrase ("measure of the Scriptures") in the two texts cited in note 38 above, is one thing. The Coptic ("that which is established") in the first text cited in note 39 above, is something else. The use of *regula* by Jerome in both cases is consequently mistaken since the word meaning "measure" (*psi*) is translated by him elsewhere by *mensura.* See Boon 53:9. As to the *monasterii disciplina* of the first text cited in note 40 above, this expression has nothing to correspond with it in the Coptic text.

42. See the Prols. of PI and PJ. Cf. Praec. 51; Boon 27:2: *juxta euangelii praeceptum.*

43. A. Veilleux, *La Liturgie dans le cénobitisme pachômien au quatrième siècle,* Studia Anselmiana 57 (1968): 263–266. See in particular L. T. Lefort, *Les vies coptes de s. Pachôme* 95:6 (Bo 23): "Il (Pachôme) leur fixa, d'après les saintes Ecritures, des règles." Cf. A. de Vogüé, "Le monastère, Eglise du Christ," *Commentationes in Reg. S. Benedicti,* Studia Anselmiana 42 (1957): 31, note 29 and pp. 34–35.

cannot doubt that Pachomius and his successors, in establishing the rules of the *Koinonia,* shared the same thought as Augustine or Basil: their own ordinances were, in their eyes, only the point of impact of the rule of the Scriptures upon the concrete day-to-day life of the communities.

The Plurality and Unity of the Rules

Holy Scripture, especially the example and the teaching of the Apostles, is then at once the historical origin and the first theological foundation of the rules for monks. These were born out of a desire to make the Word of God penetrate into the very existence of such or such a group of men and they drew their authority before all else from their conformity to this Word. This fact leads us to a corollary of some importance. If all the monastic rules have the same origin and the same foundation, their multiplicity is not opposed to the unity of monasticism but is rather at its service.

The historians who study the first three or four centuries of Latin cenobitism are often struck by the apparently anarchical phenomenon of the proliferation of rules.[44] In fact, we can count almost thirty of them, from the Rule of Augustine and the first translations of the Oriental texts to the Spanish, Irish and Frankish documents of the seventh century.[45] But the impression of anarchy which this diversity of rules displays is misleading. Besides the multiple connections of literary dependence which unite the texts—we will return to the subject later—it is evident that their common reference to Scripture binds them very closely together. The particular elements which distinguish them are less striking than the strong homogeneity of their doctrines and their respective observances, all of them being derived from the same divine source.

If, for the rest, the rules are multiple, this very multiplicity is demanded by the diversity of locales and times, of charisms and needs, of men who make the laws and of communities to whom

---

44. See, for example, H. I. Marrou, *Nouvelle Histoire de l'Eglise,* vol. I (Paris, 1963), p. 681.

45. See our ed. of RB, Intro. I, I, no. I.

these laws are directed. The rule of Scripture is unique but it must apply itself to different situations. The monastic rules in this regard play a role analogous to that of the modern "Declarations," diverse and changeable vis-à-vis the Rule of Benedict. These various commentaries, each one insistent on such and such a text or aspect of the one matrix-rule, are necessary in order that the latter might act upon such and such a community according to its potentialities and its own particular needs.

This profound unity of the ancient monastic rules in Latin cenobitism doubtlessly explains why the ancient monks scarcely seemed to be moved or affected by their multiplicity. They were very conscious of their substantial homogeneity as well as of the necessity to respond to the various situations, so much so that they would hardly take it amiss if bishops and founding abbots would legislate individually for their own foundations.[46] Only Rufinus and Cassian raised any protests, one in a discreet way, the other with vehemence, against the variety of observances in the monasteries of the West in their own times.[47] In presenting to the Latin cenobites two great traditions, that of Cappadocia and that of Egypt, they both hoped that the West would rally in unity around these Eastern models. What actually happened did not respond to their expectations. It was neither the Basilian Rule nor the Institutes of the monks of Egypt which would realize in the West a certain formal unity, but rather the Benedictine Rule, a document Latin in every respect, which would impose itself in the West only four centuries after the attempts of Rufinus and Cassian and then less by the unanimous adhesion of the monks themselves than by the will of an emperor. In the meanwhile the written rules were being multiplied but this proliferation did not prevent the monasteries from considering themselves all members of the one and same body, united by a common profession.

46. Of particular interest in this regard are the Prols. of Caesarius (*Reg. uirg.*), of Isidore and of Donatus in their respective Rules. See also *Regula Pauli et Stephani,* 41. Cf. our ed. of RB, Commentary, 1, 2, notes 222–229.

47. Rufinus, *Pref. in Regulam S. Basilii;* PL 103:486b; Cassian, Insti. Pref. 8; 2:2–3.

The Master and Benedict seem to have shared this profound feeling of unity with a certain indifference to the diversity of rules. When they reproach the Sarabites for not having been "proven by *any rule*,"[48] they suggest that their own legislation was by no means a monopoly. More clearly still, the Master speaks of a postulant who enters the monastery "already proven by *some rule*."[49] In other words rules were not lacking and it was hardly important whether one was formed or proven by this rule or that rule, for they all resembled one another. The important thing was effective submission to one of these authentic and authorized rules of which a good number existed.

THE SECOND FOUNDATION OF THE RULES: AUTHORITY OF THE LEGISLATORS

We have just encountered the word "authorized." This quality required of all monastic rules brings us into the presence of the second theological foundation of these documents: the personal authority of the legislator. It is not sufficient, in fact, that the rule would be rooted in Scripture and in tradition. There is further need that it emanate from a person with a mandate from God to legislate for the intention of such and such a group of men.

This quality of authority which the text assumes because of its author is more or less clearly indicated according to the rules themselves. The Master, for example, insists very much more on this than does Benedict, which might be seen in the prophetic claim that he makes in his Prologue—"It is not I who speak to you, it is God himself"—or by the repeated affirmation that he is writing under the "dictation" of the Lord,[50] or again by the initial formula, *Respondit Dominus per magistrum*, which gives an oracular tone to each of his chapters. Obviously, the Master is conscious of his right

---

48. RM 1:6 = RB 1:6: *nulla regula approbati.* Cf. above, note 18.

49. RM 92:57: *aliqua regula approbatus.*

50. RM 11:T; 13:65; 22:12. Cf. *La Règle du Maître,* 1:194–197.

and his duty to legislate, doubtless because he knows that by his title of a regularly ordained abbot he is an authentic "doctor," whose authority is analogous to that of a bishop, but also because he has received the grace that is proper to a founder.[51] The author of a rule should not only be instructed in the Scriptures and tradition; it is also necessary that he have the authority to establish and prescribe. God ought to have made him *capable* in the eyes of all to make a rule.

This mission of abbot-legislator has been celebrated by Faustus of Riez in his panegyric of Honoratus, the founder of Lerins. Happy those who have lived under the abbacy of that saint! But "no less happy is he who observes the holy rule brought forth by him and which Christ has set up by his intermediary to found on a solid foundation this community."[52] In this role of institutor of a rule, Honoratus is compared to Moses, that other legislator of the desert. As Moses brought down the two stone tablets from Mount Sinai, the holy abbot took on the mountain of virtues (the teachings of the Egyptian Fathers) the "precepts of the apostolic rule, drawn from the two Testaments," and then carried them down to his community of monks, the new Israel.[53]

In this subtle allegory where each detail is significant, what is of paramount interest to us is the global analogy between the abbot-legislator and the mediator of the Old Covenant. The rule of

---

51. As was natural, the majority of the rules were written by the founders of the monasteries, abbots and bishops.

52. Faustus of Riez, Ser. 72; PLS 3:690. This follows a development on the theme *non aliter potuit docere quam uixit* (Cf. Gregory, Dial. 2:36). Allusions to *regula* in Faustus are found in Ser. 37, 42, 43; PL 50:840b, 851d, 855b. There is nothing to prove that Faustus is thinking of a written rule. The same is true for the canon in the Council of Arles (around 455), in Labbe, *Sacrosancta Concilia* 4:1024e: *regula quae a fundatore ipsius monasterii dudum constituta est in omnibus custodita.*

53. Faustus of Riez, Ser. 72; PLS 3:693: *erit nobis Moyses, quibus per felicem ducatum eremi patefecit ingressum, quibus . . . apostolicae regulae praecepta ex utroque composita testamento, uelut duas tabulas detulit de institutione aegyptiorum patrum, tanquam de monte uirtutum.* The allusion to the two Testaments recalls the *Versus Simplicii*—L. Traube, *Textgeschichte der Regula S. Benedicti* (Munich, 1898), p. 92.

Honoratus was not his own invention, no more than the Law was the personal discovery of Moses. Both legislations are the Word of God. Honoratus played the same indispensable role of mediator between God and his people just as Moses had done. A man was necessary to gather up the divine Word of God and to transmit it to the people. This man ought to have been chosen by God and commanded by him in view of such an apostolic mission. The rule, though apostolic and drawn from the two Testaments, still has need, in order to have force, of a man of God who might bring it to the community in the name of the Lord.

Personal Character of the Ancient Rules

This necessary mediation of an authorized spokesman imprints on the majority of the ancient rules a personal quality which surprises us today. The monastic or the quasi-monastic rules of the twentieth century hardly ever show that they are the work of one man. Whatever else might be said of the Directory of Charles de Foucauld,[54] or the rule of Taizé,[55] or the regulations of some Canadian hermits,[56] or the rule of the Brothers of the Simple Life recently published at Ligugé,[57] or the Spiritual Guide of Father Placide Deseille,[58] it must be noted that all of these documents have been drawn up in an impersonal fashion. Only a discreet dedication or an editor's note will sometimes reveal the name of the author. The text itself avoids all affirmation of any personal authority, even when

54. Charles of Jesus, *Directoire* (*Text of 1909–1913*) (Paris, 1933). It is not the case with another text of this spiritual family, *La Règle de vie des Petits Frères de Jésus* (roneotype, 1950) whose intro. signed by Br René (Voillaume) has a very personal quality about it which is found again in the body of the work.

55. *La Règle de Taizé* (Taizé, 1965). Dedication of R. Schutz: *"A mes frères."*

56. (J. Winandy), *A Manual for Hermits* (Courtenay, 1964).

57. *Livre de vie monastique,* Suppl. to the *Lettre de Ligugé,* no. 137 (1969). No less anonymous is the Rule of the Brotherhood of La Vierge des Pauvres. See *Au coeur même de l'Eglise. Une recherche monastique: les Frères de la Vierge des Pauvres* (Paris, 1966).

58. P. Deseille, "Guide spirituel," *Collectanea Cisterciensia* 31 (1969): 271–315.

all evidence shows that it does proceed from a charismatic personality. None of these authors would ever dream of speaking as an
inspired master who commands in the name of God. On the
contrary, it seems as if the only way to make these rules acceptable
and convincing is to present them as the fruit of an anonymous
wisdom or the result of some community experience.

Opposed to this attitude, it would seem that the ancient rules
were all the more acceptable when they proceeded from a well-
known personage who enjoyed a reputation for sanctity. If some of
them have in fact remained anonymous,[59] it is still a fact that the
majority of these ancient rules present themselves as the work of
some given person. It is of slight importance if that person would
actually name himself,[60] or that his name would appear in only the
Incipit and the *Explicit* of the copyist,[61] or that the name remained
hidden under one or several pseudonyms,[62] and even sometimes
remained completely anonymous.[63] The important thing is that the
work displays itself as a discourse of one or several persons and
these show no fear in asserting their existence.

In this regard, the beginning of the Benedictine Prologue is
typical: "Hearken, O son, to the precepts of the master . . . the
admonitions of a loving father."[64] From its very outset, the Rule of
Benedict presents itself as the *praecepta* and the *admonitio* of a certain
wise man, at the same time a master and a father. As regards the
Rule of the Master, not only does the author present himself from
the first words of the Prologue as some sort of prophet, but the
personal character of the work constantly asserts itself into the

59. So the *Regula Orientalis,* the *Tarnatensis,* the two *Regula cujusdam Patris.*

60. So Caesarius (*Reg. uirg.*), Ferreol, Aurelian, Isidore (at least according
to PL 103:555a) and Donatus.

61. So Augustine, Basil, Pachomius, Caesarius (*Reg. mon.*), Benedict, Paul
and Stephen (?), Columban and Fructuosus.

62. So for the Four Fathers (Serapion, Macarius, Paphnutius, Macarius) and
the author of the *Regula Macarii.*

63. So the authors of the Second and the Third *Rule of the Fathers,* those of
the *Regula communis* attributed to Fructuosus and above all the Master.

64. RB Prol. 1. For these expressions which can mean the author as well as
the Lord, see our ed. of RB, Commentary, 1, 1, no. 2.

rubrics of the "question" and "answer" which are inserted into the title of each chapter.

The Augustinian Rule begins with a phrase which makes it somewhat like the Rule of Benedict, an ensemble of "precepts" from a given person: *Haec sunt quae ut obseruetis praecipimus in monasterio constituti.*[65] And the *Explicit* of the most ancient manuscripts give to the rule not the title "The Rule of Hippo"—and in this instance I am thinking of the "Rule of Taizé"—but rather the "Rule of Augustine." Already the Rule of Basil, *Regula Basilii*, had presented itself as a personal work, not only by the rubrics of questions and answers, albeit more brief and less explicit than those of the Master, but also and above all in the Prologue where Basil frankly declares that he will speak as a priest with the grace and the authority of this sacred function.[66] In his own turn, Rufinus, in his "Preface of the Translator," presents Basil as a jurist who interprets the divine Law.[67] The competence and the prestige of the author are evidently implied in this image: the authority of his consultation depends on the recognized worth of the jurist himself.

Very impersonal in itself, the Rule of Pachomius takes on the same personal aspect from the solemn titles which we read in the translation by Jerome and which go back perhaps in part to the original Greek and Coptic;[68] these articles or regulations are the *Praecepta Pachomii*, an expression which we have already come across in Benedict and Augustine. A fair number of the later rules, as those of the Four Fathers, Caesarius, Aurelian, Ferreol and Isidore, bring out this personal character in such an evident way that it is pointless to insist on it here.

The Rule as a Monument of Tradition

The authority of the legislator can then be considered as the

---

65. Augustine, R 1:1; Verheijen, 1:417.
66. Basil, Prol. *Humanum genus;* PL 103:487 (see above note 37).
67. Rufinus, *Pref. in Reg. S. Basilii;* PL 103:485b.
68. See Boon, p. 13 (Praec.) and 53 (Pl). The titles in PJ (p. 63) and *Praecepta ac Leges* (p. 71) are less solemn but they also mention Pachomius. See the response of the first of these four titles in the Greek *Excerpta* (p. 170). No title corresponds to the second in the Coptic (CSCO 160:80, line 1).

second foundation of our rules from the theological point of view. However, this foundation preserves its entire solidity only in the particular case which up to this point we have kept constantly in mind, namely, that of the communities to whom the rule is directed and the very age in which it was actually written. What will happen in the case where the rule extends itself to other communities and in other times? What kind of authority can it enjoy in monasteries which were not founded by the author of the rule, or which actually having indeed been founded by such an author, now find themselves in a situation more or less different from that of the time of their origin?

This question brings us to the point where we must distinguish two roles which a monastic rule can play: that of the rule properly so called and that of a monument of tradition. As a rule properly so called, that is to say, in so far as it is a code obligatory in all its details and more or less exclusive of all other legislation,[69] the rule would scarcely be able to apply itself except in the monasteries for which it was written and at the time in which it was written. Outside of these precise situations, it appears rather as a document of tradition along with others like it.

Such, for example, has been the fate of the Rule of Benedict in the Frankish monasticism of the seventh century. At Luxeuil and in the numerous monasteries founded or influenced by this center, the Rule of Benedict does not appear alone but in company with other rules, above all that of Columban, from which it seems to be inseparable.[70] Without being obliged by religious bonds which unite them in a personal way to Benedict, but rather in virtue of a free decision, the founders of these monasteries chose to place themselves under the Rule of Benedict and at the same time under the Rule of Columban. They then borrowed a part of the doctrines and observances from one legislator, and a part from the other. In

---

69. The exclusiveness supposes that the rule was fairly complete, which is far from always being the case with these small rules often occasional and fragmentary. The RM and the RB are among the more complete rules.

70. See F. Prinz, *Frühes Mönchtum in Frankenreich* (Munich-Vienna ,1965), pp. 273–282. Cf. our ed. of RB, Intro. 1, 5.

such a combination the Rule of Benedict will be retained not in its entirety, but only partially.[71] Therefore the superiors of the Frankish monasteries in the seventh century enjoyed a double freedom in relation to the work of Benedict, freedom to adopt or not this Rule and freedom to take what they wanted from it and to leave the rest aside.

More generally, this manner of using an earlier legislation reasserts itself throughout all the literature on the Latin monastic rules. Once the first generation has passed, the generation of the original texts, each new rule re-uses the pre-existing material. Sometimes the borrowing is done on a small scale as in the case of the Rule of the Master which scarcely used anything but Cassian. In other instances, the dependence is much more remarkable, as in the case of Benedict vis-à-vis the Master, of Caesarius in relation to Augustine, of the *Tarnatensis* in relation to both Augustine and Caesarius. The *Regula Orientalis* is practically a cento of Pachomius and of the Second Rule of the Fathers, and the Rule of Donatus breaks itself loose still less from the three models that it uses. It is possible to find pure and simple centos such as the florilegium of *Parisianus Latinus 12634.*

These borrowings, incessant and multiform as they are, make of the collection of Latin rules, a veritable family whose genealogical tree is a very complicated thing indeed.[72] But above all they show perfectly this concept of the monastic rule as a monument of tradition which we have already seen at work in the Frankish monasticism of the seventh century. The authors of the new rules acted in the same way as did the founders who placed their monasteries *sub regula sancti Benedicti et sancti Columbani.* They also treated the ancient rules with a mixture of veneration and freedom. Certainly none of them ever made any pretenses of complete liberty or of absolute originality. On the contrary, they borrowed from their predecessors all that they could, a little through laziness

71. A patent example of this is found in the Rule of Donatus.

72. This genealogical tree remains to be constructed. Summary indications are given in our ed. of RB, Intro. 1, 1, no. 1.

perhaps as well as a lack of creativity, but certainly also and pre-dominantly because they were under the sway of a profound sense of tradition; for them it was not a question of doing something new, but a question of setting up a monastery which would be traditional.

Nevertheless, this fidelity to the Fathers did co-exist with a certain freedom. No legislator felt himself to be a slave to this or that earlier document. When they took up the pen, they were conscious of their right and their duty to make a work which would be relatively personal, first of all by choosing from the writings of the Fathers those things which seemed to them to be particularly appropriate for the actual situation of their community and then, where there was need, by correcting and completing what they had borrowed according to the same criterion.

So each legislator might take from the common treasury of monastic rules what he wished and then in his own turn enrich it with some new addition. The work will not, in fact, disappear with the particular conditions of time and place for which it had been conceived. Outside of this limited framework in which it will have played the role of a rule properly so called, the rule will survive as a monument of tradition. Then this rule will no longer be observed integrally or exclusively but will be utilized in a free and partial way, conjointly with the other traditional documents. The legislator thus becomes *quidem Pater*, one of the Fathers.[73] His rule takes its place among the *Regulae Patrum*,[74] those rules of the Fathers which each abbot and each community had to follow in their great common lineaments which constitute the axis of tradition, while at the same time remaining free to choose from among the particular regulations those which suited their own situations the best. We might say that the monastic rule thus lost its individual authority

73. Two anonymous rules are known as *Regula cujusdam Patris* (see note 59 above). In his Commentary on the RB (PL 102), Smaragdus frequently used the expression *quidam Pater* to indicate the Master and other legislators.

74. Three rules have come down to us under this name (see notes 62–63 above), without taking into account the RM which is also designated in this way by its *Explicit*. For the attitude of the monks vis-à-vis the *regulae Patrum*, see in particular the texts cited above in note 46.

and acquired a part of the collegial authority which all these rules exercised together.

THE RULE AND THE ABBOT

We have just considered the fate of the monastic rules after their death as rules properly so called. It is now necessary to return to their first role, that of rules, in the strict sense, the unique role which their authors ordinarily intended them to play. In this properly normative function, the rule will find itself in collusion with the abbot, as we could foresee from the formula which we commented on at the beginning of this study, namely, *militans sub regula uel abbate*. It is now indispensable to study and examine the relationship between the two principles of government, *regula* and *abbas*, in order to make the nature and the limits of authority inherent in the rule more precise.

The Two Pillars of the Political Order

If we admit that we are faced with a question of two different principles and not simply one,[75] we will find ourselves in the presence of a written law and of a living person, this latter being placed after the former. Now we are no longer contemplating an abbot free to make himself the rule of this monastery, using for this purpose whatever would please him in the *regulae Patrum*, but rather of an abbot who must submit himself to a determined rule just as did the first successors of the Master and Benedict.[76] In this perspective, the rule does not emanate from the abbot, but exists independently of him and before him. He receives it and must conform himself to it.

At first blush, the couplet rule-abbot constitutes a formula of complete and balanced government. The law serves as a foundation and as a guide to the authority of the head which prevents it from decaying or degenerating into tyranny. Reciprocally, personal

---

75. See above, note 18.
76. RM 93:15; RB 3:11; 64:20. Cf. Caesarius, *Reg. uirg.* 47, 64.

authority allows the law to remain at the service of life and of the Spirit, without extinguishing it or becoming a dead letter. As time never ceases to bring with it new problems and modify the conditions for which the rule has been written, it is indispensable that this should be continually completed, interpreted, even corrected, by a living person.

Two Modes of the Presence of Christ

However, the rule and the abbot are not only the two pillars of a political and wisely tempered constitution. Beyond this natural meaning attached to the formula, it is difficult for Christian ears not to detect the echo of another couplet of an almost antithetical character which occupies a well-known place in the Pauline epistles: the Law and Christ. Indeed, on this point, the Master and Benedict are formal: the abbot represents Christ.[77] On its side, the rule is for them a "law,"[78] and we have noted from the beginning of this study that the resonances of such an appellation would always be present, at each epoch, for the readers of the Old and the New Testament.[79] Today more than ever, we would be inclined without doubt to consider law, that is to say, the rule, with a suspicious eye, sensitive as we are to the proclamation of Christian liberty as made by St Paul. We know indeed that Christ has freed us from the curse of the Law.[80] The living authority, that of a man who speaks in the name of Christ, is this not for us the only authority that is acceptable?

Without entering into a profound examination of the question, let us simply remark that the idea of law is far from having lost all its importance after Christ. Certainly, it is in the Person of the Son that it has pleased God to offer his ultimate revelation to the human race and thus to save it. Person, and not law, is then the center of Christianity. But law does not cease to exist for all of this. It only became, from the time of Christ, subordinated to that Person and has been endowed with a personal character: henceforth it will be

77. RM 2:2; RB 2:2; 63:13.
78. RM 93:15: *legem Dei hanc regulam* (cf. RM 10:72–73); RB 58:10, 15.
79. See above, note 2; cf. note 31.
80. Gal 3:13.

called the "law of Christ,"[81] for Christ is the one who gives it,[82] and is the one for whom it is observed, its origin and its end. Hence there is no reason to oppose rule and abbot, law and person, as if the first was only some anachronistic left-over from the Old Covenant and that the second alone would represent Christ. Such an opposition would be all the more unfounded since the Patristic Age, whence comes this formula *sub regula uel abbate,* was fond of considering the New Covenant itself as a "law."[83] Moreover, we have seen that the rules have their historical origin and their religious foundation in the teaching of Christ and of the Apostles which they aim simply at concretizing for the use of this or that monastic community. It follows from this that the rule as well as the abbot can and ought to be regarded as emanating from Christ and representing him. Both the *regula* and the *abbas* are two modalities of the one and unique presence of Christ.

God is, in fact, both Law and Persons.[84] Christ also is the Incarnate Word, the eternal Law made flesh and at the same time the divine Person of the Son in the nature of man. These two aspects of Christ, the Law and the Person, manifest themselves in the rule and in the abbot. Both of these principles of cenobitic authority are equally sacred, equally important. Christ is not present in his fullness in the monastery unless these two elements are united.

The Relation of the Two Principles

This manner of uniting the rule and the abbot, by referring both of them to Christ, is certainly that of the ancient monks whose thought we have to try to penetrate. Neither the Master nor Benedict, nor any monastic author seem to have opposed these

81. Gal 6:2.

82. One may think here of the iconographic theme of the Patristic Age: *Christus legem dat.*

83. Cf. preceding note. See also RM Th:23 and the note. When Benedict wishes the abbot to be *doctum lege diuina* (RB 64:9; cf. RM 15:35), he is thinking certainly of the New Testament as well as the Old.

84. As regards the eternal law, *summa ratio in Deo existens,* see St Thomas Aquinas, *Summa Theologiae,* I-II, q. 93, a. 1, which is based on St Augustine.

principles. Putting aside certain tensions of which we shall soon speak, the harmony between the rule and the abbot is, for all, the natural, normal and almost constant perspective.

The abbot is the minister of the rule which he should read and comment upon for the postulant,[85] and impose on the community day after day and year after year.[86] In it, after the Holy Scriptures,[87] he finds the principal source of his doctrine. What the Master calls *ars sancta* and Benedict calls *instrumenta bonorum operum,* is nothing else but a collection of maxims positively meant to serve the abbot as a guide in his teaching.[88] More generally, the entire rule is both the book of the master and the manual of the students in this *scola Christi* which is the monastery. Inversely, the rule establishes the authority of the abbot and defends it, both against activity from the outside[89] and insubordination on the part of the monks.[90]

The Weaknesses of the Abbot

This habitual alliance of these two powers, however, knows some vicissitudes, either through the weakness of the abbot or from the insufficiency of the rule. It can happen, first of all, that the abbot is derelict in his duty and disobeys the rule.[91] In this regard, the Master and Benedict differ. The former never foresees any such eventuality, the abbot and his subalterns being thought impeccable. Contrariwise, Benedict becomes rather disturbed at the failings to which superiors are subject. He puts the abbot on his guard against such faults, enjoining him to obey the rule in all things.[92] This

---

85. RM 87:3; 90:5, 64. RB 58:9, 12, 13. In Benedict it is not certain if the reading of the Rule was done by the abbot in person, as in the Master.

86. See note 76 above.

87. RM 15:35; RB 64:9. Cf. RM 2:4–5 = RB 2:4–5: Scripture, called *praeceptum Domini* and *iustitia diuina,* should be the norm for the teaching of the abbot.

88. RM 2:51.   89. RM 83:7.

90. RM 93:43–45 and 69–70; RB 62:2–11; 65:1–22.

91. Caesarius, *Reg. uirg.* 47, 64; Aurelian, *Reg. mon.* 43; *Reg. cujusdam* 20.

92. Faults of the abbot: RB 2:33; 3:6, 11; 4:61; 61:13; 63:2; 64:16; 65:22. That the abbot should obey the Rule: RB 3:11; 64:20.

attitude is the fruit of experience which has shown to the legislator that there is indeed reason to be fearful of incapable and unworthy superiors. At the end of the century, the Letters and the *Dialogues* of Gregory will attest to the seriousness of this danger. It is evident that such a state of affairs would certainly influence the balance of the couplet rule-abbot. As time reveals the frailty of the superiors, the prestige of the rule will consequently grow, its strict observance appearing as the only means to palliate the weakness of abbots and to save the monasteries from decline.

The Weaknesses of the Rule

The abbot, however, is not always the only one at fault. If, in principle, the rule cannot be at fault, it sometimes happens that it is no longer adapted to the circumstances and can no longer furnish answers to the questions posed by real life situations. It is self-evident that in such a case the abbot ought to supply for the rule, but the legislators have not all foreseen this eventuality.

Once again we come across a difference in the two authors, the Master and Benedict. The Master for all practical purposes does not allow much liberty to the abbot.[93] His Rule is so precise and so detailed that a superior who is bound to follow it would scarcely ever have the occasion of deciding something by himself. On the contrary, the Rule of Benedict leaves a certain margin for the initiative of the abbot. This is not merely the result of abridgment which prevents the legislator from entering into too many details and obliges him to create a certain amount of imprecision. Besides this *de facto* situation, the Rule of Benedict also explicitly appeals to the judgment of the abbot in several cases.

In the place of himself indicating all that should be confided to the care of a *custos*, as the Master did in his Rule, Benedict invites the abbot to share all this among several guardians "as he will judge suitable."[94] Instead of simply determining, as does the Master, what the brethren should wear in winter and in summer, Benedict

93. See *La Règle du Maître,* 1:121, notes 1–2.
94. RB 32:1–2. Cf. RM 17.

begins his chapter *De vestiario* with a short preamble which makes this a decision of the abbot, taking into account climatic conditions. The suggestions which he will then give are not imperative. It is simply a question of indicating what the clothing might be in a "moderate" region.[95] At the end of the same chapter, Benedict confides to the abbot the care of distributing all the necessary objects "to each one according to his needs" thus conforming to the sentence of the Acts of the Apostles so dear to Augustine.[96] "Unequal,"[97] this distribution supposes that the abbot will take into consideration the particular needs of each person.[98] This is something that goes beyond the prevision of the legislator. The living person alone, the superior, is both to discern them and to satisfy them. This is something that the Master does not think of and thus he limits himself to regulate in his Rule those things which the brethren ought to receive.

In Benedict then there is a new sense of diversity, either of places or of persons, and this leads him to stand back as it were behind the living authority of the abbot in charge. Thus the abbot's authority can extend itself into the field left free by the Rule. Consequently, if both Rules define cenobitism by the couplet *regula-abbas*, it would seem that the accent would be somewhat heavier on the Rule for the Master, and on the abbot for Benedict, at least if the real power of each element is taken into consideration.

If we associate the two points we have just made, we can say that in comparison to the Master, Benedict is both less sure of the abbot and more liberal towards him. If he insists on the abbot's obedience to the Rule, he also grants him a new latitude for personal decision in certain cases. This freedom left to the superiors is without doubt one of the reasons for the historical success of the

95. RB 55:1–6. Cf. RM 81.   96. RB 55:18–22.   97. RB 34:T.

98. RB 34:1–5; 55:21. It is probably to this solicitude of the abbot for individual cases that RB 22:2 has reference to: *Lectisternia pro modo conuersationis secundum dispensationem abbatis sui accipiant.* Cf. RM 81:31–33 and RB 55:15 which simply indicates bedding suitable for all. Benedict even invites the abbot to see that the habits fit those by whom they are to be worn (RB 55:8). The Master never thought of this.

Rule of Benedict. By it that Rule was more supple and more adaptable than the Rule of the Master. Evidently, Benedict could not foresee the advantage that his work would have down the centuries. Nevertheless, this unforeseen success is due to an understanding of local and personal situations which seem to be a quality proper to Benedict when one compares him to the Master.

CONCLUSIONS AND APPLICATIONS

The Three Meanings of "Regula"

These considerations on the couplet rule-abbot will have a validity, as will be remembered, only in the particular case of an abbot subject to a written and well-determined rule. It is now important to enlarge once again our perspective and by way of a conclusion to also see in a general view all the different realities which have come into focus in the course of this study. We can do this by placing side by side the three principal meanings of the word *regula* which we have encountered up to this point.

Regula can mean first of all the authority of the abbot himself. As we have learned from Jerome, from Sulpicius Severus, from the biographer of Fulgentius, from Gregory the Great, this principle of authority can suffice to characterize in a summary fashion the cenobitic life. To live *sub regula* means then nothing else than obeying an abbot, who is the depository and the organ of tradition, the living rule of his monastery.

In the second place, *regula* can mean the "common rule" of all the *coenobia*, that *disciplina coenobiorum* which, according to Cassian, goes back to the Apostles. It is thus a question of tradition itself, inseparable from Holy Scripture. Apart from Scripture, the *regula* does not evoke, as in the preceding meaning, any notion of written text. "Universal" and "apostolic," it remains at the same time oral. Of course, we cannot give credence to Cassian when he asserts the apostolic origin of the *coenobia* and the unity conserved by Egyptian cenobitism since its origin. But the concept of a common rule of cenobitism which he developed from these theses is far from being proper to him alone for it is a question of a reality perceived and expressed by more than one author after him.[99]

Finally, the word *regula* can designate a written rule,[100] proper to a particular time and place, to a monastery or a group of monasteries. Such would be, among many others, the Rule of the Master and the Rule of Benedict. In this case, the *regula* is not all tradition, but it is a particular crystalization of it. It does not identify itself any longer with the authority of the abbot, but forms with him a couplet of complementary forces. The written rule, once it has gone beyond its primitive framework, can enter besides into a new relationship, either with the authority of the abbot, or with tradition. Having become one of the *regulae Patrum* it takes on a value proper to a traditional monument, in the midst of a group of analogous documents which each individual legislator or abbot should know, respect and use with discernment.

The first two realities covered by the word *regula* are both absolutely indispensable. No Christian community can exist without this law which flows from the Gospels and this personal authority which represents Christ.[101] One might even say that these two elements are sufficient in themselves. Many monastic writers,

---

99. In particular by Gregory, Ep. 5:1 = R 5:1: *monachica regula;* Ep 5:33 = R 5:33 and *Hom. Eu.* 38:15: *regularis districtio;* Ep. 7:35 = R 7:32 and Ep. 8:9 = R 8:9: *regularis disciplina;* Ep. 9:37 = R 9:107: *regularis ordo;* Ep. 8:5 = R 8:10: *norma regularis; Hom. Eu.* 38:16: *regulariter;* Dial. 2:3: *regularis uitae custodia,* etc. Same ref. to the common rule of monks in Bede, *Vita Cuthberti* 16; PL 94:754b: *regula monachicae perfectionis;* 754c: *monachica . . . regula* (Bede cites Gregory, Ep. 11:64; PL 77:1184b: *monasterii regulis,* a text of doubtful authenticity, cf. Jaffe, 1843); 755a: *instituta monachica* and *regularis custodia;* 755b: *regula.*

100. In order to be complete it would still be necessary to distinguish from this the particular rule of a monastery, but a non-written one, which seems to have been the rule instituted by Honoratus at Lerins (see note 52 above). If it is a question of a non-written rule, it could not become a monument of tradition.

101. Even Basil who scarcely insists on the role of the superior as the representative of God cites Lk 10:16 ("Who hears you, hears me."), in R 70; PL 103:519b = PR 38; PG 31:110b.

beginning with Cassian,[102] do not even conceive of a written rule, and many monasteries before the sixth century and even afterwards went without a written rule completely.

The third reality, the written rule, is not then necessary and is still less self-sufficient. However, it can be very useful, either to concretize the universal rule according to particular conditions which obtain in this or that community,[103] or to aid the abbot in establishing his authority and guiding him in the use of this authority or, finally, by its posthumous role, if one may so speak, when its author becomes a member of the venerable senate of the Fathers and continues to exercise a more or less marked influence on the cenobitic movement.

A Contemporary Problem: the Rule of Benedict and Ourselves

These general conclusions will permit us to bring forth one last question: What is the Rule of Benedict for us today? Written as it was for some Italian monasteries in the sixth century, can it still, properly speaking, be the rule of our monasteries in the twentieth century, scattered all over the surface of the earth and placed in a very different cultural milieu? Under the second form, the question would evoke quite evidently a negative response: the Rule of St Benedict has not been written for us and in the proper meaning of the word, it cannot be our rule.

For the rest, without wishing the monks of today to put themselves at a greater distance from the Rule of Benedict than they have already done, it seems to me that simple honesty obliges us to recognize that the Rule of Benedict, *in fact*, is not our rule.

---

102. It is true that in writing the Insti., Cassian's thought was to furnish the monasteries of the West with the rule they needed (see note 47 above). In fact, Bks. 1–4 will be transformed into the *Regula Cassiani*. It remains that the *regula monasteriorum* which he applied himself to describe (Insti., Pref. 8; 1:1, 2, 3; 3:1, etc.) is a "common" and "universal" rule.

103. For Benedict, this first role of the rule consists more precisely, given the state of decadence of contemporary monasticism, in establishing the minimum of common observances which are absolutely necessary. Cf. RB 18:22–25; 40:6; 49:1–2; 73:1–9. On the relation of this concept of the rule to that of the law in Cassian, see above, note 31.

Half or three-quarters of the code are no longer in practice and we observe a quantity of laws and usages that come from elsewhere.

It will be said that while abandoning the material element in many of the observances, we keep at least the spirit of St Benedict, the spirit of the Rule. An easy and fallacious distinction! Where is the spirit if not in the observance which incarnates the spirit? Furthermore, we would deceive ourselves in believing that the Prologue and the first seven chapters of the Rule remain for us a heritage completely intact. Not so! The doctrine of these treatises is, in fact, as different from our real spirituality as the prescriptions of the following chapters are from our behavior. Certainly we practice obedience, but is it really the prompt obedience, unconditional and without reflection, which is proposed in Chapter Five of the Rule of Benedict? We practice silence, but is it for the two motives indicated in Chapter Six of the Rule of Benedict? We practice humility, thanks be to God, but how meaningful for us are the last four degrees on the Benedictine ladder—those eyes cast down to the ground, that gravity, that abstention from laughter, that silence which is maintained until one is questioned?

The facts, therefore, verify, whether we wish it or not, what reflection would permit us to infer. The Rule of Benedict does not play in our monasteries the role of a rule properly so called, as was the case for Monte Cassino about the year 550, because it neither could nor was meant to play such a role. Like all other rules similar to it, it has ceased with the passage of time to fulfill the function of a rule in the strict sense of the word while taking on another function. What the Rule is for us now is somewhat akin to what it was for the Frankish monasteries of the seventh century or for the legislators who used these various rules in their own compilation: a monument of tradition, a part of our heritage and our treasury, a source of our rule. Or to express it in a better way: rather than one source among many, it is in truth *the* source of our rule, to an eminent degree which puts it above all the other traditional documents.

As the reader may have observed, what I have called "our rule" is the law which our monasteries observe in fact and which differs with each one of them. When I do this I am conscious of the fact that I am thereby separating myself from the accepted terminology according to which all the monks live "under the Rule of St Benedict," but who are free to complete and modify this unique and immutable "Rule" by a multiform and variable legislation: Declarations, Constitutions, Decrees of Chapters, usages and customs of monasteries and congregations. I do not wish to contest the ground of this juridical fiction but only to point out that it is fictitious in character. If we consider the true role of a rule, to effectively regulate the common life, it would be necessary to say that our rule consists in the Declarations, Constitutions and other laws which are really normative for us, while the Rule of Benedict is the source of this concrete rule we observe.

The Rule of Benedict: Mirror of Tradition

When we do this we do not diminish the authority of the Benedictine Rule but we define it more exactly. There is no question of weakening the influence of this venerable Rule. On the contrary, it should be listened to today with all the more attention as we are attempting to infuse a new life into monasticism.

Several reasons would suggest that the Rule should keep its role as a privileged monument of tradition, the only one which it has in reality played for many centuries. First of all, there is the historical fact of paramount importance: the Rule of St Benedict, conjointly with his Life, has constantly exercised, from the Frankish seventh century down to our own day, an incomparable influence on the monasteries of the West. It has become a common denominator and a common language for all generations and a veritable axis of an entire tradition.

As regards this first title which remains in the extrinsic order, there might be added the exceptional value of the Rule of Benedict as a witness to ancient monasticism and cenobitism. It is in fact a remarkably clear mirror of the monastic life of the first centuries. The image which it reflects is not complete, certainly, but it would be difficult to find a Latin document which would be as representative as is the Rule of Benedict. Depending mostly on the Master, and through him also on Cassian, Benedict borrows also from other traditions, from the work of Augustine notably. Of considerable amplitude, when one compares it with the majority of its sisters,[104] the Rule of Benedict is relatively complete and organic, very rare qualities among the ancient rules, and Benedict owes this without doubt to the remarkable framework furnished by the Master. At the same time, Benedict completes and corrects the all too simple, almost absurd, schema of the latter, in particular by the new attention which he gives to fraternal relationships.

The Rule of Benedict has then considerable value, perhaps unique, as a representation of the cenobitic life of the first generations. This quality of its historical witness constitutes in all probability its principal advantage. In any case, to ask this excellent image of the past to give what it is able to give seems to me more fruitful and more secure than to boast of some of its other privileges and advantages which are more or less unverifiable, be it "an abbreviated doctrine of the Gospel"—may Bossuet forgive me!— or as a specific remedy for the evils of our time. In order to recommend it to men who in our time wish to be monks, there is no need to attach to it some intemporal quality or some particular affinity to contemporary man. It suffices that it is in fact one of the best images which can come to us from the origins of this monastic movement to which we pretend to belong.

We are indeed vowed by our profession, we monks of the twentieth century, to this historical form of religious life which has developed in the Church since the fourth century and which is called monasticism. Far from diluting its original content into a mixture in the fashion of today, it is rather necessary to purify and strengthen it according to the suggestions of our own tradition if we wish to be something of interest and of use in the Church today. What the Church expects of us is not that we place ourselves in unison with a standardized religious life, but that we take our

---

104. Out of thirty such rules, the RB is the third longest (after the Master and Basil). It exceeds by almost a third the Rule of Donatus which is the fourth longest and which is itself much longer than those which follow (Pachomius, Waldebert, Isidore, Ferreol and Caesarius).

own proper and irreplaceable part as monks in the contemporary chorus of voices which sing to the Lord.

It is thus a matter of our redoubling the intelligent fidelity to the monastic tradition from which we have issued, of understanding it and cultivating it not only in the spirit, but also—and here let it be remembered that monasticism is essentially a practice—in its institutions and fundamental observances of which this spirit has need in order to express itself.[105] This is why a document such as the Rule of Benedict is more precious to us and more indispensable than ever. This Rule is indeed the best means at our disposal for remaining in contact, either with the primitive tradition which it has rather happily gathered together, or with the later tradition which it has so strongly influenced.

To Unite Benedict and the Fathers

One should not believe, however, that the Rule alone is sufficient to render such a service. To suitably fulfill the function of a mirror of the ancient monasticism, the Rule of Benedict should not be considered solely and independently of all other ancient monastic literature of which it is a part. For too long a time we have been content, we sons of St Benedict, both Black and White Monks, to read it in isolation without taking care to consider its sources and parallels, or what amounts to the same thing, with the view of opposing it to these latter. It was thought that St Benedict was being given added grandeur when there was attributed to him a

---

105. It would be necessary to suspect certain overly simple distinctions: spirit and institutions, tradition and historicity. I can hardly believe it possible to separate the spirit from the institutions, to isolate a pure tradition, detached from all historical contingency. In fact, the two elements are inseparable in a great measure. Historicity cannot and should not be conceived as a garment that the spirit puts on and takes off at will, while still remaining itself. This would be something akin to docetism. The Incarnation goes much further. If there is something intemporal in tradition which survives certain passing realizations, one should not overlook the fact that the historical forms themselves are bearers of spiritual elements which can appear only in such concrete institutions.

F

"revolution in monachism."[106] In this perspective, it would seem to be legitimate to take the Rule of Benedict alone, as a solitary masterpiece sufficient in itself. Such an attitude, however, would lead us to read into the Rule of Benedict whatever one would wish to find there, to project upon this ancient work the tendencies of modern spirituality. Isolated from his milieu, Benedict would appear without any difficulty as a precursor who would have genially anticipated the concepts which hold sway today. This would shore up the original message of the Fathers for whom Benedict wished to be nothing more than the spokesman.

It is then necessary to preserve for the Benedictine Rule its privileged place, but this must be done by situating it in the ensemble of patristic literature from which it cannot be separated. The Rule of Benedict obtains all its meaning from the fact that it is a synthesis of ancient cenobitism. Now this synthesis cannot be perceived as such nor correctly interpreted unless its elements are known. A fruitful reading of the Rule of Benedict supposes as a consequence that it is to be clarified as much as possible by those documents which belong with it. Thus it would be no longer considered as a manifesto of a school of new spirituality and the instigator of our own modes of thought but rather as a vehicle of an ancient monastic attitude of mind, alien in some way from our modern spirits, which ought to inform and fecundate these, sometimes even by provocation.

In this taking the Rule of Benedict *with* the other writings of the Fathers, we will draw from its reading a real enrichment. Reciprocally, this Rule will assert itself as an excellent guide for penetrating into the world of the ancient monks. Nothing facilitates such a penetration so much as the recognition by heart, and here is meant not only by memory but cordially, of a limited text, but a very full one as is the Rule of Benedict. It is a fact that the monk who has listened to the Rule thirty or forty times, who loves it and willingly goes back to it in his search for God—it is a fact that such

106. C. Butler, *Benedictine Monachism,* 2 ed. (New York: Barnes & Noble, 1924), p. 45. See my ed. of RB, Intro. 1, 1, no. 6.

a man is marvelously prepared to listen to and assimilate the teaching of the Fathers.

An Example: the Question of the Habit

In conclusion, I would like to illustrate the necessity of reading the Rule of St Benedict *with* the literature which it represents by means of a precise example. This example is furnished to me by the question of the habit. Modest in appearance, this question takes on real importance for monks and nuns, for the way in which a man or woman dresses expresses what they wish to be in society, and by the fact what they really are in their heart and soul. The monastic life, let it be repeated, cannot by-pass such signs, and it is a fact that the habit has always been an integral part of the monastic life.[107]

If we consult only the Rule of Benedict on this point, we will hardly find anything there except a list of articles of clothing which are to be worn by the monks: *tunica, cuculla, scapulare, etc.*[108] If the Rule does give some directives, very useful in themselves, on the adaptation to the climate and adoption of the material which is the easiest to obtain in the locality, it does not give any indication on the meaning and the sense of the religious habit and on the general norms to which it should respond.

Consequently, the modern monk who contents himself with reading the Rule of Benedict will not find there an adequate answer to the questions which have been posed in our own days. Taken in isolation, the Benedictine text can only lead him to debatable solutions. There will be variations in the letter according to the subjective interpretations of the text which will suggest to the monk his own personal inclinations.

If he is conservative, he will find satisfaction in the fact that we

107. See the study of P. Marie-Felix, *Recherche et réflexions à propos de l'habit monastique* (Sept-Fons, 1970). We share the author's opinion, but we would insist more clearly on the opportuneness of a reform of the monastic habit. In our opinion, it is necessary and sufficient that the monks of today *have a habit* which presents the principal characteristics indicated by St Basil.

108. RB 55:1–14.

still wear the pieces of clothing indicated by Benedict: "tunic," "cowl," "scapular." Unhappily, as is well-known, only the names correspond exactly to what Benedict indicates in his rule. The things themselves are very much different, whether it is a question of the cut and shape of these garments or of the use we make of them. More than that, our modern monastic wardrobe contains a quantity of objects foreign to this list which are hidden under the "monastic clothing" or cover it, or what is more often the case, replace it.

The monastic habit which we wear in fact has only a pseudo-fidelity to the Rule which cannot be satisfying except for the less demanding of spirits. Along the same line, some more enlightened monks might be found who would look for ways to restore the authentic form and usage of the garments listed by Benedict. Even supposing that this was materially within the bounds of realization, the attempt would lead us to an artificial restoration at which one could only smile.

At the other extreme, one can hear it said that the habit as it is prescribed by the Rule was simply what was worn by the peasants in the environs of Monte Cassino and, consequently, the monks of today should dress exactly like secular workmen who live around us, retaining only a choir robe to be put on over the secular clothes when they go to pray in choir. Benedict does in fact seem to lend support to this theory when he prescribes that the used articles of clothing should be put into the wardrobe *propter pauperes*:[109] if the clothing was to be worn by a poor man would not the article necessarily have the ordinary appearance of what was actually being worn by people in the world?

Here we put a finger on the insufficiency of a strict exegesis of the Rule which would consider it in isolation and does not take into account all the ambient literature.[110] To cite only two witnesses

109. RB 55:9.

110. Such is unfortunately the case of the article by D. De Bruyne, "Note sur le costume bénédictine primitif," *Rev. Bénédictine* 33 (1921): 55–61. It is regrettable that this study would be made an authority and serve to justify decisions in this matter.

close to Benedict, one before him and one after him, neither the
Master nor Gregory would allow it to be called into doubt that
the monastic habit of their time, as close as it was to the clothing
of poor men, still did not have some distinguishing trait which
would separate it clearly from all secular clothing. The Master says
that by the reception of the habit, the postulant appears in the eyes
of all as the property of God.[111] Worn outside the cloister, the
"holy habit" drew to itself the veneration of pious persons and the
ridicule of the faithless.[112]

As far as Gregory is concerned, he habitually characterized the
entrance into religion and monastic profession by expressions such
as *sanctae conuersationis habitum quaerere*,[113] *conuersationis habitum
suscipere*,[114] *monachicum habitum . . . suscipere*,[115] *monachicum habitum
sumere*,[116] *religiosam vestem induere*.[117] His other references to the

---

111. RM 90:74–76. Strictly speaking, *omnibus* (90:76), can mean the brothers
of the monastery: those alone would recognize the new brother as one of their
own. Still this recognition implies that the habit, in one way or another,
makes the brother known for what he is.

112. RM 95:19–21. It will be noted that the articles of clothing enumerated
in RM 81 are almost the same as those mentioned in RB 55. The only original
piece of clothing in the Master is the *pallium*. Would this piece of clothing be
the distinctive element by which the monk would be recognized? In this case,
its absence from the clothing list mentioned in RB 55 would serve to confirm
the thesis of D. De Bruyne. It is certain that the wearing of the *pallium*
characterized the monk (Conc. of Gangres, can. 12 = no. 70; PL 67:158c), to
such a point that *pallium accepisse* meant "to become a monk" (Conc. of
Orleans I [511], can. 21; Mansi, 8:347). However, the *pallium* is far from
figuring in all the descriptions of monastic habits given by the ancient texts
(see our ed. of RB, Commentary, 7, 3, notes 122–135), and it is doubtful that
it was the only piece of clothing by which the monks were characterized. The
texts of Gregory cited below attest that the monks were recognized by their
habit. The absence of the *pallium* would change nothing of this. At the most
its absence would make it easier to distribute the used garments to the poor
(RB 55:9).

113. Gregory, Dial. 2, Prol.; Moricca 72:3–4, which corresponds to Dial.
2:1 (76:7): *ei sanctae conuersationis habitum tradidit.*

114. Dial. 3:21 (188:21–22). It is a question of a nun living alone.

115. Gregory, Ep. 8:5–R 8:10. The context twice mentions *ecclesiasticus
habitus.*

116. Ep. 12:3 = R 9:114.   117. Ep. 10:32 = R 9:3.

"habit of the monk,"[118] "the monastic habit,"[119] "their habit,"[120] show abundantly that the monastic state meant for him the wearing of a distinctive apparel. It is difficult to see how Benedict could separate himself from a usage in his own day and age so well known and accepted and understood: the monk should be defined by his habit. If there is a phrase of his which might give a contrary impression,[121] this fact only shows up what errors can be made in any attempt to interpret the Rule without reference to contemporary documents.

If instead of limiting oneself to the remarks of the Rule of Benedict, one would turn towards the great authors, the reading of which Benedict himself recommended, there will be found among several of them exposés which would furnish one with what is being sought: a *doctrine* of the habit. Certainly, the allegorizing consideration of Cassian will be rather useless for us,[122] but a passage of the Basilian Rule responds exactly to our expectations.[123]

According to Basil the habit should be simple and poor, suitable for manual labor. It should distinguish a Christian consecrated to God from other men, in such a way that this consecration is recalled constantly to his mind. It ought to be the same for all the brothers, as a sign of fraternity and of their common service to the Lord. It should also be the same for all circumstances, whether in the monastery or outside of it, for the man who thus clothes himself is simply himself in the gift of his entire being to God. Let it be

118. Ep. 12:24 = R 12:6: *habitus monachi.*

119. Ep. 1:34 = R 1:33: *sub monachico habitu.* Cf. Ep. 7:32 = R 7:29: *sub sanctitatis habitu.*

120. Ep. 11:36 = R 11:25: *ad habitum suum redire.* Cf. Ep. 8:9 = R 8:9: *religiosis uestibus . . . religiosum habitum.*

121. It will be noted that RB 55:9 does not necessarily mean that *all* the articles of monastic clothing could be worn just as they are by the poor. Distribution of clothing to the poor: see Caesarius, *Reg. uirg.* 43 (the used clothing of the nuns); Gregory, Dial. 4:23; Moricca 261:10: the abbot Soranus gives to the refugees *uestimenta sua ac fratrum omnia.*

122. Cassian, Insti. 1.

123. Basil, R 11; PL 103:502–504 = GR 22–23; PG 31:977–981.

noted in passing that Basil did not envisage a special garment for prayer. The other ancient legislators did not think in such terms either. In their eyes, the monk is consecrated to God without reserve, and the distinction of profane and sacred does not make sense to him.

It is principles such as these of which we have need, it would seem, in order to resolve in a suitable way the question of the habit and other similar problems which at the present time are presenting themselves. Sometimes the Rule of Benedict does give us these principles, and when it does not, it refers us to other sources where we will find the principles we need. The aim of the Rule is not to have us stop at itself, but rather to introduce us to the writings of the Fathers wherein is displayed the fullness of the traditional doctrine.[124]

Adalbert de Vogüé OSB

Pierre-qui-vire,
France

DISCUSSION

There was general agreement with many of the points in Fr de Vogüé's paper. Some found especially helpful the distinction between the Rule as a legislative code and the Rule as a monument of tradition, but not all agreed as to the precise way Father applied this distinction.

In the discussion which followed several questions were proposed: 1) How will the community interpret the Rule and what will be the role of the abbot in this effort of the community? 2) Is the difference between the authorship of rules in the early centuries by an individual and in contemporary times by a group not a normal evolution due to the fact that we have become aware of the responsibility of the community as such? 3) If the written Rule is neither sufficient nor necessary for monastic life, could not the opportuneness of such a written rule be questioned in our times of constant and rapid evolution?

Fr de Vogüé placed emphasis on the abbot as having the charism for interpreting the Rule. Yet it was maintained that the community also had

124. See RB 73.

its role in the task of interpretation. Each member of the community has the charism of his own call or vocation, just as the community as a whole has its charism. The abbot needs to be aware of the community and in harmony with it in exercising his charism. He has no monopoly on charism. In a word neither the Rule nor any interpretation of it should be merely imposed upon all by the superior. There must be collaboration between the community and the abbot in making decisions, but there must also be leadership, one who can exercise authority. One should not treat the abbot and community as if they were two distinct entities. They are closely interrelated. The abbot retains the role of teacher, a teacher of life who assists the community in making decisions in the Holy Spirit.

The fact that a rule was written by an individual did not preclude the fact that it also had to be received and accepted by a community in order that its authority might be truly efficacious.

A rule and the Rule retain their value even today. Dom de Vogüé saw the vow of "*conversatio morum secundum regulam S. Benedicti*" as a promise to live according to monastic tradition, using RB as a guide to understand that monastic tradition. The Rule is one interpretation of Scripture, it is a partial interpretation, yet it is a valid one. No epoch can pretend to have and to live the fullness of the Scriptures; such a fullness can never be embraced by any one period.

Some saw the Decree on Unity and Pluralism (Cistercian General Chapter, 1969—see Appendix II) as an excellent expression of the role the Rule should play in Cistercian life. By a prudent adaptation in the application of RB to changing circumstances, the abbot and community prevent it from smothering life while employing it as a means for welcoming the Spirit who will lead monks to an intuitive perception of the monastic ideal which they share with St Benedict.

In the course of the discussion Fr de Vogüé indicated some other significant conclusions emerging from his extensive study:

—one can assume that St Benedict gives the same meaning to a text as the author of the RM unless there are contrary indications.

—there are no positive reasons for questioning the authorship of RB; few documents of the early periods are as well authenticated.

—RB was the fruit of a lived experience, developed over a period of time; it was not written all at once.

A SCRIPTURE SCHOLAR LOOKS AT THE RULE OF ST BENEDICT

I HAVE BEEN INVITED TO PROPOSE ANSWERS to two questions in this essay. First: what do Scripture scholars do to discover the timely and timeless message of a document that was written many, many centuries ago? Second: how would a Scripture scholar comment on St Benedict's use of Sacred Scripture? To be perfectly frank, I was both honored and dismayed by Father Basil's graciously worded and gently persuasive invitation. I disclaim at once the title of scholar. To be sure of my reasons for avoiding a term that seemed to me to denote great learning, extensive erudition, unusual competence, special expertise I betook myself to a dictionary and found that "scholar" can mean many things including the humble claim of "one who can read and write." As a scholar, therefore, as one who has read a lot and written a little I now address you reluctantly because: 1) I can claim the distinction of being the one in this room who knows the least about the Rule of St Benedict; 2) my own experience is more in the line of Biblical theology.

My talk will be divided into three parts: Scripture scholarship in the sixth century; Scripture scholarship in the twentieth century; Scripture as I see it in the Rule of St Benedict.

SCRIPTURE SCHOLARSHIP IN THE SIXTH CENTURY

Scripture scholarship in Italy in the sixth century shines with no clear and distinctive light. Internal disturbances within the Italian peninsula, caused and increased by barbarian invasions, with all the consequent economic maladjustments, continuing political dissensions and the consolidation of new and rival forces in Constantinople did not provide a suitable situation for advances in learning. But few historians today would concur with the once widely held opinion of this and later centuries:

> We approach the subject of medieval exegesis with every desire to judge it in the kindliest spirit; but we are compelled to say that during the Dark Ages, from the seventh to the twelfth century, and during the scholastic epoch, from the twelfth to the sixteenth, there are but a few of the many who toiled in this field who added a single essential principle or furnished a single original contribution to the explanation of the Word of God. During these nine centuries we find very little except the "glimmerings and decays" of patristic exposition.... Not one writer in hundreds showed any true conception of what exegesis really implies .... They give us folio volumes of dogma, morality and system, which profess to be based on Scripture, but have for the most part no real connection with the passages to which they are attached.[1]

This is not only an exaggerated, but also a totally incorrect picture.

Nineteenth- and twentieth-century research has done much to correct this once widely accepted idea. It is true that Biblical criticism as we know it does not begin until the middle of the seventeenth century. Prior to that time reverence for the inspired Word of God favored the acceptance of its record of events and its moral pronouncements regardless of their cultural and historical setting. Men failed to see the importance of the role of the sacred author, of the possibility of development of Old Testament

1. F. W. Farrar, *History of Interpretation*, Bampton Lectures, Oxford, 1888. See B. Smalley, *The Study of the Bible in the Middle Ages* (University of Notre Dame Press, 1964), pp. xii–xiii.

revelation. Criticism was dogmatic and theological. Differences due to the distance in time, place and culture between the sacred authors and their exegetes were ignored. Questions about ethnology, anthropology, archaeology and linguistics were not even asked, much less answered in the sixth century.

Yet, St Benedict and his contemporaries had much more than pieties and platitudes, "glimmerings and decays," to guide them in the use of the Bible. Many men had been working in this field for centuries. Which of these men aided him most we do not know, but there is much that was available in the sixth century. For example, it was Marcion (ca. 150) who challenged his second-century contemporaries by rejecting all of the Old Testament and much of the New, forcing the Church to take a definite position and affirm the contents of the canon as St Benedict knew it and we know it today. Another pioneer was Tatian (ca. 175) who wove the strands of the four Gospels into a single, continuous narrative. His *Diatesseron* did much to influence the art and prayer of the early medieval centuries. Origen may serve as an example of one who was concerned with establishing a true Biblical text. The great Alexandrian (ca. 185–254) made some notable contributions to Scripture scholarship. His six-columned edition of Old Testament books marked the beginning of Old Testament textual criticism. This *Hexapla Biblia*, or sixfold book, in most manuscript copies that we possess was usually arranged in six vertical columns: (1) the Hebrew consonantal text which had been standardized two centuries earlier; (2) this text transliterated into Greek characters; (3) Aquila's Greek translation of the Hebrew made about 130 AD; (4) Symmachus' independent translation made fifty years later; (5) the Septuagint, a good edition; and (6) the Theodotian Old Testament, compiled largely of recensional material which had been prepared in the first century.

These few examples show that St Jerome had wide possibilities open to him when, at the request of Pope Damasus at the close of the fourth century, beginning of the fifth, he began to work on the Latin Vulgate. In fact Jerome, who died in the year 419, declared that in his day there were "as many forms (of the Latin text of the Bible) as there were readers."[2] Jerome's Old Testament was a correction and adaptation of the Old Latin with emendations suggested by the best Greek manuscripts.

What evidence is there in the Rule as to what Biblical text St Benedict used? I can summarize much research briefly and inconclusively: (1) Vulgate—though not yet in universal use—especially passages found in lectionaries; (2) *Vetus Latina*; (3) quotations from the Rule of the Master and other Rules; (4) *Florilegia*— collections of appropriate texts; (5) quotations from the Fathers; and (6) quotations from memory. At times he quotes Scripture exactly; at other times he paraphrases; frequently, he makes verbal modifications in the text to meet the needs of his own sentence structure.

How did St Benedict and his contemporaries interpret the Bible that had been so painstakingly prepared for them? This is the question of methodology, or hermeneutics, a term most popular today. The Greek word *hermeneia* was used to describe the many steps in the work of interpretation. Reduced to its simplest elements, in the fifth century this meant the search for the different senses of Sacred Scripture. This work was begun in the early Church. Men like Justin and Tertullian did it soberly. Yet in their eagerness to locate Christological proof-texts in the Old Testament they read into many passages what they were looking for, in their exegesis going far beyond the literal meaning. Men like Clement and Origen went still further. In the Alexandrian school to which they belonged, there was a basic belief in a Christian *gnosis*, that is, the presence of an occult truth hidden behind the plain words of a text. Only an elite could reach this secret meaning. Their key was allegory. This fanciful exegesis is based on a belief that every detail of a literary composition signifies some reality. It was used by early Christian apologists who tried to show the Jews, who denied that Christ is the fulfillment of the Old Testament, that Old Testament persons, institutions or events are types, images, models, prefigurings of persons, institutions or events in the New Testament.

2. St Jerome, *Praef. in IV Evang. ad Damasum;* PL 29:526–527.

Recently several attempts have been made to re-evaluate Origen's exegesis favorably (H. de Lubac,[3] J. Daniélou[4]) but it is difficult to see that this is a move in the right direction. Fortunately for Christian spirituality Origen was much sounder in his other doctrines than in his exegesis. The same statement also seems to be true of his successor, Evagrius of Ponticus (346–399), but it was men like Hilary (d. 367), Ambrose (d. 397) and Augustine (d. 430) who ensured the popularity of the allegorical method in the West.

Augustine's words were normative in the sixth century: "The New Testament lies hidden in the Old; the Old Testament is illuminated in the New."[5] Jerome (d. 419) early fell under the influence of Origen but his later commentaries tended to stress the literal as opposed to the typical or spiritual sense.

It was John Cassian (d. 435) who supplied the final form to exegesis as we find it in the sixth century. He distinguished four senses of Sacred Scripture: (1) the historical or literal; (2) the allegorical or Christological; (3) the tropological or moral, sometimes called the anthropological; and finally (4) the anagogical or eschatological.[6] Several centuries later a Scandinavian Dominican named Augustine crystalized this doctrine of the meaning of Sacred Scripture in an often-quoted distich:

> *Littera gesta docet, quid credas allegoria,*
> *Moralis quid agas, quo tendas anagogia.*[7]

Cassian supplied a simple illustration that you probably know well. When Jerusalem is named in the Bible, in its literal sense the reference is to the Jewish city founded by David; allegorically the reference is to the Church founded by Christ; tropologically the

---

3. H. de Lubac, *Exégèse Médiévale,* Part I (Paris: Aubier, 1959), c. 3, 5, pp. 207–219.

4. J. Daniélou, *Origen,* trans. Walter Mitchell (New York: Sheed and Ward, 1955), Part 2, c. 2, pp. 139–173.

5. "*In vetere novum lateat; et in novo vetus pateat.*"—*Quaest. in Heptateuchum,* 2:73; PL 34:525.

6. Cassian, Conf. 8:3; 14:1–2.

7. H. de Lubac, *op. cit.,* Introduction, pp. 23–24.

reference is to the soul of man; anagogically the reference is to the heavenly city that is above.[8] It was these more-than-literal senses that were highly valued in the sixth century and influenced much monastic thinking and writing.

Let us turn now to the twentieth century and see how scholars look at the sacred books today.

SCRIPTURE SCHOLARSHIP IN THE TWENTIETH CENTURY

The twentieth century has been the reversal of much that was cherished fourteen centuries earlier. In his methodology the scholar today not only enjoys greater freedom, but his techniques and tools should enable him to come closer than ever before to the meaning of the original authors. Imagination is no longer allowed to dominate. The literal meaning is not neglected in a desire to express an elaborate symbolism. The *New Hermeneutic* is concerned with the way God's Word is understood by man. It draws heavily on the later philosophical writings of Martin Heidegger. However, there is a willingness on the part of many scholars in favor of a more-than-literal exegesis. As Krister Stendahl expresses it, two questions must be asked: "What *did* Scripture mean when it was written?" and "What does this text mean to me?"[9] Both explanation and understanding should be sought: historical criticism can help to explain what the meaning of the text originally was; Biblical theology can help to understand the meaning of the text to the Christian today.

Encouraged by Pope Pius XII in his 1943 encyclical, *Divino Afflante Spiritu*, the Catholic exegete sets out "to discern and define that sense of the Biblical words which is called literal . . . so that the mind of the author may be made clear."[10] Or, to put it another way: "The literal sense is the one which the author directly in-

8. Cassian, Conf. 14:8.

9. K. Stendahl, "Implications of Form-Criticism and Tradition-Criticism for Biblical Interpretation," *Journal of Biblical Literature* 20 (1958): 33–38.

10. Pius XII, *Divino Afflante Spiritu,* Sept. 30, 1943. Official English translation, Part 2, par. 23.

tended and which his words convey."[11] This means that the exegete in looking at an ancient document is concerned not only with the author's thought, but also with the message he conveys. This message should include the theological doctrines of faith and morals and the spiritual sense when it is patently intended by God, but figurative senses should not be propounded as the genuine meaning of Sacred Scripture. The exegete should employ history, archaeology, ethnology, linguistics and every other useful ancillary science that will enable him to know as much as possible about the authors, their times and their circumstances, and most especially about their language, their thought patterns and their favorite literary forms.

Another difference between the sixth and the twentieth century can be seen in the field of textual criticism. Our knowledge of the preservation and transmission of the books of the Old Testament is more detailed and accurate today than ever before. This is due to the unforeseen and startlingly valuable manuscript discoveries in the area of the Dead Sea since 1947 and the Greek papyri since 1920. It is the result of vastly improved printing and photographic techniques making possible exact and inexpensive reproductions of early and rare manuscripts. Here the New Testament scholar is much better off than the classical scholar. Textual criticism of the New Testament literature can in no way be compared with first-century Greek and Latin literature. The number of classical manuscripts earlier than the thirteenth century is scarcely more than two or three for any single author such as Vergil, Horace, Ovid. Whereas, there are more than 4,500 manuscripts of the New Testament available for scholars. Of these 240 are uncials, 2,500 are cursives, 75 are papyri; 1,800 are lectionaries (fifty-three of these lectionaries contain the entire New Testament).

Another advantage enjoyed by the Scripture scholar is the development of form criticism which seeks to study the origin and history of the pre-literary, oral tradition behind our Gospels. The premise of form criticism is that after the death of Christ much of

---

11. *Ibid.*, Part 2, par. 26.

what he said and did was treasured and repeated in the first Christian communities before the Gospels were written. The form critic asks three questions about each pericope: What was its *Sitz im Leben Jesu*? What was its *Sitz im Leben der Kirche*? What was its *Sitz im Evangelium*?

The third question marks the transition from form criticism to redaction criticism.[12] This is the most recent development in form criticism. It claims that the needs of the early Church and its desire to win acceptance from the pagans were instrumental in shaping the early tradition. The early Christian community creatively combined to form our Gospels (not create out of nothing), the episodes and discourses reportedly derived from those who had known Christ.

Three great names dominate the form critical school: K. L. Schmidt, M. Dibelius and R. Bultmann. Demythologizing is the latter's contribution. His manifesto, *The New Testament and Mythology*, appeared in 1941. Myth, he explained, was being used by him in a special sense. Myth was not an imaginary story or fanciful fairy tale, but the use of images and tales to express the other-worldly in terms of this world. Demythologizing is not the rejection of the theological meaning of the New Testament, but the only way he could see to bring its saving message to modern man so that such a man can make a decision for Christ.

This contrast between Scripture as studied in the sixth century and as studied in the twentieth provides the background for the study of Scripture in the Rule of St Benedict. It is obvious that three conclusions follow: (1) It would be impossible to expect St Benedict to have or to use the same texts and methods that are known today; (2) It would be unrealistic to expect him to employ Scripture as it is employed today; (3) It is possible to use present-day methods to discover the meaning of the Scripture passages in the Rule.

12. Example: Mk 8:31 (turning point in Mark's Gospel): "Son of Man must suffer—be killed—after three days rise again."—(1) one of three Marcan predictions of passion: 8:31, 9:31, 10:33. (2) 8:27–9:1: Bethsaida to Caesarea Philippi. (3) Marcan purpose in Gospel—Passion Story with an Introduction. (4) "Son of Man." (5) Theology of the Cross. (6) Cf. Mt 16:13–28.

SACRED SCRIPTURE IN THE RULE OF ST BENEDICT

When I carefully reread the Rule of St Benedict in preparation for this meeting, I closed the book with something like awe. Monks, I said to myself, should not be called monks—a more accurate title would be "men of the Bible." The Rule is Biblical in its inspiration, in its demands, in the opportunities it offers. The rest of us, those not living under this Rule, run the risk of being dilettantes in Sacred Scripture—in comparison to anyone who seriously studies and lives the full implications of all its demands.

To indicate briefly how rich this Rule is in its Scriptural content let me just enumerate how many times each Book of the Bible is quoted:

OLD TESTAMENT

Gen 4	Job 5	Jer 2
Ex 2	Judges 1	Ezek 3
Lev 1	Ps 65	Dan 2
Deut 1	Prov 16	Wis 6
Kings 6	Eccles 1	Sir 13
	Is 9	

NEW TESTAMENT

Mt 40	Gal 5	2 Tim 2
Mk 3	Eph 5	Tit 1
Lk 20	Phil 4	Heb 2
Jn 3	Col 1	Jas 4
Acts 8	1 Thess 6	1 Pet 7
Rom 10	2 Thess 1	1 Jn 2
1 Cor 14	1 Tim 4	Jude 1
2 Cor 7		Rev 1

Looking as an "outsider" at your Rule I see its passages radiant with the light of the inspired Word. I see the life it presents as shaped and fashioned by the Bible: prayer, work, fraternal rela-

G

tions, role of the abbot, reception of guests—all these are understood in a Biblical context.

Modern scholarship might justly challenge the use of some key
texts. One which puzzles me is in Chapter Five, "Obedience": "He
who hears you, hears me." Two points: strict exegesis would not
allow us to apply these words to the command of a superior. Yet
the whole scientific methodology of Sacred Scripture teaches us to
approach a text to learn the meaning intended by the author.
Certainly St Benedict's desire here is to inculcate reverence for a
superior's expressed will leading to a prompt fulfillment of the
same. This intention is clear. The words he quotes from Scripture
assert this even though this is not a Sacred Scripture proof-text. His
desire cannot on these grounds be disregarded.

Modern scholarship and *Divino Afflante Spiritu*[13] warn against
Biblical fundamentalism. Perhaps Biblical fundamentalism is one
of the most vicious kinds of error. If I think that God actually spoke
to me as De Mille made out in the film on the Ten Commandments,
then it is obvious to us all that God has long since ceased to speak to
us. In fact, God is dead. If, on the contrary, God has spoken from
within history to reveal himself through the rather unimpressive
historical events and experiences of one nation—Israel—then we
can see how he still speaks to us today, through the experiences of
the Church and our own experience in life. The value of demythologizing for the study of the Rule is that it can help to show how
to keep tradition alive by *aggiornamento*. I mean that the socio-
cultural, religious and economic aspects of the world view of St
Benedict must be restated in function of the world view of the
modern mind if the monk is to find a meaningful norm in the Rule.

Redaction criticism has drawn scholarly attention to the religious
message of each inspired author. It is this which transfigures St
Benedict's Rule in my eyes—even when he is quoting Sacred
Scripture with unexpected meanings.

For this reason I think that a great new creative era—a springtime
in the Cistercian Order—might be heralded by a profound study of

13. Pius XII, *op. cit.,* especially pars. 27, 50, 54.

Sacred Scripture—every monk an exegete. An exegete of great gravity and depth because of the all-pervading Biblical context in which his life is to be lived.

Yet, I must pause, *gnosis*, a pseudo-kind of intellectualism, is not what I am advocating. St Benedict had an intimate understanding of the Paschal Mystery in its totality—that is my prayer for you. Darkness. Now. Dawn for the whole Church made possible by your deepening understanding of the beauty of the Biblical dimensions of your life as I have seen them in your Rule.

Kathryn Sullivan RSCJ

Manhattanville College,
Purchase, New York

DISCUSSION

As a fruit of Mother Sullivan's study of the Scriptural sources employed by St Benedict, Fr Thomas Smith brought out how St Benedict adopted the Sapiential style. He saw himself as a "scribe instructed in the Kingdom of God" and shared his knowledge with his monks. He begins his Rule with "Listen, my son . . .," the well-known device of the Wisdom writers. He frequently quotes from the Sapiential literature, especially the Book of Proverbs. (See above, Mother Kathryn's listings.) Chapter Four of the Rule seems to be his own shortened version of this book of the Bible. It might therefore be questioned whether Benedict in the Rule is primarily trying to "legislate" or whether he is not more concerned in transmitting monastic wisdom, the monastic tradition.

Fr Paulinus Chu-Cong felt that this Scriptural study showed that it is necessary to go beyond the letter of the Rule. In Chapter Sixteen St Benedict seems to fall into Scriptural literalism when using Ps 118:164 (Vulgate version) as a basis for the seven hours of prayer in the divine office. Cassian understood the text, to pray seven times, to mean to pray without ceasing. Modern interpretation validates his understanding, showing that seven need not be taken numerically, but means rather many times. In this way, modern interpretation makes us conscious of what was actually at the heart of Benedict's thought regarding the Office. Modern techniques aim primarily at discovering the literal sense, through which we attain to the more-than-the-literal sense, the timeless meaning that is contained in the text, its application to our changing life circumstances. Like the literal sense of Scripture, that of the Rule has virtualities which can gradually unfold and be brought out in succeeding periods of history.

Realizing that St Benedict and the Fathers in general did not have the same concern for the literal meaning of the text that Biblical scholars now have, it was asked whether the ancient interpretations of Sacred Scripture should today be regarded merely as archaic. Mother Sullivan replied that the old interpretations still have an enriching value for us today. Modern Scripture scholarship may be regarded as the further development and the fruit of all the exegetical efforts of the past. Some of the old interpretations may have to be set aside today, others are only partially acceptable, but at times it is possible to synthesize the old exegesis with the new. We can still learn something today from the Scriptural interpretations of successive past ages. Along this line Pius XII, in *Divino Afflante Spiritu*, exhorted modern exegetes to combine today's professional erudition with the religious spirit of ancient writers.

THE EARLY CISTERCIAN EXPERIENCE
OF LITURGY

THERE WAS ONCE A TIME when even the specialist in a subject was expected to preface his remarks with an apology for his lack of competence in the matter at hand. Prefaces of this sort are no longer as fashionable as they used to be; but even nowadays, simple honesty occasionally calls for an initial apologetic note; which is the present case.

My topic is the early Cistercian *experience* of the liturgy. If I were dealing simply with the origin and evolution of this or that Cistercian liturgical book, there would be little problem: the facts could be cataloged, analyzed, schematized and controlled with a fair amount of scientific objectivity. But once we situate ourselves at the level of human *experience*, much of the data tends to escape clear analysis and careful control. Since I am not a historian of culture, nor a psychologist, nor even a sociologist, I can bring to our present topic little of the scientific background and disciplined methodology called for by the subject. So I insist, not humbly, but simply truthfully, on the modest scope of the following reflections. I wish only to share with you a few of my own personal and not always scientific reflections about the early twelfth-century Cistercians and their liturgy.

Sources: Cistercian "Culture" seen in Cistercian "Civilization"

As men created after the image and likeness of God, we share in something of God's creativity. God created the universe, and he

77

saw that it was good. And it was good because God is good, and his works reflect the truth and beauty and goodness which are in God himself. So too with us. *We create outside ourselves a material world which reflects rather faithfully our inward, spiritual physiognomy.* In recent decades, some scholars have referred to this interior state and vision of reality in terms of "culture"; and they use the word "civilization" to describe the material expression of our spiritual experience.[1] Just as philosophers and theologians examine God's works and learn something about God's inner life and attributes, so also we can learn a great deal about the inner life and spiritual experience of the Cistercian Fathers if we examine the environment or "civilization" they created. And if we wish to study specifically their liturgical experience or liturgical "culture," then we must begin with their liturgical "civilization," that is to say, the texts, the rites, the music, the buildings, and everything else they used to express, sustain, and deepen their experience of the Christian mystery in its sacramental dimension.

But first a word of caution. It rarely happens that a material civilization is a perfect and direct expression of a spiritual quality or type of experience. An analogy from music might help explain —even though, like all analogies, this one limps.

Arnold Schönberg has compared the composer's activity to that of a creator. "A creator," he writes, "has a vision of something which has not existed before this vision. And a creator has the power to bring his vision to life, the power to realize it."[2] The author then remarks that in the case of God the Creator, vision, will and accomplishment coincide: God spoke, and it was made.

1. Thus J. Laloup and J. Nélis, throughout the entire first chapter of their book, *Culture et civilisation: Initiation à l'humanisme historique* (Tournai, 1955). Not everyone accepts this distinction. T. S. Eliot, for example, admits that there are contexts where one word obviously fits and the other does not, but his final judgment is that the distinction is artificial. See his *Notes towards a Definition of Culture*, 2nd ed. (London, 1962), p. 13.

2. A. Schönberg, *Style and Idea* (New York, 1950), p. 102. This and the following citation are taken from the essay "Composition with Twelve Tones," first delivered as a lecture at the University of California, March 26, 1941.

"Alas, human creators, if they be granted a vision, must travel the long road between vision and accomplishment; a hard road where, driven out of Paradise, even geniuses must reap their harvest in the sweat of their brows. . . . It is one thing to envision in a creative instant of inspiration and it is another thing to materialize one's vision by painstakingly connecting details until they fuse into a kind of organism."[3]

The application to the Cistercian Fathers is fairly obvious. They might have had some sort of creative vision which led to the founding of a new monastery, and eventually to the founding of a new Order; but their vision by no means produced its total, concrete effect instantaneously. Their passage from inward experience to lucid objectification was gradual; and just as a composer is often less than 100 per cent successful in giving concrete expression to his creative idea, so also the Fathers might not have been 100 per cent successful in actualizing their own creative idea. We ought not to be surprised, then, if our study of the early Cistercian liturgy reveals an occasional contradictory element, or an element of instability.

Liturgical Books and Liturgical Reforms[4]

For our present purpose, we can note within an eighty-year period no less than three programs of liturgical reform.

The *first period* began almost with the foundation of the New Monastery in 1098, and extended over an indefinite number of years. It was an incredibly rich period; and it was in these years that our liturgical books and monastic ritual assumed their characteristic shape. A *second period* of liturgical reform ended sometime around 1147.[5] Its scope included the revision of both the texts and

3. *Ibid.*

4. A great deal of material touched on in this paper is based on unpublished documentation and private research. Most of this will eventually become available to the general public through occasional notes and articles in *Liturgy OCSO* or other monastic publications.

5. For the date of the *terminus ad quem* of this liturgical reform, see C. Waddell, "The Origin and Early Evolution of the Cistercian Antiphonary: Reflections on Two Cistercian Chant Reforms," CS3, note 5.

the music of the earlier liturgical books; but the new repertory was in basic continuity with the old, and it was more a question of an editorial revision than a new beginning. The *third and final period* was more a period of slight re-touching than of revision or reform; and it can be safely assigned to some year after 1175 and before 1182 or 1183.[6]

First Period of Reform

In 1099, perhaps towards mid-year—the date is under discussion —Hughes de Die, Archbishop of Lyons and Papal Legate to France, arranged the details of St Robert's return from the New Monastery to his former abbey of Molesme. The legal document drawn up on this occasion[7] specifies that Robert's *capella* or chapel

6. J. Leclercq has discovered in a 12–13th-c. ms., Laon, Bibliothèque Municipale, Ms. 471, f. 102ᵛ, a list of General Chap. statutes dating from 1182, among which occurs the following ref.: *Lectionarium, Missale, Textus, Epistolare, Collectaneum nuper emendata sunt.* See his art. "Epîtres d'Alexandre III sur les Cisterciens," *Revue Bénédictine* 64 (1954): 77. That such a revision actually took place is borne out by comparison of the Cist. epistolaries and evangeliaries which can be dated before 1182 with the corresponding sections of the famous Cist. ms.-type, Dijon, Bib. Municipale, Ms. 114 (olim 82), written in or after 1185 (the calendar provides for St Thomas à Becket, whose feast was adopted by the Order in 1185; see J. M. Canivez, *Statuta Capitulorum Generalium Ordinis Cisterciensis*, vol. 1 (Louvain, 1933), Anno 1185, Statute 36, l. 102). Variants between the ms.-type and the earlier mss. point to a revision effected between 1175 and 1185. The text discovered by Dom Leclercq narrows the extreme dates to 1175 and 1182.

7. It is included in the dossier of official documents which make up part of EP. It may also be found in J. Marilier, *Chartes et documents concernant l'abbaye de Cîteaux 1098–1182*, Bibliotheca Cisterciensis 1 (Rome: Editiones Cistercienses, 1961), no. 15, pp. 39–40. Is EP safe to use as a source? Marilier, in his book, rejects as spurious several of the documents included in this compilation; and J. Lefèvre, in his several studies dealing with EP, adopts the position that the compiler is more pamphleteer and satirist than objective historian. See, for instance, "Le vrai récit des origines cisterciennes est-il l'Exordium Parvum?" *Le Moyen Age* 61 (1955): 79–120. But even such an ardent demythologizer of Cist. myth as is Lefèvre, distinguishes between the "pièces diplomatiques," which have all the characteristics of authentic documents, and the allegedly tendentious narrative sections. See his remarks in the art. cited, p. 119, as well as in his later art., "St Robert de Molesme dans l'opinion monastique du XIIIᵉ et du XIIIᵉ siècle," *Analecta Bollandiana* 74 (1956): 58. The text under present discussion belongs with the unimpeachably authentic documents.

—that is to say, the sacred vessels, vestments, linens, and books used in divine worship[8]—was to remain with the brethren at the New Monastery. The sole exception was a certain breviary which was to be retained for copying purposes, and then returned to the community of Molesme by the feast of St John the Baptist.[9] The conclusion is inevitable: the earliest liturgical books in use at Cîteaux were liturgical books from Molesme.[10]

Among these books only one is known to have survived—a psalter popularly known as "St Robert's Psalter."[11] Since eleventh- and twelfth-century psalters differed textually only slightly one from the other, this single manuscript can tell us next to nothing about the earliest Cistercian liturgy. But from a mid-twelfth-century summer breviary from Molesme, we can learn a great deal not only about the Molesme Office, but about the earliest Office texts used by the first Cistercians.

8. For an all but exhaustive discussion of the various meanings of the word *capella* in the course of its semantic evolution, see J. Van den Bosch, *Capa Basilica Monasterium et le culte de s. Martin du Tours: Etude lexicologique et sémasiologique*, Latinitas Christianorum Primaeva 13 (Nijmegen, 1959), with special ref. to pp. 25-34.

9. *De capella etiam predicti abbatis roberti et de ceteris rebus quas a molismensi ecclesia recedens secum (tulit) et cum eis cabilonensi episcopo atque novo monasterio se reddidit, id statuimus, ut fratribus novi monasterii salva permaneant, preter breviarium quoddam, quod usque a festivitatem sancti iohannis baptiste retinebunt ut transcribant, assensu molismensium.* Text taken from the transcription of the ms. Zürich, Zentralbib., Car. C. 175, f. 73^r, in Van Damme, *Documenta*, p. 9.

10. Even without the explicit text in Hugh's decree, the theory of continuity between Molesme and Cîteaux would be tenable. Cîteaux was founded by men formed in the Molesme tradition. The foundation of a new monastery without at least those books needed for the celebration of the liturgy would have been unthinkable. Indeed, one of the reasons for the return of the breviary discussed above might well have been the need of such books for one of the frequent Molesme foundations. Molesme was a mother no less fruitful than Cîteaux. For a listing of her multitudinous offspring, see J. Laurent, *Cartulaires de l'abbaye de Molesme*, vol. 1 (Paris, 1907), pp. 208-275.

11. Originally written for use in the church of St Vaast, Arras. Two of the Molesme monks who pioneered the foundation of Cîteaux were originally from St Vaast. Cf. V. Leroquais, *Les psautiers mss. latins des bibliothèques publiques de France,* vol. 1 (Paris, 1940-1941), p. 178. This ms. is now in the possession of the Bib. Municipale, Dijon, where it is catalogued as Ms. 30 (olim 12).

Our manuscript—now in the possession of the Bibliothèque Municipale of Troyes, where it is cataloged as Ms. 807[12]—represents only the summer section of what was once a complete breviary. Unfortunately, it has no chant notation. But both in itself and in conjunction with other manuscripts it offers us a wealth of material which has yet to be exploited.

I wrote: "In conjunction with *other* manuscripts." Which other manuscripts? Manuscripts chiefly from the monastery in which St Robert lived for many years before undertaking the foundation of Molesme, that is to say, Montier-la-Celle, an ancient Benedictine abbey located in the vicinity of Troyes.[13] Our one Molesme manuscript, when carefully collated with the three extant breviary manuscripts from Montier-la-Celle,[14] reveals that the antiphons and responsories and similar texts are all but identical.[15] Thus, the earliest Cistercian breviary has its roots in the tradition of Montier-la-Celle, a tradition represented also by similar manuscripts from

12. Not included in the present discussion is Ms. 124 of the Bib. Municipale, Evreux. Though at least major sections of this composite ms. are from Molesme, there are leaves interpolated from a somewhat different Benedictine tradition. The material included in the hodge-podge consists of a complete Molesme calendar (ff 1–6), a complete psalter with canticles, a long litany of saints (non-Molesme), and a mixture of summer season masses and offices from the temporal cycle. The description given in V. Leroquais, *Le Bréviaires mss. des bibliotheques publiques de France,* vol. 2 (Paris, 1934), pp. 106–107, is not always accurate.

13. For a summary *curriculum vitae S. Roberti,* see K. Spahr, *Das Leben des hl. Robert von Molesme: Eine Quelle zur Vorgeschichte von Cîteaux* (Freiburg in d. Schweiz, 1944), pp. xliii–xlvii; or J. Laurent, *op. cit.,* 1:146–153 (to be corrected in points of detail, but reliable in general). For Montier-la-Celle, see *ibid.,* p. 147, note 2 and H. Cottineau, *Répertoire topobibliographique des abbayes et prieurés,* vol. 2 (Mâcon, 1937), pp. 1952–1953.

14. Troyes, Bib. Municipale, Ms. 1974, a complete 13th c. breviary (2nd half), without chant notation; Ms. 109 of the same library—a winter season breviary of roughly the same date, with full chant notation; finally, Châlons-sur-Marne, Bib. Municipale, Ms. 360, a lacunose, shabby ms. tossed together from 14th- and 16th-c. material. Descriptions of the first 2 mss. are to be found in Leroquais, *Les bréviaires,* 4:253–256 and 212–214; the third ms. is described in 1:253–255.

15. The lectionary and prayer-texts, however, seem to belong to different traditions.

Ste-Trinité de Vendôme, St-Faron de Meaux, and St-Melaine de Rennes.[16]

Anyone expecting to find an extravagant, decadent type of office at Molesme will be severely disappointed. Indeed, the tradition in question is so hopelessly sane and sound that it is a bit difficult to find any really distinguishing features. The hymn repertory is absolutely standard. The structure of the office is evidently Benedictine, and of the most prosaic type. Antiphons and responsories are for the most part classical; and offices of a later vintage can hardly be said to be present in excessive numbers. The sanctoral cycle is a simplified form of the more exuberant sanctoral cycle of Montier-la-Celle; and, for practical purposes, the Molesme calendar and the early Cistercian calendar are very much the same as regards the saints represented.[17] Though I have been able to identify most of the sources drawn upon for the patristic lectionary, I prefer to pursue my research a bit further before drawing any precise conclusions; but I can assure you even now that the vast bulk of the material is standard, or else in perfect harmony with the sort of readings we find in the lectionaries of Paul the Deacon and Alan of Farfa.[18] The office prayers likewise derive from standard sources, and can be identified for the most part with the help of the

16. Vendôme, Bib. Municipale, Ms. 17E, complete breviary (with chant notation), middle 13th c.; Meaux, Bib. Municipale, Ms. 4, 15th-c. breviary of St Faron; Abbaye St Pierre de Solesme, Bib., printed breviary (1526) of St Melaine de Rennes. In a series of comparative studies involving hundreds of mss. and printed sources, R. Le Roux has consistently discovered a near identity of the mss. comprising this group. The studies referred to are: "Aux origines de l'Office Festif: Les antiennes et les psaumes de Matines et de Laudes pour Noël et le 1er janvier," *Etudes grégoriennes* 4 (1961): 65–170; "Les Répons de Psalmis pour les Matines, de l'Epiphanie à la Septuagésime," *ibid.* 6 (1963): 39–148; "*Guillaume de Volpiano: Son cursus liturgique au Mont Saint-Michel et dans les abbayes normandes,*" *Millénaire monastique de Mont Saint-Michel,* vol. 2 (Paris, 1967), pp. 417–472.

17. The list of saints was basically the same, but many of the saints feasted at Molesme with 12 lesson offices enjoyed only a commemoration and mass at Cîteaux.

18. A recent valuable tool in this area of research is R. Grégoire, *Les homéliaires du Moyen Age: Inventaire et analyse des mss.,* Rerum Ecclesiasticarum Documenta, Series Maior: Fontes 6 (Rome, 1966).

indexes of modern editions of gregorian sacramentaries and of sacramentaries belonging to the francogelasian branches of tradition. Almost the only texts to be read with raised eyebrows are isolated passages in a few of the sanctoral cycle offices.

Nevertheless, the early days of the New Monastery witnessed the beginnings of a long-ranged liturgical reform.

The Holy Rule and Cistercian Liturgy

The first indications of liturgical changes are vague and summary. In the letter written on behalf of the monks of the New Monastery and addressed to Pope Paschal II by Archbishop Hugh of Lyons, the Papal Legate notes that the new community, having left Molesme in order to live a stricter, holier way of life according to the Rule of St Benedict, has abandoned the usages of certain monasteries, judging themselves too weak to stand up under so great a burden.[19] The usages or customs thus abandoned are not specified, but they could hardly have failed to have concerned at least in part the liturgy; and, indeed, the early Cistercian liturgy did appear far less demanding than was the case in even the smaller Benedictine communities. If authentic, this letter would have been written in midsummer of 1100.[20] The so-called "Roman Privilege," dating from October 19, 1100, from Troja, Italy,[21] and taking the New Monastery under the protection of the Holy See, is followed in the *Exordium Parvum* by a detailed catalog of statutes formulated upon the reception of the Roman Privilege, and meant to ensure a more faithful observance of the Holy Rule.[22] Here again, references to the liturgy are only general; but the import is clear enough:

19. . . . *depositis quorundam monasteriorum consuetudinibus, imbecillitatem suam ad tantum pondus sustinendum imparem iudicantes.*—EP, p. 11. Other mss. wrongly substitute *iudicantium* for the final word, probably to avoid reproducing a text which asserts that the first Cist. were too weak (!!!) to support the burdens which were part and parcel of life in communities of Black Monks.

20. Marilier, *op. cit.*, no. 19, p. 47, presents the text as of doubtful authenticity. His reasons seem (to me) astonishingly gratuitous. Fortunately, the text in question is not essential for our knowledge of the early Cist. liturgy.

21. *Ibid.*, no. 21, pp. 48–49; EP, p. 12.

22. EP, pp. 13–14.

Thereupon the abbot and his brethren, mindful of their vows, unanimously decided to establish and keep the Rule of Saint Benedict in that place. They rejected what was contrary to the Rule. . . . In thus taking the rectitude of the Rule (*rectitudinem regulae*) as the norm of conduct for their whole way of life (*supra cunctum vitae suae tenorem ducentes*), they fully complied with its directions in ecclesiastical as well as in other observances. . . .[23]

This principle of "conformity with the Rule in ecclesiastical as well as in other observances" was to have monumental effects on the liturgy of the White Monks. Among the immediate consequences for the liturgy were the following.

There was a radical elimination of many of the traditional elements which had become part of the Benedictine daily *pensum servitutis*. The author of the *Exordium Magnum*, though writing perhaps a full century after the events described,[24] is quite accurate when he says that the early Cistercians "excised and rejected all the appendages of psalms, prayers, and litanies which the Fathers (the pre-Cistercian Fathers), acting less discreetly, had added (to the office) simply because they wanted to do so."[25] He goes on to explain—and this is important for our understanding of the Cistercian experience of the liturgy—that, with the traditional office, even the more zealous monks could pray only with lukewarm, careless dispositions.[26]

This is probably a gross exaggeration. At this point, the Cistercians traditionally remark that there were days at Cluny when no less than 215 psalms had to be said; they catalog the various daily processions, litanies and prayers; nor do they fail to note that the whole long book of *Isaiah* was sometimes spread out over only

23. EP, p. 13. Trans. from Larkin, pp. 262–263.

24. Conrad of Eberbach (earlier a monk of Clairvaux), the compiler, redacted the final sections sometime after 1206. See EM, pp. 32–34.

25. . . . *recisis penitus et reiectis cunctis appendiciis psalmorum, orationum e letaniarum, quae minus discreto patres pro velle suo superaddiderant.* . . .—EM 1:20, p. 75.

26. *Ibid.:* . . . *ob multiplicitatem sui non solum a fastidiosis, sed ab ipsis quoque studiosis omnino tepide et negligenter persolverentur.*

six Advent night offices,[27] and that prime with its litany lasted as long as the whole Cistercian daily office, minus the mass and vespers.[28] And this, we conclude, is the interminable sort of thing the Cistercian Fathers, faithful to the Rule, wished to disavow. This attitude involves a distortion of the facts, and it should be remarked that Cluny was quite unique. None of the monasteries dependent on Cluny could boast a liturgy even approaching the heroic proportions (usually grossly exaggerated)[29] of Cluny. Still, an examination of representative monastic customaries from the eleventh and twelfth centuries gives us a picture of a rather ample style of celebration.[30] In the summer season, vigils was generally preceded by the fifteen gradual psalms with versicles and a few collects; and the last thirty-two psalms served the same function in many places during the winter season. The night office proper was followed by four or five psalms said for friends and benefactors. Vigils, lauds, and vespers of the dead were part of the ordinary liturgical fare. And, apart from compline, all the other hours had as their conclusion a group of psalms such as those which followed vigils. Prime was generally lengthened by the Athanasian Creed, the penitential psalms, and the litany of saints. Two daily conventual masses were standard. A special office of All Saints seems to have

27. For a somewhat material account of the liturgy at Cluny, see the art. by P. Schmitz, "La liturgie de Cluny," *Spiritualità Cluniacense,* Convegni del Centro di Studi sulla Spiritualità Medievale 2 (Todi, 1960), pp. 85–99. But surely we should approach the liturgy at Cluny against the background sketched by J. Leclercq in the same vol., "Spiritualité et culture à Cluny," pp. 103–151.

28. An often repeated commonplace first perpetrated in the Dia, where the Cluniac happily remarks: . . . *sola nostra Prima, cum Letania et sibi adiunctis superat omne servitium vestrum, quod Deo exhibetis in oratorio per totum diem praeter missas et vesperas.*

29. See the judicious remarks of J. Leclercq, "La 'psalmodie prolixe' de Cluny," *La liturgie et les paradoxes chrétiens* (Paris, 1963), pp. 238–241. The c. in which this material is found was originally published as "Prière incessante: A propos de la 'laus perennis' du Moyen Age," *La Maison-Dieu* 64 (1960): 90–101.

30. A useful catalog of such customaries can be found in K. Hallinger, ed., *Corpus Consuetudinum Monasticarum,* vol. 1 (Sieburg, 1963), pp. lix–lxxiv.

been quite usual; but the daily office of Our Lady became widespread only later in the twelfth century.

All these "extras" the Cistercian Fathers abandoned—at least in the beginning. William of Malmesbury, writing around 1124, describes the spartan Cistercian office, but mentions also an additional "Vigils of the Dead,"[31] whereas an anonymous Benedictine—probably Hugh of Reading—in replying to St Bernard's *Apologia* only a few years later, around 1127 or 1128,[32] specifically refers to the absence of such an office in the daily Cistercian round of prayer.[33] Be that as it may, the earliest extant redaction of the Usages shows that by 1134, the daily office of the dead had regained admittance in the Order.[34] The daily office of Our Lady in common took longer to gain a strong foothold; but a statute of the General Chapter for 1185 deals with this office both *in conventu et in infirmatorio.*[35]

---

31. *Gesta Regum Anglorum* 4:336; PL 179:1289b: *Horas canonicas indefesse continuant, nulla appenditia extrinsecus adjicientes, praeter vigiliam pro defunctis.*

32. See A. Wilmart, "Une riposte de l'ancien monachisme au manifeste de saint Bernard," *Revue Bénédictine* 46 (1934): 296–344. Though the attribution to Hugh has been questioned by J. Bouton in "Bernard et l'Ordre de Cluny," *Bernard de Clairvaux* (Paris, 1953), p. 200, note 31, Dom Wilmart's proposals as regard author and date have been convincingly defended by C. Talbot, "The Date and Author of the 'Riposte,'" *Studia Anselmiana* 40 (1956): 72–80.

33. Wilmart, *ibid.,* p. 335.

34. See B. Griesser, "Die '*Ecclesiastica officia Cisterciensis Ordinis*' des Cod. 1711 von Trient," *Analecta S O Cist* 12 (1956): 170–172, where he discusses the Cists. and their obligations to the dead. Explicit ref. to a *daily* office of the dead is found in c. (lxiii) I: *Quibus diebus et quo ordine celebrandum est officium defunctorum,* p. 214. This ms. can be dated 1130/1134, according to Griesser, p. 174. Unfortunately, F. Kovacs in his excellent study, "Relation entre l'Officium Defunctorum feriale et la liturgie cistercienne primitive," *Analecta S O Cist* 7 (1951): 78–84, had at his disposal only part of the documentation for a complete treatment of the subject.

35. See R. Trilhe, "Cîteaux," *Dict. d'archéologie chrétienne et de liturgie* 3/2:1792; J. Canivez, "Le rite cistercien," *Ephemerides Liturgicae* 63 (1949): 300; B. Kaul, "De Kalendario Cistercensis ejusque revisione instituenda," *Analecta S O Cist* 5 (1949): 37–40. The remarks of A. Presse, "Les observances adventices dans l'Ordre de Cîteaux," *Revue Mabillon* 20 (1930): 229, should be read with caution. First prayed privately by individuals, then in common by monks and

All of which suggests that the liturgical pruning done in the early days of the Order proved to be a bit excessive, though certainly in the right direction. If the average Benedictine liturgy was ample, it was ample because it answered a real spiritual need. If there were times when the tendency was towards a less ample form of prayer, this too answered a real need. Liturgy springs from life.

The Cistercian Fathers managed to retain a number of liturgical practices which have little or no foundation in the Rule, but which, on the other hand, are not particularly incompatible with the Rule. Thus there was from the beginning of the Order a daily conventual mass, and even two on Sunday and feasts when there was no work. It is also true, however, that when the work load was heavy, the community went *en masse* to the work at hand, and left only the sick and infirm to assist at the mass after prime.[36] The Lord's Prayer and the Apostles' Creed before vigils and after compline were prayed silently. The Athanasian Creed was also retained, but only at Sunday prime, after the dismissal verse. St Benedict apparently makes no provisions for commemorations within the office. The Cistercian solution was to retain commemorations, but only *after* the official conclusion of the office with the standard *Benedicamus Domino*.[37] Neither was there any difficulty about the quite ample chapter prayers after prime, or the grace procession to church after dinner. But all these elements were kept separate from the office proper.

Once the *Deus in adjutorium* had been intoned (or the *Domine*

---

abbots on the road or at granges, the little office eventually was authorized for common prayer in the infirmary, then in the community at large. Pertinent 12th-c. General Chapter statutes are found in Canivez, *Statuta,* 1:60, 101-102, 171, 197 (1195 is a repetition of 1185).

36. Griesser, "Die '*Ecclesia stica officia,*'" c. (cviii) lxxxiv, pp. 248-249.

37. The *Benedicamus Domino* was repeated after the versicle, antiphon and prayer of the saint. See B. Kaul, "Auf den Spuren des alten Cistercienserritus in Spanien," *Cistercienser-chronik* 55 (1948):228. (The practice here described is still followed by the Carthusians.) Special blessings for the kitcheners (after Sunday lauds) or for monks returning from a journey likewise followed the office but were in turn followed by the commemoration of the saint or saints. See Griesser, *op. cit.,* c. (cxxx) cviii, p. 268; c. (ci) lxxviii, p. 244.

labia mea aperies at vigils), nothing was allowed to interfere with the prescriptions of the Rule as interpreted by the first Cistercians. Even during the Sacred Triduum, when all other Benedictine monks adopted an archaic form of the office in compliance with the universal western practice, the Cistercians maintained the ordinary ferial day structure.[38] Neither general custom nor ecclesiastical law could persuade the White Monks to drop the office *alleluia* at Septuagesima instead of at the beginning of Lent.[39] And a curious interpretation of the Rule's prescription for the lauds psalmody (c. 13) resulted in the adoption of a single lauds antiphon to replace the traditional five.

Again, since St Benedict had failed to distinguish between festive psalms and ferial day psalms at vespers, the Cistercians retained even on the greatest feasts the ferial day vespers palms.

Referring to the readings at vigils, St Benedict speaks of the Scriptures and the commentaries on the same by well-known and orthodox Catholic Fathers;[40] but he nowhere mentions hagiographical writings. The Fathers took their cue from this, and banished this type of literature from the office to the refectory and to private *lectio divina*. The result was an extremely rich but very sober night office lectionary, drawn for the most part from the material included in the collection of homilies attributed to Paul the Deacon.[41]

---

38. In Peter Abelard's Ep. 10, addressed to abbot Bernard of Clairvaux around 1132, and containing a catalog of objectionable Cist. liturgical novelties, the maintenance of the ordinary ferial day structure for the last days of Holy Week comes in for Abelard's condemnation. See PL 178:339d–340a.

39. Cf. RB 15: *Alleluia quibus temporibus dicatur. A Pentecoste autem usque caput quadragesimae . . . dicatur.* The dropping of the Alleluia at Septuagesima became law in the decrees of the first Synod of Aix-la-Chapelle. See Hallinger, 1:465. Abelard did not fail to draw attention to this Cist. innovation, Ep. 10; PL 178:339d.

40. RB 9.

41. The careful study by B. Griesser, "Das Lektion- und Perikopensystem im Stephans-Brevier," *Cistercienser-chronik* 71 (1964):67–92, calls for reserves. Griesser used for his studies only breviary mss. in which the readings have been reduced to mere snippets, whereas the office lectionaries were bulky tomes with enormously long (by modern standards) readings. The scribes responsible for the breviaries were relatively free to produce their "token

A rather literal interpretation of St Benedict's term *ambrosianum* used to designate hymns in several chapters of the Rule[42] resulted in the radical rejection of the sober, traditional Molesme hymnal, and the adoption of the chief items in the Milanese hymnal, since these had all been composed, it was thought, by St Ambrose himself.[43] Unfortunately, the Milanese hymnal provided only one vigils hymn; but the Cistercians preferred (at least for a time) to sing the same vigils hymn for Christmas, Good Friday, and Easter, rather than sing a hymn not invested with the authority of the Rule.[44]

In keeping with the Rule, the Cistercian summer season *cursus* began with Easter Monday, instead of the Monday after Trinity Sunday, as was the general practice outside the Cistercian Order.[45]

Though the Molesme calendar of saints was retained in substance, the rank of celebration accorded each saint was either a twelve–lesson office (with one or two masses), or else a simple commemoration at lauds and vespers (*after* the office proper) with a conventual mass[46]—evidently because the Rule makes no provisions for a feast-day office less elaborate than the Sunday-type structure.

All the preceding examples concern specific elements of the

---

readings" from the material at hand and not all scribes went about it in the same way. Thus, the breviary-mss. provide a risky basis for us to gain a secure knowledge of early lectionaries. Fortunately there are at least two choir lectionaries which can be dated to a period before 1147—a winter season lectionary which passed from Clairmarais to Clairvaux and is now at Troyes, Bib. Municipale, Ms. 394; and the temporal cycle lectionary, Ms. 869 of the same collection, and of Clairvaux provenance.

42. RB 9:4; 12:4; 13:11; 17:8.

43. For a brief discussion of the primitive Cist. hymnal derived from Milanese sources, see *art. cit.* note 5, with a special ref. to notes 36–42.

44. Cf. Abelard, Ep. 10; PL 178:339b-c.

45. The result was a great loss in terms of the Easter Season patristic and Biblical readings. Standard Benedictine sources (represented also by the Molesme mss.) provide 3 Biblical or patristic readings for all the days of Eastertide.

46. A study of pre-1147 sacramentaries and evangeliaries of the Order reveals that a commemoration at lauds and vespers automatically called for a proper conventual mass. Between 1175 and 1182 about a third of these "commemoration-masses" were dropped.

Cistercian liturgy determined by a particular exegesis of the prescriptions of the Rule. But the markedly simple, even poor *style
of celebration* characteristic of the early White Monks might also be
said to have been at least in part a consequence of the Cistercian
interpretation of the Rule. The Christian values of humility,
poverty and simplicity inculcated by the Rule could not fail to
affect the liturgy as well as the general life style. The compiler of
the *Exordium Parvum* links the name of St Stephen Harding with a
period of further refinements adopted in the name of humility and
poverty: painted wooden crosses rather than gold or silver ones, a
single iron candelabra, copper or iron censers, elimination of copes,
dalmatics, tunicles, silk vestments, gold- or silver-embroidered
linens.[47]

There is nothing specifically "Cistercian" about this humble
style of celebration. Abelard's *Rule for Religious Women*, written
for Heloise and the nuns of Le Paraclet, contains liturgical prescriptions as austere as anything in the Cistercian tradition;[48] and the same
can be said of the Carthusians and so many other similar groups.
The specifically "Cistercian" elements of the early liturgy were
chiefly matters of detail based on an interpretation or even mis-
interpretation of the Holy Rule.

For it must be admitted that the Cistercian Fathers were faced
with an almost impossible hermeneutical problem. Even with the
help of the refined tools of comparative liturgiology, modern
scholars are often at a loss in their attempts to interpret this or that
point of the Rule's liturgical prescriptions.[49] Nor should we be so

47. EP 16, pp. 14–15.
48. Critical ed. T. MacLaughlin, *Medieval Studies* 18 (1956): 241–292. For the
description of the oratory and its liturgical appointments, see p. 263.
49. A single impressive ex. of the difficulties involved is to be found in the
excellent study of O. Heiming, "Zum monastischen Offizium von Kassianus
bis Kolumbanus," *Archiv für Liturgiewissenschaft* 7 (1961): 89–156. In situating
the "Benedictine Office" in its historical context, and in studying the data of
the Rule against the background of the interpretations of other reputable
scholars past and present, he himself throws much new light on many particular
points; though much of this light only serves to reveal how many other
points remain shrouded in darkness. The interpretation of the liturgical data
in the Rule is not as easy as it might seem.

naive as to think that, since the Fathers were eight centuries closer to St Benedict than we are, theirs was a more direct link with tradition. Not at all. In spite of evidence for the early diffusion of the Rule,[50] and in spite of intermittent attempts to assign the Rule a primacy of place in various monastic reform attempts, this sixth-century monastic code seems to have been observed only in parts, or in fruitful conjunction with other monastic rules.[51]

And even in the case of the Cistercian Fathers, there was never a question of "the Rule and nothing but the Rule." The starting point of their reform had been a concrete, living, complex tradition tributary to multiple sources. What was rejected was not this tradition as a whole, but only those elements judged incompatible with fidelity to the Rule and with the exigencies of reason.[52]

50. For a select but sufficient bibliography on this subject, see Hallinger, 1:79, note 2. Of special interest is G. Penco, "La prima diffusione della Regola di S Benedetto," *Studia Anselmiana* 42 (1957): 321–345.

51. Monte Cassino was destroyed by the Lombards around 577. When it rose from its ashes under Abbot Petronax sometime after 717, the new community was recruited gradually from various groups which had had no contact with the ancient abbey. J. Chapman, "La restauration du Mont-Cassin par l'abbé Pétronac," *Revue Bénédictine* 21 (1904): 74–80; and G. Penco, *Storia del Monachesimo in Italia* (Rome, 1961), pp. 136–137. Dom Penco corrects the dates given by the earlier writer. Not even at the restored Monte Cassino was the Rule observed in all its "purity." J. Leclercq summarizes the general trend in the following passage taken from his art. "Mérites d'un réformateur et limits d'une réforme," *Revue Bénédictine* 70 (1960): 236: *L'observance sera fixée par une Règle. Or il n'est pas sur qu'en ce Xe siècle celle-ci soit partout celle de saint Benoît, et nous avons pu relever quelques nouveaux indices des lenteurs de sa diffusion. Longtemps ont persisté des équivoques, ou plus exactement—car ce terme est péjoratif—des alliances fécondes entre les deux grandes institutions d'ascèse et de prière qu'étaient le monachisme et la vie canoniale. De plus en plus néanmoins, orsqu'on substitue une règle à une autre, c'est au profit du code bénédictine.*

52. A. Schneider has rendered an enormous service by the publication of his doctoral dissertation, *Cîteaux und die benediktinische Tradition: Die Quellenfrage des Liber Usum im Lichte der Consuetudines monasticae, Analecta S O Cist* 16 (1960): 169–264; 17 (1961): 73–114. A comparative study of various redactions of the usages with dozens of parallel Benedictine sources reveals that the Cist. usages are rooted in the ground-bed of Burgundian monasticism of the type styled "Cluniac." Commenting on the significance of Fr Schneider's thesis J. Hourlier writes in *Studia Monastica* 4 (1962): 246–248: . . . *on a trop volontiers opposé Cîteaux à Cluny . . . alors que les similitudes l'emportent en nombre et sont*

Exigency of Authenticity

Important decisions touching on the early Cistercian liturgical reform were made not only with reference to the Holy Rule, but with reference to the *exigencies of the authentic*. Whereas some basis for the adoption of Milanese hymns could be found in the Rule itself, this was not the case with the other liturgical books used in the Cistercian liturgy. In his *Prologue to the Cistercian Antiphonary*, written around 1147, St Bernard writes that "the chanting of the divine praises according to the most authentic version" was among the chief concerns of the founders of Cîteaux.[53] This passion for the authentic led to a whole series of new options in the choice of liturgical books.

In passing we may mention a treatise on Latin accentuation written by Abbot Lambert of Saint-Pierre de Pothières at the request of St Alberic and the brethren of the New Monastery, and dating from the early part of the twelfth century;[54] also the famous attempt of St Stephen Harding to establish a "critical" text of the Vulgate—though this textual revision was a purely local project with no influence on the Order's liturgical books.[55]

Much more significant, however, is a whole series of liturgical

---

bien plus importantes en valeur. Le constater n'enlève rien à la personalité de Cîteaux, mais permet de mieux apprécier la position du Nouveau Monastère dans l'histoire de monachisme. And J. Leclercq in "Une thèse sur Cîteaux dans la tradition monastique," *Collectanea OCR* 24 (1962): 358: De plus en plus on s'aperçoit que Cîteaux ne fut pas un commencement absolu: rien, dans sa constitution, dans ses attitudes envers Dieu, la Vierge Marie, l'Eglise, la societé, ne se comprend si l'on ignore ce qui le préparait, ce qui, autour de lui, évoula dans le même sens.

53. Critical ed. of the Latin text in Leclercq-Rochais, *S. Bernardi Opera*, vol. 3 (Rome, 1963), pp. 511–516; trans. with intro. C. Waddell in *The Works of Bernard of Clairvaux*, vol. 1, CF 1 (Spencer, Mass.: Cistercian Publications, 1970), pp. 153–162.

54. Text established with the help of 3 12th-c. mss. and published in Marilier, no. 17, pp. 41–46.

55. The popular notion that this textual revision served as a ms.-type for the Order's liturgical books is without foundation. The best recent study which deals chiefly with the text remains that of A. Lang, "Die Bibel Stephan Hardings," *Cistercienser-chronik* 51 (1939): 247–256, 275–281, 294–298; 52 (1940): 6–13, 17–23, 33–37.

books, which I can here only enumerate and describe in a few words.

The *sacramentary* as contained in the two earliest manuscripts I could find—both dating before 1147[56]—is almost pure Gregorian in its repertory of texts. The question of the origins and evolution of the so-called Gregorian Sacramentary is enormously complex and does not concern us here. My only point is that, with only extremely few exceptions, the sacramentary prayer-texts have been taken from a very pure source of the type styled "Gregorian." (The Cistercian calendar, derived from the Molesme calendar, included a large number of saints not found in the Gregorian sacramentaries. This was no problem, since these saints were simply given formulas already found in the Gregorian sources.)

The *collectaneum*—the book containing *capitula* and collect texts sung by the hebdomadary of the office—repeats the mass collects. But the Cistercians, like almost all other monastic groups of the period, also had special collects for sext and none. These additional collects likewise derive from the same Gregorian source tapped for the sacramentary.[57]

The *antiphonary* of the office is based on the prestigious Metz antiphonary, which enjoyed the reputation—undeservedly, alas— of being "authentically Gregorian."[58] Though the Metz tradition

---

56. Paris, Bib. Nationale, Ms. lat. 2300—a pre-1147 sacramentary from Landais (filiation of Cîteaux); a collection of masses follows the common, and these mass texts have been revised by a second hand so as to bring the earlier text into conformity with the Cist. revision of ca. 1147. Rheims, Bib. Municipale, Ms. 310 is from an unidentified Cist. monastery, probably in the vicinity of Rheims. For a while the sacramentary was used in a Benedictine monastery, as is evidenced by a number of late marginal additions in several places.

57. I have been unable to locate a *collectaneum* dating from the early, pre-1147 period. However, all the material which constitutes a *collectaneum* is included in breviary mss. We providentially have still extant a virtually complete Cist. breviary ms. of ca. 1132. Until recently catalogued as Ms. lat. in octavo 402 in the Westdeutsche Bib. Marburg a.d. Lahn, the ms. has since been transferred to the West Berlin State Library. An analysis of this ms. gives a clear idea of the contents of the *collectanea* of the same period.

58. For a more detailed treatment of the Metz-derived Cist. antiphonary, see Waddell, "The Origins and Early Evolution," CS3, pp. 190–223.

definitely had its roots in authentic sources, the melodic tradition had degenerated by the early twelfth century into something of a local "chant dialect." Still, the antiphonary in question enjoyed the reputation of being an "authentic" source; and it was on the basis of this reputation that the Cistercian Fathers adopted it as the source of their own office chants.

For the lack of early documentation the *gradual* has till now been largely an unresolved problem. I recently had the good fortune of identifying several mutilated folios used as guard-leaves in a twelfth-century collection of St Bernard's sermons now in the Bibliothèque Nationale, Paris.[59] The folios in question are nothing less than fragments from an early Cistercian gradual written before St Bernard's reform of around 1147. The melodic characteristics are the same as for the antiphonary, so that we can safely conclude that the Fathers went to Metz not only for the antiphonary, but for the gradual as well.

The *evangeliary* and *epistolary*[60] are based on a calendar which could be termed "classical."[61] Later and more local saints are relegated to the common, so that these two books are without any truly regional characteristic. In recent years, great strides have been made in sorting out the various families of gospel- and epistle-lists; but there remain many complex problems, and I prefer for the moment not to attach the Cistercian series to a specific type.

59. Paris, Bib. Nationale, Ms. lat. 2546, ff. 1-2v. The folios (only one of which is mutilated) contain mass propers for the 3rd and 4th weeks of Lent.

60. Two evangeliaries: Colmar, Bib. Municipale, ms. 107, from nearby Paris; and Paris, Bib. Nationale, Ms. lat. 1128, from Villers-Betnach, near Metz. Both these mss. pre-date 1147. The only epistolary which I have been able to work with is Troyes, Bib. Municipale, Ma 1095—a Clairvaux ms. dating from between 1176 and 1182. The epistle-list, however, agrees with the incipits indicated in the margin of the corresponding masses of the ancient Hauterive gradual formerly at Oelenberg but now in the possession of Tre Fontane Abbey, Rome.

61. A fairly detailed study on the early Cist. calendar is in the course of preparation and will probably appear in 1971 in *Liturgy OCSO*. A curious fact is to be noted in all our early liturgical books: the body of the ms. excludes all refs. to the saints of more recent or more local import. These were relegated to the common.

I should like to insist, however, that there is every indication of a sober, classical, and ancient exemplar.

We have already seen that the primitive Cistercian *hymnal* was composed from "authentic" Ambrosian sources; and that the substance of the *night office lectionary* is certainly taken from the collection of material assembled by Paul the Deacon at the request of Charlemagne.

From the above enumeration, it seems clear that St Bernard was writing the gospel truth when he remarked that the Fathers wanted to use only the most authentic sources in their liturgy.

Second Period of Reform: ?*–ca. 1147*

At an unknown date, the peculiar "chant dialect" of the Metz-derived antiphonary and gradual proved intolerable, and so much so that the General Chapter decided upon a complete reform of the Order's chant books.[62] The *Life of St Stephen of Obazine* gives a brief description of this reform,[63] and the author remarks that, while some liturgical books had to be entirely rewritten, other books survived the purge with only occasional emendations.

The earlier books which escaped virtually intact were the *sacramentary*, the *night office lectionary*, the *collectaneum*, the *epistolary*, and the *evangeliary*.

The *hymnal* underwent a strange sort of revision. The bulk of the Milanese melodies were not exactly "standard" outside the direct sphere of Milanese influence, and the melodies often failed to conform with the ideas on chant theory held by the chants experts active in the reform effected at the request of the General Chapter under the personal aegis of St Bernard. And yet, in the light of the Cistercian exegesis of the prescriptions of the Rule, there was no possibility of rejecting the earlier Milanese-Cistercian hymnal. The following solution was adopted: 1—All the Milanese

62. See St Bernard's *Prologue to the Cist. Antiphonary, loc. cit.*, p. 161. The ed. in PL 182:1121–1122 is non-critical, but reliable.

63. Edited by E. Baluze in 1683 and then re-printed in the same scholar's *Miscellanea*, vol. 1 (Lucca, 1761). The pertinent section occurs in Bk. 2, c. 13, p. 161 of the Lucca ed.

texts were retained. Since there was only one vigils hymn, however, a system of dividing the vespers feastday and seasonal hymns was devised, so that a portion of the hymn could serve as a proper vigils hymn. 2—Many of the Milanese melodies were rewritten in the interests of conformity with Cistercian ideas on chant theory; about seven Milanese melodies were entirely replaced by new, specifically Cistercian compositions. 3—Around sixteen traditional and popular *non*-Milanese hymns were introduced. Providentially, St Benedict had limited his use of the term *ambrosianum* to the hymns of vigils, lauds, and vespers. St Bernard and his collaborators were thus able to assign the newly adopted popular hymns to terce and compline. This was an absolutely novel sort of innovation; but it seemed that drastic measures were taken in order to make good the inadequacies of the older "authentic" but barely tolerable Milanese hymnal.

Something rather similar happened in the case of the *antiphonary*. Many melodic revisions were made in the interests of Cistercian chant theory. But a large number of melodic changes—in fact, most of them—simply brought the Metz melodies more in line with the standard repertory as it was sung in most parts of monastic Europe. Textual revisions corrected numerous repetitions and "gaucheries" of the older repertory. Also, a significant number of *new* texts and *new* melodies were introduced. Perhaps typical of the newly introduced material was the beloved Marian antiphon, *Salve Regina*, and the series of antiphons assigned to several of Our Lady's night offices, and inspired by texts from the *Song of Songs*.[64]

Lack of documentary material makes it prudent not to say too much about the shape of the *gradual* reform. It would seem from corrections I found in an early, non-noted Cistercian "missalette" included in our oldest extant Cistercian sacramentary[65] that there were changes made in a number of introit versets; and there was even the adoption of some later mass chants such as the then

64. For a more detailed discussion, see Waddell, "The Origin and Early Evolution," CS3.

65. The Landais Sacramentary, Paris, Bib. Nationale, Ms. lat. 2300.

relatively recent *Alleluia. Dulce lignum.* But the greater number of changes concerned the melodic text.

In the light of these occasionally drastic revisions, are we able to hold that the primitive, chaste, wonderfully "authentic" earlier liturgical books were really in line with the spiritual and aesthetic needs of the first Cistercians? I think it immensely significant that the bulk of the changes introduced around 1147 tend to align the Cistercians with their contemporaries. In fact, the "Bernardine" reform is in part a return to the Molesme-type of monastic office.[66]

In a sense, the pure, chaste lines of the earlier books were admirable; and I should like to insist that the earlier classical dimension survived intact in the reformed books. Thanks to the earlier, strong reform, the Cistercian books were to remain for a long time uncluttered by the wilder sort of musical and emotional excesses found in many manuscripts of the period. But thanks to Bernard and his collaborators, the aesthetic and spiritual needs of the ordinary "monk in the pew" were to be more adequately provided for by the Order's liturgy.

There is a sad little story in the lovely *Life of David of Himmerod,* who died in 1179.[67] The author tells how the venerable old monk had a special love for a young novice, and that the novice repaid David's affection by singing him "sequences and certain sweet songs about Our Lady."[68] It is too bad that David and others like him were unable to find in the liturgy of the White Monks the full answer to their aesthetic and spiritual needs. And those of us

66. In an interesting study, "Analogie e contrasti fra Cîteaux e Cluny," *Cîteaux* 19 (1968) : 5–39, R. Cortese Esposito notes details in the reforming decrees of Peter the Venerable which seem to be of Cist. inspiration. When I first studied the collection of Peter's statutes several years ago, my conclusion was that the Cist. reformers were the ones who were dependent on Cluny for a number of liturgical revisions, e.g., the series of Johannine antiphons for the Thursdays in Lent, the substitution of the opening section of St Mark's Gospel for the account of Jesus' entry into Jerusalem, etc. On the whole, however, the points in question are matters of mere detail.

67. *Vita B. Davidis Monachi Hemmenrodensis,* intro. and ed. A. Schneider, *Analecta S O Cist* 11 (1955): 27–44.

68. *Ibid.,* pp. 41–42.

who are concerned—and rightly so—for values of simplicity, poverty, and monastic gravity, should not forget David; nor should we look on Bernard's contributions as foreign to the spirit of the Order.

Third Reform: 1180–1182

I mention this third and final period[69] only on its relative unimportance. "Reform" is perhaps too ambitious a word, since the changes were modest in scope, and were chiefly a matter of textual revision. The common of the night office lectionary was somewhat simplified; the Sundays after Epiphany were reorganized. An occasional text was emended. Rather more significant was the purge of some forty-eight masses celebrated in honor of various saints who enjoyed a commemoration at lauds and vespers.[70] Since all these masses had been inevitably taken from the common, perhaps it was the constant repetition of the same mass formularies which paved the way for this rather drastic simplification.

Not directly connected with this revision, but symptomatic of the trend in general, are the overly exuberant and wildly unclassical office of the Holy Trinity adopted in 1175 and the office of St Bernard adopted not long after his canonization in 1174.[71] It is a bit ironic that the infamous *Dialogus Duorum Monachorum*, written not too many years before the canonization of St Bernard, mentions the Feast of the Holy Trinity as an example of what should be excluded from a monastic liturgy.[72] Within a few years, the White Monks were happily celebrating an office which had once served as an example of the excesses of Cluny! Mention could also be

---

69. See above, note 6.

70. The names of the saints concerned have been barred or scraped away in the older mss., and they no longer appear in the ms.-type, Dijon 114 of ca. 1185.

71. For the Holy Trinity office, see Canivez, Statute 1 for 1175; for St Bernard, Statute 2. His canonization seems to have taken place the preceding year, rather than in 1175 as is sometimes claimed.

72. Dia 5:1586.

made of almost a dozen new feasts added to the calendar in the last half of the twelfth century.[73]

If we wish to sum up some of the most evident facts which emerge from this rapid survey of these twelfth-century reforms, we should include at least these points: the Cistercian Fathers and their successors were concerned for Christian values of poverty, simplicity and authenticity. But possibly they tended to push a good thing too far, because they were also children of their time, and had basically the same aesthetic aspirations and spiritual-psychological needs as their fellow-Christians and fellow-monks of other persuasions, as is indicated by the reform of 1147 and later developments.

If this is so, we should rejoice. There is something admirable, perhaps, about a pure, classical style of celebration identified with no particular time or place, but open to every age and culture. Still, the more general or universal, the less particular and relevant is the impact (at least, in many instances). Our southern gothic writer, Flannery O'Connor, once expressed her reaction to the cosmopolitan type of person she often met at dinner parties in New York literary circles: "You know what's the matter with all that kind of folks? They ain't *frum* anywhere!"[74] This is the sort of remark we might be able to make about the earliest Cistercians as judged on the basis of their liturgical books. The same remark would hold less in the second half of the century. I do not suggest that we should wallow in our provincialism. But, after all, as monks we should be humble, unpretentious, unsophisticated, ordinary people, more concerned with the love of God and neighbor than with the authenticity of liturgical forms. And if the early Cistercian liturgy was a living liturgy, it was so less because the texts came from the Gregorian Sacramentary, than because the monks themselves were alive in Christ, and filled with love and zeal.

73. Cf. B. Backaert, "L'évolution du Calendrier cist.," *Collectanea OCR* 12 (1950) and 13 (1951).

74. Quoted in R. Drake, *Flannery O'Connor: A Critical Essay* (Grand Rapids, 1966), p. 11.

The Cistercian "Prepared Environment"

More important than the question of liturgical books and rubrics is the question of the actual environment in which the early Cistercians lived and celebrated the liturgy. In recent times, no one has done more than Dr Maria Montessori to call attention to the importance of what she calls a "prepared environment." The function of the prepared environment is to help the growing child to achieve liberty of spirit and full satisfaction of his intellectual, moral, social and religious needs. As the child passes through his various sensitive periods of development, he is placed in that environment in which his budding talents and aptitudes can best come to full growth.[75] Indeed, Dr Montessori defines a school as a "prepared environment in which the child, set free from undue adult intervention, can live its life according to the laws of its development."[76]

Neither St Benedict nor the early Cistercian Fathers would have had difficulty in transposing this concept to the monastic context. "The monastery is a prepared environment in which the monk, set free from undue constraint from within and from without, can live his own life in Christ according to the law of the Spirit."

The early Cistercian monastery provided a prepared environment of effective solitude, silence, fraternal openness, serious ascesis, meditation and study, and unremitting prayer. The ideal effect of such a regime (not always realized, alas!) should have been to open the individual more and more to the realities present in word and action in the liturgy. There is nothing the least bit specifically "Cistercian" in all this; but it is important, I think, for an understanding of the experience of the liturgy in early Cîteaux. Everything was geared to make the monk come alive and grow in Christ within the context of a living community experience.

Along the same line of thought, we might note how rarely we

75. For the non-specialist reader, an excellent exposé of this and related ideas developed by Dr Montessori may be found in E. M. Standing, *Maria Montessori: Her Life and Work* (Fresno, 1957). See in particular, c. 16. pp. 243–259, where the concept of the prepared environment is discussed in detail.
76. *Ibid.,* p. 99.

can find expressed in twelfth-century Cistercian literature any kind of a conscious, clearly articulated attitude towards the liturgy as such. The monk seemed content simply to live in an atmosphere sustained and permeated by the liturgy.

Cîteaux and the Unity of the Life of Prayer: God's Word made Fruitful

In recent centuries, the relationship between liturgical prayer and contemplation has become a question of major importance.[77] The problem, however, seems to be a relatively "modern" one; and scholars of the stature of a Dom Jean Leclercq OSB, can rightly assert that, for the period under discussion, the "problem" seems to have been all but non-existent. I have found nothing in my study of Cistercian sources which would suggest a different conclusion; and I can do nothing better than to quote Dom Leclercq *verbatim*:

> If we are to grasp well the characteristic feature of the prayer of the older monks, we should recall this fact: prayer is essentially a meeting with God in Holy Scripture. Prayer feeds upon and finds expression in the Word of God, always living in the Bible. God speaks to us in the Scriptures; in order to speak with him, we have only to read, listen, ruminate, meditate, tell God in our turn what he has told us; we have only to repeat the words which he himself suggests, to let our thought, our desire, and our love flow in the formulas which he teaches us, and to give our consent to them by making them our own. In the Middle Ages, it was normal for one to pronounce the words, not just interiorly, but with the lips as well. . . . Every prayer was at one and the same time vocal and mental. . . .[78]

William of St Thierry provides us with an incredibly beautiful

77. J. and R. Maritain, *Liturgie et contemplation* (Bruges, 1959); trans. *Liturgy and Contemplation* (New York, 1960) occasioned a revival and deepening of discussion on the topic. For a copious bibliography of the related literature see the 3 issues of *La Maison-Dieu* dealing chiefly with questions of spirituality and liturgy, 69 (1962), 72–73 (1963).

78. "Culte liturgique et prière intime dans le monachisme au Moyen Age," *Aux sources de la spiritualité occidentale* (Paris, 1964), p. 295. This art. first appeared in *La Maison-Dieu* 69 (1962): 39–55.

expression of the general approach when he prays to the Holy Spirit at the beginning of his great *Exposition on the Song of Songs*, and asks that "what we read may actually take place within us": *ut agatur in nobis quod legitur a nobis.*[79] Or again, to quote a contemporary masterpiece of monastic literature, consider what Mother Genevieve Gallois OSB has little Saint Placid say to describe what the office means to him: "To sing one's life and live one's song. What is this song and what is this life which it opens up for us? . . . Little Placid found himself placed objectively before God. The liturgy put into his mouth words he never dared utter. His words formed his thought and his thought formed his being. And so, the liturgy enfolded him as in a mold, and when it had transformed him, then rose to God as the expression of his own being, Little Placid."[80]

The primacy of the word as a factor in the twelfth-century liturgical reforms has still to be appreciated. Mention has already been made of the Cistercian Fathers and their efforts to secure the most authentic texts possible. And though the reform of around 1147 has heretofore been studied chiefly from its musical aspects, the revision of the texts was of no less importance than the revision of the music. All textual oddities and incongruities were removed, so as to render it possible for the monk to make the texts his own without any reservation.[81] I have even encountered instances of musical changes being made in the interests of a better accentuation of the text.[82]

---

79. No. 4, ed. J. M. Déchanet, SC 82 (Paris: Cerf, 1962), p. 74; trans. C. Hart, *The Works of William of St Thierry,* vol. 2, CF 6 (Spencer, Mass.: Cistercian Publications, 1970), p. 7.

80. *The Life of the Little Saint Placid* (New York, 1956), the pages are not numbered.

81. See St Bernard's *Prologus, Opera,* 3:515; trans., CF1: 161–162; but more especially the entire first section of the anonymous treatise explaining the editorial principles operative in the reform of the Cist. antiphonary, *Cantum quem Cisterciensis,* ed. several times (always badly), but most easily accessible in PL 182:1121ff.

82. The transition from the classical Latin prosody to the rhythmic, often rhymed verse of the Middle Ages has frequently been traced. See, e.g., William

Until the present time, rather much has been written about the Cistercians and their ideas on the theory of music.[83] But Bernard and his fellows saw music not only as an ordered discipline pertaining to the *quadrivium*, but also and especially as a means of coming into a more fruitful contact with the text to be sung. As Bernard himself expressed it, the music should not "void the text of its meaning, but rather make the text more fruitful."[84] Thus, liturgical chant had to be in the service of the word. Virtuoso vocal display and badly composed music were bad because they obscured the life-giving word, and rendered its impact less effective. Unless the music deepened one's experience of the word and helped to intensify the quality of the spiritual experience, it quite simply failed in its proper function.

The Classical Structure of Early Cistercian Culture

We have already seen that the first Fathers apparently had a predilection for classical sources. Possibly this was in part tributary to the need they felt, like most of their contemporaries, for order, proportion and harmonious balance. I suppose that one can make out an argument in favor of the Cistercians as heralds of *devotio moderna* and the religious emotionalism of a later period. While I do not personally accept this view, I gladly admit, and even insist on the warmth and lyricism characteristic of the early Cistercian literature; but I further insist that this warmth and this lyricism are rooted in an experience marked by order, discipline and harmony.

Beare, *Latin Verse and European Song* (London, 1957). The later medieval concept of the Latin tonic accent was different from the earlier generations which saw the rise of the traditional chant repertory. Many of the attempted "corrections" of later musicians actually denatured the authentic reading of its proper qualities.

83. For a brief bibliography, see Waddell, "The Origins and Evolution," CF3, note 6; to which should be added P. Gümpel, "Zur Interpretation der Tonus Definition des *Tonale Sancti Bernardi*," *Abhandlungen der Akademie der Wissenschaften und der Literatur* (Jahrgang 1959), 2:29–51.

84. Ep 398; PL 182:611a. The letter is an excellent commentary on the nature of liturgical texts and music as seen by one of the foremost spokesmen for the White Monks. Trans. with intro., M. B. Pennington, *Liturgy OCSO* 4 (1970): 18–20.

Perhaps others have shared the intense annoyance I used to feel each Feast of St Bernard, when we sang the untranslatable first responsory of the night office:

R7. The first virtue to be noticed in this holy man was the harmony of his bearing and his perfect self-mastery. * Nothing could be discerned in him which might give offense.

℣. Everything about him was well-ordered; everything bore the mark of virtue and was a model of perfection. [85]

The point of this text is *not* that Bernard was the perfect gentleman. Rather, it tells us, as I now realize, that Bernard's inmost being so radiated the splendor of harmony and the unity of truth, that even his outward bearing reflected something of his spiritual qualities.

In the twelfth century, no one would have thought for a moment of denying to the universe and to man's spiritual microcosm an order based on divinely willed harmony and proportion. That the world was in fact disordered, no one denied. But this was due to the intrusion of sin. The redemption was understood as a restoration of the broken order; and man's ascetical effort was aimed at escaping from the region of unlikeness and disorder in order to be re-formed anew in the perfection of man's original harmony and beauty. In the words attributed to St Stephen Harding at the very beginning of the Cistercian reform, "By reason the Supreme Creator has made all things; by reason he governs all things; by reason the fabric of the world revolves; by reason even the planets move; by reason the elements are directed; and by reason, and by due regulation, our nature ought to conduct itself," [86] and Stephen goes on to explain that the function of the Holy Rule is to bring fallen men back to the divine order of reason. In brief, God's

85. The text is Bernard's own—but written originally in praise of his friend, St Malachy of Armagh, *Vita Sancti Malachiae,* c. 19, no. 43, *Opera* 3:348.

86. William of Malmesbury, *Gesta Regum Anglorum* iv, n. 334, PL 179: 1287c. Trans. *The Portable Medieval Reader,* ed. J. B. Ross and M. M. McLaughlin (New York, 1949), p. 56.

I

universe is ordered, and each element therein finds its perfection in finding its proper place. This is classicism at its purest.[87]

It is in the context of this spiritual universe of harmony and proportion that we should consider the Cistercian chant reform of *ca.* 1147. The particular details of Cistercian chant theory are interesting enough—at least, to the specialist. But the general spiritual postulates which under-gird the theory are much more interesting. Music, like all the arts and like every form of human activity, should be an expression of order, proportion, truth. Music has an inner nature, a *ratio*; and the great tragedy is that music in the concrete so often runs counter to its truest nature. The whole thrust of the 1147 chant reform was directed towards restoring the chant to its deepest and truest nature. It was a failure, of course, but a glorious failure. The essence of chant cannot be reduced to a few formulas based on mathematics, and most of the Cistercian "corrections" justified only in terms of chant theory are actually mutilations of the original melody. But the basic intuition is of perennial significance: in a world disordered by sin, we should become at every level of our being what we are in our deepest reality.

A somewhat different but related idea about music was that it necessarily had a moral "ethos," a moral evaluation. The listener was affected whether he liked it or not; for music was an instrument for the promotion of the individual in good or for his debasement in evil.[88]

---

87. Even a summary bibliography of the Augustinian idea of a universe created in measure and number and weight would run to many pages. For an excellent description of the background against which Cist. architecture and chant theory should be studied, see O. Von Simson, *The Gothic Cathedral: Origins of Gothic Architecture and the Medieval Concept of Order,* Bollingen Series 48 (New York, 1956), pp. 21–58. The author makes numerous mistakes in points of detail, but his general presentation is of exceptional merit.

88. See P. Hindemith, *A Composer's World* (Cambridge, 1953), pp. 1–13, with special ref. to the author's discussion of Boethius' dictum (cribbed from Plato), "Music is a part of our human nature; it has the power either to improve or to debase our character," pp. 7ff. For an equally stimulating, but rather more systematic presentation of much the same material, see E. Routly, *The Church and Music* (London, 1950), pp. 41–108.

Cîteaux and the Spirit of Celebration

In a late summer issue of the *Herder Correspondence* in 1967, the editor devoted several paragraphs to a remarkable discussion of the spirit of celebration. This spirit, he wrote, "is an outgrowth of a particular kind of life: the life of people who, caring deeply for their lives together, feel themselves well cared for, and are habitually content."[89] The author then reflects that, nowadays, many of us neither care deeply for our lives together, nor feel ourselves well cared for; indeed, "the most basic assumptions underlying the contemporary status quo are that our existence on this earth is a sorry business."[90] Thank God for the exceptions—those who "possess that profound contentment with their lives which issues habitually in thankful wonder. But lack of encouragement from the social environment stifles incipient celebration in the weakest of these; the strongest are condemned to live with it—forever incipient, never realized—in frustrating solitary confinement. Celebration, being deeply human, is necessarily a social growth."[91]

Gloomy lines. They never could have applied to the first generations of Cistercians; because their whole life-situation was geared to draw forth, sustain, and deepen a spirit of celebration.

For the White Monks cared deeply for their lives together. They believed intensely in their reform; and to the extent they remained generous in their commitment, they understood and marveled at God's goodness and love. William of Malmesbury tells us that St Stephen Harding sometimes used to pretend that, out of his love for the brethren, he was thinking of easing the burden of the Rule they bore. They themselves would have none of this. They intended to persevere, come what may, and leave a good example for those who would come after them.[92] In a social dimension and community experience such as this, it is easy for joy, wonder, and the spirit of celebration to spring forth.

It is both interesting and significant that in the more unpreten-

89. "No Wonder No Celebration," *Herder Correspondence* 4 (1967): 198.
90. *Ibid.*   91. *Ibid.*
92. *Op. cit.*, no. 337 *in fine*; PL 179:1290b-c.

tious Cistercian literature of the twelfth century, so many of the
visions and spiritual experiences present us with a community at
prayer, as if it is in this aspect of their life that they most perfectly
express what they really are. Typical is the experience related by
Christian, the holy, semi-literate monk of Aumône, who once
had a vision of the community of Cîteaux and of their venerable
abbot, Raynaud. The community was arranged as for choir; above
them was gathered another choir—the choir of angels, among
whom was the abbot of Cîteaux.[93] This is the author's way of
telling us that the monastic liturgy is a participation in the liturgy
of the angels, and that this community is essentially a community
of prayer and praise, a community of celebration.[94]

The Balanced Life of the First Cistercians

There is a rather curious story in the *Exordium Magnum* which
makes an important point for our understanding of the early
Cistercian liturgy. The novice master of Grandselve had been a
champion athlete of the spiritual life. As such persons often did, he
made a spectacular return appearance shortly after his death. His
bodily appearance resembled nothing less than clear crystal blazing
with the purest light—except, alas, for a dark blotch on the ap-
parition's foot. Why the blotch? Well, the holy novice master, in
spite of his merits, had had a single fault: he was a bit less fervent
than he should have been when he went with the brethren to the
daily common work. The narrator piously adds the moral: "It is
certain that *every* practice of the Order is holy and pleasing to God,
and that no one can be neglected without serious danger to the
soul."[95]

The story is a bit crude, but it remains true that the strength of

93. EM 1:34, p. 95. A different redaction of the same story is included in the
complete version of the *Vita Christiani Monachi,* ed. J. Leclercq, *Analecta
Bollandiana* 71 (1953):42.

94. A common-place in monastic writings. For an excellent presentation
accompanied by rich bibliographical refs., see J. Leclercq, *The Life of Perfection*
(Collegeville, 1961), c. 1: The Angelic Life, pp. 15–42; as well as E. Peterson,
The Angels and the Liturgy (New York, 1964), pp. 22–40.

95. EM 2:24, p. 125.

Cistercian life lay, at least in part, in balance. The Acts of the Apostles describe the life of the primitive Christian community in terms of devotion "to the Apostles' teaching, to the fellowship, and to the breaking of bread and the prayers."[96] Exegetes differ in their commentaries; but a general picture emerges of a community united in the same faith and teaching, in the same concern for effective charity, and in the same prayer and sacramental life. In both East and West, monks have looked back to the primitive Church as to the model and source of monastic life at its most authentic;[97] and it can be said in a general way that, so often as *one* of the aspects of this life is lost sight of, the consequences are serious. Doctrine, social consciousness, liturgy: each is essential for a living cenobitic tradition. Thus, emphasis on the liturgy without due regard for doctrinal formation or the needs of one's fellow-man, has led at times to a caricature of monasticism. Was this true at Cîteaux?

I suggest that there was a happy balance of all these aspects in early Cîteaux. We have already considered the liturgy at length. Let us consider briefly the Cistercians and their social consciousness and doctrinal formation.

Poverty in the Cistercian liturgy was an expression of an aesthetic attitude; but it was also an expression of actual poverty and a humble way of life. The monk was, by his very state of life, identified with the poor (at least, ideally). William of Malmesbury tells us that Stephen Harding, as abbot of Cîteaux, considered his purse as a kind of source of public funds for all the poor and needy.[98] Though a few of the following lines call (I think) for a more nuanced expression, perhaps this passage from a book by the late Fr Louis Merton ocso, states the position well:

> Underlying the Cistercian insistence on manual labor was a powerful element of what some call "social consciousness." The

96. Acts 2:42; cf. 2:44–47; 4:32–35.

97. Frequent refs. in the c.: The Apostolic Life, Leclercq, *The Life of Perfection*, pp. 63–80. It is significant that EM 1:2 bears the title: *Quod a primitiva ecclesia communis vitae traditio coeperit et quod hinc monasticae religionis institutio principium sumpserit.*

98. *Op. cit.*, no. 337, PL 179:1290a.

poverty and labor of the early Cistercians had explicit reference to the social situation in which they lived. Besides being a return to St Benedict and the Gospel, their way of life was also a protest against the inordinate wealth of so many of the great feudal abbeys.

One of the strongest criticisms leveled by Cîteaux against the Cluniac regime was that it was rooted in social injustice. The Cistercians could not accept the notion of a life of contemplation in which the interior peace and leisure of contemplation were luxuries purchased by the exploitation of serfs and the taxation of the poor.[99]

As for doctrinal formation and spiritual culture, it is clear that not every Cistercian was a St Bernard or an Isaac of Stella. Our monasteries had their massive proportions of illiterate and semi-literate monks, and one ought not to generalize on the basis of a handful of luminaries, most of whom were well formed intellectually and spiritually before they entered the Order. Yet, it is impossible to ignore the cumulative picture which emerges from serious works of scholarship such as Fr Louis Lekai's *The White Monks*,[100] Fr Bouyer's *The Cistercian Heritage*,[101] Fr Anselme Dimier's monographs on Cistercian art and architecture,[102] to say nothing of works by Dom Jean Leclercq too numerous to be listed. Though the vast majority of the brethren were perhaps intellectually quite ordinary, their general environment was one of sound doctrine and healthy spirituality.

We can better appreciate this balance of doctrine, social con-

99. *The Waters of Siloe* (New York, 1949), p. 17. As it stands, the passage quoted is a bit naive in presenting the "Cluniac regime" as a single, monolithic structure. Many, if not most of the "great feudal abbeys" had only tenuous connections with Cluny itself: moreover, Cluny may well be pointed to as a model of generosity to the poor. See J. Leclercq, "Culte et pauvreté à Cluny," *La Maison-Dieu* 81 (1964): 33–50.

100. (Okauchee, 1953). Subsequent French and German versions have introduced revisions and additions to the original English version. A major section is devoted to various aspects of Cistercian culture, pp. 145–284.

101. (Westminster, Md., 1958); trans. of *La spiritualité de Cîteaux* (Paris: Flammarion, 1955).

102. Best represented by his contributions in *L'art cistercien*, Zodiaque: La nuit des temps 16 (Pierre-qui-vire, 1962).

sciousness, and liturgy in the early days, if we look at the situation less than a hundred years later. One of the great monastic figures of the thirteenth century, Stephen, abbot successively of Stanley, Savigny, and Clairvaux, wrote to a fellow abbot around 1333–1334 that he knew of one monastery in which at least seven monks were guilty of formal heresy, and that public heretics had won the support of Cistercian communities in some parts of the Order. He laid the blame in part to a decline of the Order's intellectual vigor, remarking that it had been thirteen years since a real scholar had entered the Order and he quotes an unidentified person as saying that, should heresy become more general, the Cistercians would be among the first to defect from the faith.[103]

As for "social consciousness," we know how sadly the Order had declined by the mid-thirteenth century. Signs of the great old tradition are still evident; but territorial expansion, accumulation of property (always for good reasons, of course), and involvement in business and politics exacted a heavy toll on the Order's vitality. One has only to read the correspondence of Stephen of Lexington[104] or the Statutes of the General Chapters of the period to realize the extent of the malaise. Perhaps the most favored communities were those houses of nuns who followed our Cistercian customs without being completely dependent on a decaying organism such as the Order was slowly becoming. In many of the Flemish nunneries, and in convents such as Helfta,[105] intellectual life flourished, social consciousness remained keen, and the liturgy, to all appearances, was a living liturgy.

The Cistercian Laybrothers and the Liturgy

One cannot speak of the early Cistercians and the liturgy without

---

103. B. Griesser, ed., *Registrum Epistolarum Stephani de Lexington, Analecta S O Cist* 2 (1946): 116–117.

104. Published in 2 sections, *Analecta S O Cist* 2 (1946): 1–118 (dating from Stephen's years as abbot of Stanley, 1227–1229) and 8 (1952): 181–378 (from Stephen's years as abbot of Savigny, 1230–1239).

105. On the Cist. background of the nuns of Helfta, see J. Hourlier, *Gertrude d'Helfta: Oeuvres spirituelles,* vol. 1, SC 127 (Paris: Cerf, 1967), pp. 10–13.

including in the discussion the laybrothers. Monks they were emphatically not; but they were religious, and Cistercian religious.

Even with the help of excellent studies of the medieval laybrotherhood in general and the Cistercian laybrothers in particular,[106] it is still difficult for us to maintain a balanced perspective when there is question of the liturgical life of these humble men of God. Their participation in the liturgy should be gauged less in comparison with that of the monks than with that of pious laymen living in the world; and we would do well to remember that the laybrother's world was to a large extent even physically separate from that of the monks. The laybrothers had their own refectory, dormitory, chapter house, infirmary; and though they might be allowed in the back part of the church by a corridor running parallel to a wing of the monks' cloister, a specially constructed wall or screen cut them off from the monks' choir.[107] Access to the monks' cloister was forbidden on general principle, though the laybrothers did take part in the processions through the cloister on the feast of the Purification, Palm Sunday and—from 1152 onwards—the Ascension. Actual access into the chapter house was granted on the day of the individual's reception and profession; and on solemn feasts, when a sermon was preached, the laybrothers were present—but outside the chapter, next to the bay-windows which opened into the cloister.[108] Though not all the laybrothers were illiterate, books of any kind were absolutely prohibited to them;[109]

---

106. Such as J. Leclercq, "Comment vivaient les frères convers," *Analecta S O Cist* 21 (1965): 239–258; K. Hallinger, "Woher kommen die Laienbrüder," *ibid.,* 12 (1956): 1–104; O. Ducourneau, "De l'institutions et des Us des convers dans l'Ordre de Cîteaux (XIIᵉ et XIIIᵉ siècles)," *Saint Bernard et son temps,* vol. 2 (Dijon, 1929), pp. 139–201; E. Mikkers, "L'ideal religieux des frères convers dans l'Ordre aux 12e et 13e siècles," *Collectanea OCR* 24 (1962): 113–129; C. Van Dijk, "L'instruction et la culture des frères convers dans les premiers siècles de Cîteaux," *ibid.,* pp. 243–258.

107. Cf. M. Aubert, *L'architecture cistercienne en France,* vol. 1, 2nd ed. (Paris, 1947), p. 317.

108. *Ibid.,* 2:15. According to O. Ducourneau, *art. cit.,* pp. 189–190, the laybrothers were allowed entry into the chapter house on feasts of sermon.

109. Ducourneau, *ibid.,* p. 191.

and they were allowed to be taught only the Lord's Prayer, the Creed, Psalm Fifty, the doxology and a few other texts which composed the office they recited (in Latin!) at set times and in union with the office celebrated by the choir monks.[110] They were present at the back of the church for the office and the two conventual masses on Sundays and feasts when there was no work; and they assisted at the first mass on a few days which, though feasts, were also work days. But on ordinary days outside of Lent, and apart from a few special occasions (funeral masses, vigil masses, Ember Day masses), there was *no* mass for the laybrothers.[111] Communion was restricted to seven times a year, though the precise number could be increased or decreased at the discretion of the abbot;[112] and though this, by our current practice, seems to us to be infrequent it was certainly thought otherwise in the twelfth century, when the Communion of laymen was often an affair of once or twice a year. As for work, it was a dawn to dusk affair, with time out only for meals.

The lives of the early laybrothers provide us with some of the most beautiful pages in Cistercian history; and Dom Jean Leclercq osb, has synthesized much of this material in a beautiful article in which he discusses this way of life under the headings of humility, work, patience and prayer.[113] Yet, not every aspirant could live fruitfully in a regime such as this, which called for charisms of a high degree. So it is that we find not only beautiful pages in this history, but pages filled with blood, smoke, violence and corruption. One could speak eloquently of the beauty of the laybrothers' simple type of prayer in common; of their spiritual union with the monks celebrating the liturgy in the monastery church; of their sensitivity to the mystery of Christ as it unfolded year by year in the annual liturgical cycle. And one could also easily demonstrate the incompatibility of a clericalized style of liturgical celebration with the aptitude of most of the twelfth-century laybrothers. For myself, I have no intention of drawing up a score sheet. But I

110. *Ibid.*, pp. 184–185.
111. *Ibid.*, pp. 185–186.
112. *Ibid.*, p. 187.
113. Art. indicated above, note 106.

sometimes wonder whether greater possibilities in the area of intellectual formation and liturgical celebration might not have resulted in many more beautiful pages of Cistercian hagiography, and fewer pages filled with accounts of sedition, violence, moral turpitude and rebellion?

Summary

Any balanced survey of the early Cistercian experience of the liturgy will tend towards a certain complexity, because of the very nature of the material covered, which is complex. Most of the authors with whom I am familiar tend to oversimplify the picture, stressing only a few obviously important points: the early Cistercian liturgy was simple, austere, expressive of a refined, pure type of monastic experience free from emotionalism and the like. I agree. But I should like to add the following:

Fidelity to the Rule and a passion for the authentic were decisive factors in the shaping up of the early Cistercian liturgy. On the positive side, this resulted in a liturgy marked by simplicity, poverty of means, classical forms of expression. On the negative side, fidelity to the Rule and a passion for the authentic resulted in the adoption of much that could be justified at the level of abstract principle, but not at the level of living experience (the Milanese hymnal, the decadent chant from Metz, perhaps even the preponderantly "classic" repertory of early days). The liturgical reform of *ca.* 1147 did much to preserve the enriching values of the primitive period of the Order's liturgy, while at the same time it discreetly aligned the Cistercians a bit more with their contemporary Benedictine fellow-monks, and no less discreetly provided for the reasonable aesthetic needs of genuine serious monks in the age of troubadours and trouvères. Regardless of the importance we attach to the liturgical books, to the chant, and to the usages in our analysis of the early Cistercian experience of the liturgy, the vitality and authenticity of this experience were due also the the convergence of a number of favorable influences, among which we may note the following:

a—the very environment created the optimum conditions in which the monk could live at depth and grow in spiritual sensitivity;

b—unity in the life of prayer was centered in the reception and "fructification" of the word of God (liturgy = actualization of the proclaimed word of God);

c—commitment to an ideal generously embraced and a positive experience of community gave rise to and supported a spirit of celebration such as is necessary for a truly living liturgy;

d—a balanced Christian life (doctrine, "social consciousness," liturgy) promoted the well-being of the whole life style, and simultaneously fostered the well-being of each of its aspects.

I am not at all sure that St Stephen Harding or St Bernard, both in heaven, are particularly concerned as to the language in which we twentieth-century Cistercians celebrate the liturgy. I do not think they are interested in the authenticity of the sacramentary we use at Mass, or the conformity of our hymn tunes to twelfth-century ideas on chant theory. But I *do* know that they would have us find in our liturgy a means of coming alive in Christ and of living more perfectly in him. If our own primary concern lies in this direction, we shall not be too unworthy of what is deepest and best in the rich heritage bequeathed us by the Fathers of Cîteaux.

Chrysogonus Waddell ocso

Gethsemani Abbey,
Trappist, Kentucky

DISCUSSION

The period of discussion began with one of the members questioning the "social consciousness" of the early Cistercian Fathers. He asked whether we are not reading into them a contemporary problem, which would not have been so vivid for the twelfth century. It was felt that the early Cistercians were motivated not so much by the intention of identifying with the poor, as we understand this today, but rather chose poverty as an evangelical ideal. Fr Chrysogonus maintained, however, that there was a real social consciousness among the Fathers which is comparable to our contemporary mentality. It basically consisted in their identification of themselves with the poor of that period. They did not emulate the wealth of many of the great feudal abbeys. This was connected with their ideals of Benedictine humility and Cistercian simplicity.

A question then arose regarding the apparent exploitation of the lay-brothers by the early Cistercians. The brothers worked almost from dawn to compline. It was said in response that even under these conditions to be a laybrother was an advancement in that society. The mentality of the times was not as aware of the equality of persons and classes as we are today. Serfs were seen as geared to the sword and to work, while the nobles and clerics were geared to study and liturgy.

Looking for deeper underlying causes one of the respondents saw the difference in approach between ourselves and the early Cistercians as based upon a cultural difference. The Fathers of the twelfth century were classicists, for whom authenticity consisted in conformity to an ideal. Moderns, on the other hand, are more basically romanticists, for whom authenticity consists in that which produces experience.

This led to further consideration of the interpretation of the Rule for their time and for ours. The Rule of St Benedict is a particular document written at a definite period of history, in a particular place and for a particular group of persons or communities of persons. St Benedict and the monks of his time lived this Rule. It is an objectification of their experience, a record of their understanding of their monastic way of life based on the Gospel. But the Rule of St Benedict also has a message for us today. Dynamic interpretation of the Rule reveals to us not only the meaning which the Rule had for monks living in the sixth century, but also the meaning and message it has for us today. Dynamic interpretation consists not in abstract concepts, but in actual life experience. The monastic life of today —as lived on the three levels, of the Order, the local community and the individual monk—is dynamic interpretation of the Rule of St Benedict.

PROFESSION ACCORDING TO THE RULE OF ST BENEDICT

AN HISTORICAL STUDY

MONKS AND NUNS IN MONASTERIES which pertain to what is called the Benedictine Order ordinarily undertake to make a solemn commitment to live the monastic life by making profession according to the Rule of St Benedict and the constitutions of their congregation or monastery. On the other hand in the Cistercian Order they speak only of the Rule. However, they manifestly have observances which are not found in the Rule; indeed, those among them who are not "bound to choir" are dispensed, at least in part, from that divine office which holds such an important place in the Rule. The question arises then for them whether in virtue of their profession they ought to fulfill all the prescriptions of the Rule or if, for the greater freedom of conscience of some among them, their profession ought to be made equally according to constitutions which would modify the Rule.

In relation with this practical question one can place another more general one: What does it mean to make profession according to the Rule of St Benedict? In response to this one could devote himself to gathering texts and particular facts; there is not yet a complete documentation in this area, though a number of things will be found in this study. But it seems more useful to seek rather to discern through the whole course of history the directions taken and the evolution. This approach—while awaiting an exhaustive study—will imply both interpretations and hypotheses which will remain susceptible to modification. However, they will merit to be considered and reflected upon by other students in this area. This method of procedure is the only one which enables us to make progress in our knowledge of the past—on condition, however, that the information which has already been gathered is a sufficiently solid foundation for the proposed solutions or conjectures.

One of the results of this work will be to situate not only the particular question which we are trying to solve, but the whole "Cistercian fact" in the course of a history which neither began nor ended with it. In this sense, it will find itself, so to speak, "relativized." This should offset that tendency which sometimes appears, to take the initial Cistercian happening as something absolute and definitive. There were at least two great periods before it, and there are two others which follow upon its first century. One of these latter is our own, and it ought to profit by the lessons of the past.

Before going any further, it would be well to consider the terms of the formula which is the object of our present study. Two things ought to be noted:

First of all, the word "profession" designates the monastic commitment as a whole. This word is not to be found in the Rule itself. The author rather speaks of a "promise," using the noun *promissio* and especially the verb *promittere*. However, he does on one occasion use the verb *profiteri*.[1] This engagement imports what we have come later to speak of as the "vows."[2]

---

1. *Promissio*: RB 58:19, *promitti*: 4:76; 58:9, 14, 17; 59:3; 60:9; *profiteri*: 5:3.
2. In regards to the problem of vocabulary, I have given some indications in an article entitled, "S. Bernard dans l'histoire de l'obéissance" in *Recueil d'études sur S. Bernard*, vol. 3 (Rome, 1969), pp. 267–298. In St Augustine, one can find *profiteri* in regards to the clerical commitment: Sermon 355:6; PL 39:1573; in the *Regula Aureliani Arelatensis* (6th Century), 1; PL 68:388, *profiteri* is used in regards to the monk. Cassian uses *sponsio, pactio, promissio, polliceri* (*Conf.* 17:2, 8; CSEL 13:466, 469) and often *professio* (*Conf.* 17:8; 19:3, 9; CSEL 13:469, 536, 538, 543f; references to the *Insti.* in *Institutions cenobitiques*, ed. J. C. Guy, SC 109 [Paris: Cerf, 1965], *Index des mots*, p. 525), often not to designate the act itself or the commitment, but the state of life—as one might say in English the "profession"—which results from this commitment. The Spanish rules use sometimes the word *pactum*; cf. H. Leclercq, "Pacte,"

Secondly, it is good to recall that what we call the "Rule of St Benedict" or *Regula Benedicti* is a text which appeared in Gaul around the year 600. It was certainly written sometime during the sixth century. Very specialized studies are being made concerning its date and author. The extremely complex problems involved here have been sufficiently penetrated, however, as to give us a very solid probability. The Rule was only subsequently attributed to St Benedict, and this attribution is not admitted by all nor do there exist decisive proofs in its favor. According to some in so far as we can judge from the Second Book of the *Dialogues* of St Gregory the Great, the Rule followed by Benedict and his monks while they were at Subiaco was close to that of the Rule of the Master, while at Monte Cassino their Rule was much more that of the *Regula Benedicti*.[3] In order to avoid taking a position in regards to its authenticity, certain scholars have designated the Rule of St Benedict by its opening word—they speak of the "Rule *Ausculta*." But here too there are two different traditions, two forms. Certain manuscripts have rather *Obsculta*. Generally it is preferable to employ the abbreviation RB; that is what we will employ in this paper.

FROM THE ORIGINS TO THE NINTH CENTURY
THE ORIGIN AND MEANING OF THE FORMULA

RB is mentioned for the first time in relation to monastic profession in the petition, the *petitio,* which the monks in Burgundy from the end of the seventh century until 730 used to make to

---

DACL 13:1, col. 223ff. *Votum* is illustrated by a text of [the Psalm, as would also be the case with St Bernard, in the "Synodus S. Patricii," can. 17, *Mans.* 6:525. Concerning the use and meaning of *votum*, see P. Séjourné, "Voeu," *DTC* 15:2, col. 3193ff. (1950).

3. These indications are taken from J. Froger, "Remarques sur l'édition de la Règle du Maître due à dom A. de Vogüé," *Revue d'hist. ecclés.* 61 (1966): 507–509, and from A. de Vogüé, "La Régle du Maître et les Dialogues de S. Grégoire," *ibid.*, pp. 75–76.

their abbot. These monks asked to be allowed to "live under"—the Latin word is *sub* and not *secundum*—this Rule, without giving any further precision as to what they engaged themselves: *sub regula beati Benedicti vivere et conversare.* From what follows it is clear that they were considering here especially obedience and stability. This text shows up in an area where at the same time there existed Celtic monasticism. There was there a mixture of, and there could have been a conflict between, the Rule which is attributed to St Colomban and that which bore the name of St Benedict; and some monks chose the observances of the second. We could not ascertain anything else from this first document.

In the French kingdom during the rest of the eighth century the situation remained that which has been characterized by the expression of *Regula mixta.*[4] However, some monks opted for RB. Speaking of the foundation of Fulda, St Boniface in 751 said that he had "established" monks living under the Rule of St Benedict: *monachos constituimus sub Regula S. Patris Benedicti.* Note, once again the use of the word *sub.*[5] He says the same in relation to the monastery of Fritzlar in a letter written some time after 746 or 747.[6] Fifty years later in the life of St Sturmius of Fulda, RB is spoken of in relation to the "promise" of the monastic life. The sense of the formula is not very precise, but it had certainly its

---

4. See "S. Bernard dans l'histoire de l'obéissance," *loc. cit.*, pp. 276–278. The existence and the diffusion of an observance influenced by both RB and the Rule of St Columban in "irofränkish" monasticism which continued throughout the whole of the seventh and eighth centuries has been brought to light by A. E. Angenendt, *Monachi peregrini. Studien zu Pirmin und den monastischen Vorstellungen des Frühen Mittelalters* (Münster, 1970). From the first half of the eighth century there is a fragment of a commentary on RB which has been discovered and identified by K. Hallinger, "Das Kommentarfragment zu Regula Benedicti IV aus der ersten Hälfte des 8. Jahrhunderts," *Wiener Studien* 82 (1969): 211–213. It comes perhaps from Corbie or from the north of France, but in a sense it concerns itself with the general precepts contained in Chapter Four; one cannot draw anything from it in regards to the problems we are considering here.

5. "Epistle 86," ed. M. Tangl, MGH, Epist. sel., vol. 1, 2nd ed. (1955), p. 193; the letter is of 751; see P. Engelbert, *Die Vita Sturmi des Eigil von Fulda* (Marbourg, 1968), p. 92.

6. Ep., 40, *éd. cit.*, pp. 64–65.

purpose to single out this Rule in preference to others.[7] During the ninth century a layman, Charlemagne, reinforced by his authority this option on the part of certain monks in favor of RB, and he sought to impose it throughout his empire. The first text which concerns us here, that of the *Supplex libellus* addressed to him by the monks of Fulda, names St Benedict once,[8] but does not explicitly mention RB. There is only an allusion to it. The expression *secundum regulam* is used in reference to a particular point which in itself is rather vague and not in relation to the whole, that is, with the idea of "to live according to the Rule."[9] However, a little further on one finds this interesting formula: "to live according to the rule and the custom of our ancients."[10] Here we have the first of a series of witnesses which shows that in actual practice RB would always be—and it was from this particular epoch— inseparably united to a set of custons.

Among those who lived the regular life within the Empire there was not always a clear distinction between the canons and the monks; and even within these two groups there was sometimes a certain amount of confusion. To set this situation aright the Council of Aix-la-Chapelle of 816 established a clear distinction between the canonical life, which would have for its law the Rule of St Augustine, and the monastic life. In the case of this latter, it sought to eliminate the regime of the *Regula mixta*. At the instigation of Charlemagne and then of his son Louis the Pious, St Benedict of Aniane sought to have all monks adopt RB. The Council required them to study

---

7. *Porro cum fratres regulam S. P. Benedicti inhianter observare desiderassent . . .*, *Vita Surmi*, c. 14, éd. P. Engelbert, *op. cit.*, p. 145; *Regulam S. Benedicti quam se implesse promiserant, ad omnia observabant . . ., ibid.*, c. 14, p. 147. In regards to the date of the *Vita, ibid.*, p. 20. In regards to the value given to the Rule, *ibid.*, p. 93: *Sie muss tatsächlich in entscheidendem Masse als normativ angesehen worden sein.*

8. *Supplex libellus monachorum Fuldensium Carolo imperatori porrectus*, c. 16, ed. J. Semmler, in K. Hallinger, *Corpus consuetudinum monasticarum* I (Siegburg, 1963), p. 324.

9. *Ibid.*, c. 12.

10. *Secundum regulam et secundum priorum nostrorum consuetudinem.—ibid.*, c. 13, p. 325.

K

it.[11] Profession "according to the Rule of St Benedict" was then made obligatory.[12] This addition to the formula profession which was called for by RB itself was not really necessary, because the whole rite which constituted its context presupposed that the novice had become familiar with the Rule, had attempted to live according to it, and now undertook to observe it; if he now "promised" the monastic life, it could be only a life in conformity with this Rule. Why then was it necessary to add this expression? It was to single out his preference for this Rule above all the others. Certainly it is clear that it was not meant to exclude the customs which already existed, which were preserved, and which would be developed. Let us see in regards to this what the texts have to say.

There are two commentaries on the Rule of St Benedict in which these ideas are explored. The first is the one composed by Smaragdus of Saint-Mihiel sometime after 817. Explaining Chapter Fifty-eight where "the manner of receiving the brethren" is described, the author says, in speaking of the Rule, that the novices are taught the "regular disciplines."[13] If the candidate accepts the whole observance,[14] he makes his promise according to the Rule of St Benedict: *Promitto . . . secundum Regulam S. Benedicti.*[15] In the context of all that had preceded it, it is clear that the novice did not submit himself to the Rule alone but to the rules which had been gathered together, *regulis suprascriptis,* in other words, the whole of the

11. *Regulam per singula verba discutientes legant et intellegentes adimpleant.* —ed. Semmler, *ibid.,* p. 435:1; there is a more developed redaction in two other versions, pp. 441:1; 457:1. P. Riché, "Les hagiographes bretons et la renaissance caroligienne," *Bulletin philologique et historique, Année 1966* (Paris, 1968): 658, has recently cited examples of the influence exercised by the decisions of Aix even as far away as Armorica: "From 818, the Rule of St Benedict supplanted in Landevence the Celtic customs . . . Redon, founded in 832, was likewise won over to Benedictine monasticism thanks to a monk from Saint-Maur-sur-Loire (Glanfeuil)."

12. This is evident from a fragment of a text which has been brought to light by J. Semmler, "Die Beschlüsse des Aachener Konzils im Jahre 816," *Zeitschrift für Kirchengeschichte* 74 (1963): 46, no. 203.

13. PL 102:900d.   14. *Ibid.,* 901c.

15. *Ibid.* Nevertheless, in c. 5, *ibid.,* col. 796, the profession formula is found without any mention of the Rule.

"regular life" as it was lived in the monastery where he found himself. He did not make his commitment to a particular text with all its details. The meaning then is: "I promise to take the Rule of St Benedict as the fundamental law of my observance."

There is another commentary which comes from Hildemar of Corbie. It was circulated under different names and different editions from the middle of the ninth century.[16] In this commentary we learn that there was a divergence of opinion between Benedict of Aniane and Adalhard of Corbie in regards to the interpretation of the Rule on one point, namely whether one should or should not wait a year before giving a layman the monastic tonsure.[17] Although both these great abbots had adopted the RB, Hildemar does not say that the novice makes his profession "according to the Rule."[18] This expression, however, is found a little further along in relation to a detail of the ceremony.[19] There too it does not apply to RB as a whole, but rather to a particular point of its text to which it is conforming.

The same holds true for another document from the middle of the ninth century, where it is said that after his year of probation the novice conducts himself "according to what the Rule says."[20] During this time in the profession formulas mention of the Rule is sometimes present,[21] sometimes absent.[22] At St Gall, for example, it

16. In regards to the text, I have given indications in *La spiritualité du moyen âge* (Paris, 1961), p. 103.

17. See W. Hafner, *Der Basiliuskommentar zur Regula S. Benedicti* (Münster, 1959), p. 140.

18. Ed. R. Mittermüller (Ratisbonne, 1880), p. 539.   19. *Ibid.*

20. *Collectio capitularis Benedicti Levitae monastica*, c. 34, MGH, Leg. 2:1, p. 346, as cited by Hafner, *op. cit.*, p. 141: *Expleto probationis suae anno, secundum quod regula praecipit inde faciat* . . . —ed., Semmler, *op. cit.*, p. 549, c. 34 gives: *Expleto probationis suae anno secundo quod regula praecipit inde faciet*; but some manuscripts cited in the apparatus have *secundum* in place of *secundo*.

21. For example, at Reichenau, MGH, *Formulae*, p. 570, n. 30; in the letter of Theodemar of Monte Cassino to Theodoric (778–797), ed. J. Winandy–K. Hallinger, in *Corpus consuetudinum*, 1:174: *promitto me . . . secundum instituta beati Benedicti.*

22. For example, in the professions made at Saint Gall under the abbot, Andomar (720–759): ed. P. Piper in MGH, *Libri confraternitatum Sancti-Galli*, pp. 111–124.

appears progressively as an addition to a primitive text. First, it is found as an insertion towards the end of the ninth century,[23] then in the tenth it is part of a formula.[24]

In conclusion we can note several things in regard to this first period. First of all, it was the secular authority which imposed RB; western monasticism became "Benedictine" by the will of an Emperor. There was certainly a tendency in favor of this Rule, which moreover continued to manifest itself but which would only slowly triumph. But to say the least, the intervention of the Emperor was a decisive influence in this evolution. Secondly, the profession was more and more specified in regards to its object and its formula. One committed oneself to live as a monk according to the legislation of Aix-la-Chapelle, that is to say, first of all, not as a canon, and secondly, according to RB and the customs which were added to it in each particular place. In other words, the criterion for judging the value of the customs—which were necessary—was their conformity to the fundamental observances established by RB.[25]

THE TENTH AND ELEVENTH CENTURIES
THE RULE INSEPARABLY UNITED TO CUSTOMS

The Situation: Decadence and Reforms

The Carolingian Empire was divided in 843, and in the different countries the political and administrative structures which it had

---

23. *Ibid.*, pp. 125–135.

24. *Ibid.*, p. 143. The same was true at Corbie, according to a document a copy of which is found in the ms. Paris, B.N., Coll. Picardie, 16, f. 69. Other formulas of profession can be seen in Martène, *Regula commentata*, c. 58, PL 66:820; *De antiquis Ecclesiae ritibus*, 4, *De antiq. monach. ritibus*, ed. Anvers (1765), pp. 224–229; Mabillon, *Acta Sanct. OSB* 5 (Venice, 1735), p. 694; B. Albers, *Consuetudines monasticae* 3 (Monte Cassino, 1907), pp. 176–187; K. Zuemer, "Formulae Merowingici et Karolini aevi," MGH, Legum *sectio* 5, *Formulae*, pp. 569–571. In the history of the formulas and of the rites, see I. Herwegen, *Geschichte der benediktinischen Professformel* (Münster, 1912), p. 66; H. Frank, *Untersuchungen zur Geschichte des Benediktiner Ordens* 63 (1951): 106ff.; J. Semmler, *Die Beschlüsse des Aachener Konzils, loc. cit.*, pp. 46ff.

25. In regards to the value of custom in relation to the Rule, in collabora-

established began to more or less slowly deteriorate. From this time, and especially toward the end of the ninth century, monasticism like the rest of society and the Church, knew a period of decadence. There was a certain anarchy arising and the Church at Rome and elsewhere fell, as it is said, under the "power of the layman." This was true not only on the Continent but also in England. The invasions of the Normans, to which were sometimes added attacks from the Moslems, caused extensive material destruction. Temporal lords who had little interest in things spiritual came into possession of the abbeys, named the abbots, and decided directly or by subordinates who was to be admitted into the community. In regards to England, the best historian speaks of a "complete ruin of monasticism at the end of the ninth century,"[26] and also of a "disappearance of monastic life from 800 to 940."[27] There were, of course, semi-monastic communities, a description of whose life leads one to conclude that they certainly were not regular monasteries.[28] In other countries, however, especially in Italy, the decadence was not so complete. But on the whole there was not any truly regular life, that is, a life lived according to a rule. The monasteries were filled with clerics who were either "canons" or "monks" without any apparent difference between them. They were married, owned properties, and did not remain in residence. At Saint Ghislain, for example, the community was made up of married canons who made their living by exploiting the veneration of the relics.[29]

To remedy this situation two things were necessary: the monasteries had to regain their independence from the laymen who themselves were caught up in the general decadence, and they had to reintroduce a regular life. Such was the work of the reforms which began to arise during the tenth century, especially between

---

tion with R. Grégoire, I have given some indications in a review of *Corpus consuetudinum*, 1–2, in *Studi medievali* 5 (1964): 662–665.

26. *The Monastic Order in England* (Cambridge, 1950), p. 33.

27. *Ibid.*, p. v.   28. *Ibid.*, p. 36.

29. See A. d'Haenens, "Gérard de Brogne à l'abbaye de Saint-Ghislain 31–941 ?]" in *Revue Bénédictine* 70 (1960) 111.

950 and 1000. If for the history of the Church as a whole the decisive period was the time between 1000 and 1050,[30] the decisive period for monasticism was the previous half-century. It was then that monasticism prepared for the reform of the Church and made its contribution towards the reform of the nations. Now, ten centuries later, we celebrate the millennium of these reforms.[31] We speak of "reforms," using the plural, for it is not a question of a single reform such as that which Charlemagne had initiated or that which Hildebrand (Gregory VII) and his collaborators would bring about in the second half of the eleventh century. Unlike the Carolingian reform and the Gregorian reform the reforms of the tenth century did not arise from a political authority seeking to remedy the abuses in the Church and monasticism. In fact, the secular rulers and the papacy were themselves decadent. Rather we have here a spontaneous reform movement arising from among the Christian people, some of whom were civil leaders, lords, or local bishops. Reforms resulted from a confluence of their efforts in England, throughout the Empire, in France, in Italy, in Burgundy, and just about everywhere.

Each of these movements had its own characteristics yet they did not operate completely independently of each other. In England where the reform was inspired by the example and directives of the Council of Aix-la-Chapelle of 816,[32] with the tendency to return completely to RB,[33] the reformers were in touch with those who sought the same goal at Fleury and elsewhere.[34] On the Continent in general

30. According to M. D. Knowles, *Nouvelle histoire de l'Eglise*, vol. 2: *Le moyen âge* (Paris, 1968), p. 12.

31. Under the title of "Variazioni sui Millenari monastici," *Bollettino della Deputazione di Storia Patria per l'Umbria* (Perugia, 1968): 186–191 and in a résumé in c. 13 of *Aspects of Monasticism Yesterday and Today*, Cistercian Study Series 7 (Spencer, Massachusetts: Cistercian Publications, 1971) I have attempted to characterize these reforms of the tenth century.

32. See D. Knowles, *From Pachomius to Ignatius. A Study in the Constitutional History of the Religious Orders* (London, 1966), p. 9.

33. See D. Knowles, *The Monastic Order in England*, p. 38, note 4.

34. See *Variazioni sui millenari, loc. cit.,* and what I have written in regards to St Gerard in *Témoins de la spiritualité occidentale* (Paris, 1965), pp. 91–92. The interdependence between different customs was again brought to light

the aim was to replace the canons by monks, or to replace monks without rule by regular monks, that is to say, to get communities to return to a rule.

In practice this, of course, raised many delicate problems, personal, economic, and others. Often the monks who had been living without a rule of life had a certain leverage with the local authorities, ecclesiastical and civil.[35] The undertaking was not without its risks for the reformers. For example, at Farfa they had to flee with great haste in order to escape assassination by the agents of the abbot, Campo, whose monks were living each with his own family.[36] Gradually the essence of the reform began to consist in most cases in introducing RB or restoring it to practice; one reformer was even accused of trying to make himself a new St Benedict.[37]

The questions which this reform raises for us are the following: Why this desire for a rule? Why was it frequently RB without denying the possibility of adding observances inspired by one or several other rules? What meaning did one give to this adoption of RB? In what way and to what extent was it followed? Did one make profession according to it? Were not customs soon enough added thereto? What was the relationship between these and the Rule? In actual fact did not one live more according to the customs than according to the Rule even though profession was made according to RB?

The Remedy: Restoration of the Rule and Customs

The answers should come from the texts and the facts. But the

---

in the papers presented at the Week of Medieval Studies held at Saint-Benoît-sur-Laoire in July 1969, the acts of which will be published. Particular notice is to be given to that of Fr Lin Donnat. I want to thank him for the kindness he has shown me in sending me some of the references which I have used in the preparation of this present article.

35. One can find an example of this in the report given by J. Laporte, "L'abbaye du Mont-Saint-Michel aux Xᵉ et XIᵉ siècles," *Millénaire monastique du Mont-Saint-Michel*, vol. 1 (Paris, 1967), pp. 56–60.

36. G. Penco, *Storia del monachesimo in Italia*, vol. 1 (Rome, 1961), p. 191.

37. A text is cited in this sense by H. Dauphin, *Le Bx Richard, abbé de Saint-Vanne de Verdun* (Louvain-Paris, 1946), p. 232.

situations are very diverse and complex. Also, one has to take great care, for some events of the tenth century are known by accounts which were written in the eleventh century and which contain a good bit of reinterpretation.[38] It is necessary then to examine many cases. Here we can only cite some examples. Thus at Brogne it is not certain that the rule that was introduced was that of St Benedict.[39] At Mont-Saint-Michel, they followed, "knowingly, a type of monasticism distinct from the Benedictine current."[40] In the life of St Adelaid, the wife of Otto I, St Odilo reports that she founded Saint Peter of Salzburg, around 995, under the Rule of St Benedict.[41] In the *Miracles* of St Bercharius, an author of the eleventh century recounts that Gauzlin of Toul in 936 went to Fleury to seek the Rule of St Benedict, but "with the description of the whole monastic observance," that is to say with the customs which accompanied it.[42]

In the life of Odo, Abbot of Cluny from 924 to 940, John the Italian, his disciple, speaks of him going to Baume in order to observe the customs there. In connection with this, when he speaks of St Benedict, he recalls how the saint "drew his customs from all the ancient rules and became by that the one who instituted the customs which are observed still in our monasteries."[43] Further on he says clearly that the decadence of the canons of Tours became such

---

38. Two examples of this phenomenon are illustrated by J. de Smedt, "Recherches critiques sur la Vita Gerardi abbatis Broniensis," *Revue Bénédictine* 70 (1960): 5–61, and J. Hourlier, "Le Mont-Saint-Michel avant 966," *Millénaire monastique*, pp. 13–28.

39. See *Témoins de la spiritualité*, p. 91. In regard to the reforms of St Gerard of Brogne in Lotharingia, Flodoard (*Annales*, AD 934, ed. P. Lauer, Paris, 1906, p. 60) writes: "*religio regulae monachorum . . . reparatur,*" in other words, "a regular religious life was restored," without saying according to what rule. The important thing was that there was one. The expression *religio regulae monachorum* is taken up again by Hugh of Flavigny, cited *ibid.,* note 1.

40. J. Hourlier, *loc. cit.,* p. 28.

41. *Acta Sanct. OSB* (Venice, 1735), p. 861.

42. *Ibid.,* p. 863. The author of the *Gesta episcoporum Tullensium,* 31; PL 157:459, writes: "*nutu Dei regulam S. Benedicti huius regni habitatoribus omnibus ignotam, diu quaesitam, proculque inventam, sancti Apri instituit loco.*"

43. *Vita Odonis,* 1, ed. *Bibliotheca Cluniacensis* (Macon, 1915), col. 23–24.

that they abandoned their way of life and their customs.[44] Is then the Rule of St Benedict missing? It is mentioned in relation to some particular points. For example, when he was still a canon, Odo read it and in order to conform himself to it, slept with his habit on.[45] At Baume there was a guest house which was well managed as was prescribed in the RB.[46] Later on there are other allusions to RB in relation to silence and to taking the habit.[47] John of Cluny knew the text, and there are citations among his reminiscences.[48] The Rule had established an authentic way of monastic life in contrast to that of the sarabites,[49] and what it had to say was applied in various areas, for example, in regards to the care of the goods of the monastery[50] and punctuality at the office.[51]

One can gather together other witnesses of this type.[52] What is the general impression which they give? First of all, it seems that the thing that is important is to have a rule and that in fact often, indeed even generally, is RB. RB constitutes for many the point of reference which guarantees a monastic reform; it is the measure of that reform even if in practice one more or less leaves it aside. A certain liberty is taken in regard to it either to permit the fulfillment of a personal vocation or because it is necessary to adapt to the local and historical circumstances of a particular place or time. We find examples of all these things in the *Life* of Richard of Saint Vanne. He "left his monastery to go on pilgrimage." This "seemed to be contrary to the Rule of St Benedict."[53] Likewise, in the matter of abbatial election he took into consideration the fact that "the king himself assumed the right of disposing of abbeys."[54] Furthermore

44. *Ibid.*, 3, col. 42.

45. *Ibid.*, 1, col. 20.

46. *Ibid.*, 1, col. 23.

47. *Ibid.*, 2, col. 39–42.

48. E.g., *ibid.*, 2, col. 42.

49. *Ibid.*, 2, col. 41.

50. *Ibid.*, 2, col. 41.

51. *Ibid.*, 2, col. 50.

52. There is a whole series of references (to be used with critical discernment) in d'Achery's notes on the *Letters* of Lanfranc, PL 150:602–610.

53. H. Dauphin, *op. cit.*, p. 272.

54. *Ibid.*, p. 84. Further down, H. Dauphin adds that feudal lords and bishops did likewise in those foundations that were their dependencies, and that "in Lorraine, the majority of the abbeys were subject to the bishops."

the right of the founder or "patron" of a monastery is respected,[55] although the Rule says nothing on this either. Shall we say then that, in new circumstances for which the Rule has no provision, it is a case of "a procedure which was actually a return to what was foreseen by the Rule of St Benedict," or is it not rather "the application of a principle laid down in the RB"?[56] The historical context as a whole explains that such a course of action is fully justified.

The Relationship between the Rule and the Customs

Does life according to RB differ much from life according to another rule? RB shares more than one point in common with other rules. But in addition to this there is the fact that there existed a sort of middle observance which one might call "the ordinary way of life of Western European monasticism," which has been the basis of monastic customs or customary law.[57] It is indeed then a foundation upon which monks in different regions have built in diverse and sometimes contrasting ways. But "to live according to the Rule" and in particular to RB, indicates that one has adopted as a whole the monastic way of life which includes celibacy, habitual residence in the enclosure, obedience to an abbot, common ownership, and choral prayer. How these principal observances are carried out depends on the place and the local customs. Just as there is a monastic evil in being without a rule, so there is a good in having a rule; this is part of the ideal, of the theory, or if you will, of the essence which constitutes "to be a monk." But the manner of "living as a monk" according to a rule, and this includes RB, is determined by something other than the rule itself, namely the customs. In a period of decadence customs contrary to the rule—whether this be RB or some other—are introduced: marriage, private property, absence of

55. *Ibid.*, p. 88, where the references to the sources are indicated in note 4.

56. The first of these phrases was used by H. Dauphin who explained what these circumstances were: *op. cit.*, p. 243. The second phrase, rather more qualified, has since been suggested to me by the same historian.

57. D. Knowles, *The Monastic Order*, p. 44, cited in *Témoins de la spiritualité*, p. 91.

residence, of a common life and prayer, of authority and obedience. To remedy such abuses a rule was introduced, often RB, with its principal observances and with the customs which determined its practice.

What is the value of custom? Or, more exactly, what is custom? It is necessary to make a distinction between custom in general and "the customs" which are particular and local. RB speaks of these latter in regards to particular points: the "customs of the place,"[58] the "customs of fasting,"[59] or, in the Rule of Paul and Stephen, the "established custom."[60] Custom describes a usage, it does not prescribe it.[61] If it begins to prescribe something then it ceases to be a custom, it has become a law. Now there is a law: the rule, and especially RB. When custom becomes something imposed it takes the place of RB. But normally it comes in as an addition to RB rather than a replacement. Custom is an habitual way of doing things which, after it has been experimented with and has been proven beneficial, can be approved by authority. Nevertheless it never becomes fixed; its proper character is to evolve, to adapt itself to the times, to places, to circumstances. Therefore it excludes uniformity. This is clear, for example, with Cluny.[62] Thus during the period which we have been considering there was, if we can so

---

58. *"Consuetudo loci,"* RB 61:2.

59. *"Consuetudines ieiuniorum," ibid.*, 53:11.

60. *Regula Pauli et Stephani*, c. 17, ed. J. E. Vilanova (Montserrat, 1959), p. 115.

61. Texts cited in *Studi Medievali, loc. cit.*, p. 663. The notions of "custom," "customs," "law," which are proposed here are those which seem to be justified by the documents of monastic history. They do not necessarily apply to these realities as they are found in the other domains of law. It remains to the jurist to define each of them. The ambiguity of the word "custom," used sometimes in the singular and sometimes in the plural, in monastic texts makes it necessary to determine its meaning in each document. Moreover, there are the cases where custom is established without replacing the Rule. Finally, it is necessary to distinguish between a custom which is in conformity with the law, *consuetudo secundum regulam*, and that which is contrary to the law, *consuetudo contra regulam*.

62. In *Aux sources de la spiritualité occidentale* (Paris, 1964), pp. 106ff., I have cited the text.

express it, a certain "family likeness" which is common to the whole monastic order and, within that monastic order, to that which was English or Clunisian or Gorzian, and so forth, with different observances which sometimes led to "mixed customs."[63] But there existed within all this great variety certain common elements. Moreover, monastic custom is only one example of ecclesiastical custom just as monastic law is only one example of ecclesiastical law, a law which is diversified because it is for the most part a customary law.

How then to explain in this perspective the value of RB? By considering it not as a legislative document, but as a program of life leading to union with God. It is necessary to return here to the conclusion of the preceding considerations on this problem. The very diversity of the customaries proves this suppleness of the Rule of St Benedict which ought to be adapted and completed according to the necessity of each monastic group and each age, while remaining the foundation upon which everything else is built. Its permanent value comes from this that it is not a "juridical" text, in the strict sense which that word has ordinarily taken on in our days; it is rather a spiritual text.[64]

FROM THE MIDDLE OF THE ELEVENTH CENTURY TO THE MIDDLE OF THE TWELFTH CENTURY

The Reasons for a Return to the Rule

Can one live according to the Rule alone?

From the time of the Gregorian reform new factors modify the historical context. It is above all the ideas concerning legislation

---

63. See *Studi medievali, loc. cit.,* p. 665. It is here a question of the "permanent value." It is necessary to be able to establish what is that value for the men of each epoch. What value, for example, did the man of the eleventh century give to RB; for him was it a juridic document or a spiritual program? Probably, the two. Happily, no period is bound by the psychological "projections" of other periods. We are then free to ask ourselves what the Rule and custom ought to be for us; the very variations of history are sufficient to free us.

64. See *ibid.,* p. 667.

which are different from those of the preceding period. Power in the Church was becoming more and more centralized to the profit of the papacy and law tended towards a certain unification and more or less towards a uniformity. This was true in regards to Church law in general, in regards to liturgical law (think of the Romanization of the liturgy in Spain and elsewhere) and in regards to monastic law. A parallel evolution led to the formulation of "canonical collections" (some of which such as that of Gratian were practically imposed and received quasi-official authority) and to the codes which determined, sometimes down to the last detail, the observance of monks.[65] Under the impetus of this development it came about that there was not only a single rule with diverse customs, but there was a single rule with identical customs. This led at Cîteaux to the desire for conformity in the customs themselves: *eisdem usibus.* From this let us keep in mind this one lesson, that the evolution of monastic law is bound up with that of the law of the Church. One can raise the question whether this is a good or an evil. But it is a fact, and there is no reason why we should not say it is a good. Consequently, in a time such as ours when in the Church there is a decentralization of authority and the law is becoming pluralistic, monastic law also ought to move away from uniformity if this exists in it.

In regards to the history of Cistercian institutions the questions which now present themselves are these: Did Cîteaux reflect the evolution going on in the Church? In particular did its Founders want to make RB their sole and sufficient juridical text? A judgment can be made here only if we take into account another new factor of that period, the controversies.

First of all there was the controversy between the monks and the canons. The confrontation which one historian expressed in these terms: "monks versus canons,"[66] was true for more than one situation. In fact, it showed up wherever canonical life developed, that is, that form of regular life which was founded not on RB but

65. See *ibid.*, pp. 664–665.

66. J. de Smedt, *Recherches sur la "Vita Gerardi," loc. cit.*, p. 47. Also J. Hourlier, *Le Mont-Saint-Michel avant 966, loc. cit.*, p. 27.

on the Rule of St Augustine, to which there was added the *Ordo Monasterii*, customs and, soon enough, commentaries.[67] The communities of canons regular multiplied, prospered, and were fervent. During the tenth century reform monks were sent in to replace irregular canons; in the eleventh and twelfth centuries sometimes it was regular canons who replaced monks and shared with them influence and benefits. It is understandable then that in certain monastic quarters there arose a reaction and a certain anti-canonical attitude. There thus arose another reason why the monks laid greater insistence on RB: to establish a clear distinction between themselves and the canons.[68] And already there is found among certain abbots a tendency to go "Beyond the Rule." (This was a nickname given to William of Volpiano, the reformer of Trinity in Dijon, because of his penitential ways which were judged at Fécamp to be too severe.)[69] Things would be carried out with greater moderation at Cluny. But everywhere the need was experienced to clarify the nature of the life by a greater attachment to a rule which was often RB.

But here is where controversies arose among the monks themselves, and—something wholly new—they were centered around fidelity to RB. Why was that? For several reasons. First of all the customs had constantly increased until they became excessive. Monks never stopped adding new offices and new observances to those which were in the rule. In reaction to this some proposed a return, pure and simple, to RB.[70] Secondly the customs had a

67. See C. Dereine, "Chanoines," *Diction. d'hist. et de géogr. ecclés.* 12 (Paris, 1953), col. 375–405.

68. These controversies were studied by G. Lunardi, *L'ideale monastico nelle polemiche del secolo XII sulla vita monastica* (Noci, 1970).

69. J. Laporte, "Quelques documents sur Fécamp au temps d'Henri de Sully (1140–1189)," *Analecta monastica* 6, *Studia Anselmiana* 50 (Rome, 1962): 25; "Gérard de Brogne à Saint-Wandrille et à Saint-Riquier," *Revue Bénédictine* 70 (1960): 164.

70. E.g., Botho of Prüfening: *Sed Sancti praeceptoris nostri Benedicti institutio, sic per vices horarum ad elevandum fastidium psallendi, legendi et operandi tempora distribuit, ut observatores Regulae illius sub tantae discretionis moderamine nullam prorsus querelam moverent.* "De domo Dei, libri V," *Maxima bibliotheca veterum Patrum lugdunensis*, vol. 21 (1677), col. 502.

tendency, more or less according to the different localities, to become fixed. Finally and above all, they grew in importance, and this led to a double danger: on the one hand, that the customs prevail over custom, or to say it another way, the details become more important than the essential way of life, and on the other hand, the customs and custom be not founded on the Rule. And so to rectify this situation there was a desire to return to the Rule. Does not Cîteaux offer us an example of this attitude? Did it not propose to return to RB in order to free itself from the customs? This is clear from the *Little Exordium*.[71] But it is necessary to ask in what way and to what measure it succeeded. Let us note for the moment only that the circumstances which provoked this return to the Rule prepared the way at the same time for an evolution which would lead in the second half of the twelfth century to a sort of cult of the Rule (this is apparent in the commentaries on the text) and, especially from the end of the twelfth century onwards, a literalism in the interpretation of the Rule.[72] In any case the Cistercian fact and its evolution takes place within this historical context without which it cannot be understood. And it is clear that the meaning of profession according to the Rule is dependent upon this new conception of the Rule.

The Meaning and the Limits of the Return to the Rule

Why do we speak here of limits? For two reasons. First of all, because RB was not adopted by all. And secondly because where it was, it was not uniquely and without reservations.

The first fact is established by history.[73] It will suffice to illustrate it here with some examples. Thus, among the nuns, those who

71. This is what I have shown in the paper entitled "The Intentions of the Founders of the Cistercian Order," *The Cistercian Spirit: A Symposium,* Cistercian Studies Series 3 (Spencer, Massachusetts: Cistercian Publications, 1969), pp. 88ff.

72. It is in the *Exordium magnum* that the formula *regula ad litteram* appears, as has been shown by Anselm Dimier, "Les concepts de moine et de vie monastique chez les premiers cisterciens," *Studia monastica* 1 (1959): 411.

73. See above, note 40.

around 1145 adopted the institutions inspired by the customary of
Guigo the Carthusian and became "Carthusians," were previously
"Caesarines," living according to the rule of St Caesarius.[74] During
this same period at the Paraclete and in the double monasteries of
the west of France the ancient Celtic traditions, which had been
preserved in Brittany, were followed. Abelard wrote a rule for the
Paraclete and its foundations. These formed a congregation which
lasted until the French Revolution.[75] At the time of the intervention
of Hervé of Bourg-Dieu (died 1022) in the founding of Beaumont-
les-Tours and three other communities, "none of the foundation
charters of these four monasteries insisted on the Rule of St Benedict
as a norm of life. In the eleventh century, monasticism among the
women remained faithful to the early pre-Benedictine traditions."[76]
And there is no indication that this rule was introduced everywhere later on. In the sermon of Geoffrey Babion (died 1158),
written for monks, there are no citations or even reminiscences of
RB; on the other hand there is a mention of the "Rule of the Holy
Fathers."[77] Those to whom he spoke undoubtedly knew of RB,
given the influence of Cluny and of Saint-Benoît-sur-Loire in
Touraine.[78] But had they adopted it? We do not know. Further-

74. See Y. Gourdel, "Chartreux," DS 2:721. Also until the end of the
twelfth century the canons of the chapter of Saint-Lazare d'Autun lived
according to the Rule of St Chrodegang, as is brought out by L. Grille,
"Eine unbekannte Urkunde zur Illustration St Bernhard und der Orden von
Cîteaux," *Cîteaux* (1969): 103. See also M. de Fontette, *Les religieuses à l'âge
classique du droit canon. Recherches sur les structures juridiques des branches féminines
des ordres* (Paris, 1967).

75. Under the title "Ad ipsam sophiam Christum. Le témoignage monastique d'Abélard," *Revue d'ascétique et de mystique* 46 (1970), I have indicated
the characteristics of this Rule.

76. G. Oury, "L'idéal monastique dans la vie canoniale. Le Bx Hervé de
Tours (†1022)," *Revue Mabillon* 52 (1962): 23.

77. *Sermo ad monachos*, PL 171:891. This text and others have been studied
in the paper of P. G. Oury, "La vie contemplative menée en communauté
d'après Geoffrey Babion (†1158 ?)," which will appear with the Acts of the
week of Medieval Studies of July 1969 at Saint-Benoît-sur-Loire.

78. See G. Oury, "La reconstruction monastique dans l'Ouest. L'Abbé
Gauzbert de Saint-Julien de Tours (v. 990–1007)," *Revue Mabillon* 54 (1964):
69ff.

more, among those who did live according to RB, did they really differ in any great degree from the others? All the monasteries were alike at least in this that they had added to RB offices and observances which were not found in it.

With regard to those who invoked and used RB, two periods have to be distinguished. During the first period, which extended approximately from the second half of the eleventh century to the beginning of the twelfth, RB was considered as one source among others, and customs were always added to it. At Vallombrosa, founded around 1035, St John Gualbert insisted on RB,[79] but not without adding to it various customs.[80] He followed the Rule in its principal observances but not in all its details. In the twelfth-century documents concerning the monasteries of this congregation the Rule of St Benedict is mentioned but so also are the constitutions of other saints.[81] For his part St Peter Damian accepted RB reserving to himself the right to interpret it very freely. For him it was a general Rule which was followed when there was not reason for leaving it aside. He thought that St Benedict, because he was a great charismatic leader, had left not laws but directives, that he had initiated an institution which had evolved; one was not unfaithful to him in following a practice different from that which was prescribed by his text.[82] This attitude is manifest in all the legislation of St Peter Damian.[83] We find the same in the case of Guigo the Carthusian who in his Constitutions took elements from RB and from the customaries of monasteries which lived according to RB but departed from the Rule and customs in regards to his general idea of monasticism and by many of his particular prescriptions concerning

79. I have cited the text in *S. Pierre Damien, ermite et homme d'Eglise* (Rome, 1960), pp. 38–39.

80. *Secundum regulam Beati Benedicti, et consuetudinem eiusdem congregationis* —cited by D. Meade, "From Turmoil to Solidarity: The Emergence of the Vallombrosan Monastic Congregation," *The American Benedictine Review* 19 (1968): 348, note 78.

81. *Regula Sancti Benedicti sive aliorum sanctorum consuetudines monachis datas.* —*ibid.* p. 347, note 75.

82. See *S. Pierre Damien, ermite et homme d'Eglise*, pp. 41ff.

83. Some examples are cited *ibid.*, pp. 43, 47, 51, 56, 57, 62.

L

observances, some of which are very important.[84] In other words, he did exactly as St Peter Damian.

A second period begins with the end of the eleventh century and runs through the whole of the twelfth century. Two new elements appear which favor the return to RB. One was the initiative of the first Cistercians, and the other was the attitude of certain Black Monks more or less influenced by them. The attitude of the former in regard to the Rule is now well known. It will suffice to give a résumé of it in the light of several convergent studies. It is well established that they did not propose to return to the letter of RB but to its fundamental observances.[85] One can enumerate a whole series of points where, while intending to return to RB, they had in reality added prescriptions which tended to make the observance more precise or which complemented the Rule—points which were meant to be in conformity with the Rule but which were not to be found within it.[86] But what is more important than the observances is the observance, that is to say the _de facto_ practice of the principle observances of the Rule. It is in this sense that they wished to follow the Rule "in everything," but not "to the letter," an expression which appeared only at the end of the twelfth century or at the beginning of the thirteenth.[87] At the same time even the Cistercians formulated customs which were wholly inspired by the Rule,[88] but which were not in the Rule. They entered into the details which had not been fixed by the Rule.[89] Even they could not avoid adding to the principal observances of the Rule, or in other words, the observance of the Rule, prescriptions which were not in it. Were these in conformity with it? The question could be discussed while at the

---

84. Such is the conclusion of M. Laporte, _Aux sources de la vie cartusienne,_ vol. 2 (Grande Chartreuse, 1960), p. 163.

85. P. Salmon, "Monastic Asceticism and the Origins of Cîteaux," _Monastic Studies_ 3 (1965): 131ff.; and the article cited above in note 71.

86. Some examples are cited by A. Dimier, _Les concepts de moine . . ., loc. cit.,_ pp. 407f.

87. _Ibid.,_ pp. 409ff.

88. _Ibid.,_ p. 412.

89. Some examples are given _ibid.,_ pp. 412ff.

same time one can give in regards to the whole an affirmative reply. The fact remains, however, that in a new historical context the Cistercians did what all had done before them. They had the merit of centering attention on RB, of reinstating its value, and of giving it a privileged place, but at the same time they opened the way to a literalism which did not fail to develop. However, this was not the attitude of the Founders nor of that theologian, St Bernard,[90] nor of any of the great spirits of that first age, but of their disciples in the following generations.

For their part, the representatives of traditional monasticism, the Black Monks, benefited from the impulsion given by the Cistercians (who were at first called the Gray Monks, but then as they strayed more from the intentions of their Founders came to be called the White Monks). However, they reacted against the danger of a possible literalism. Thus, at the reunion which took place in Rheims in 1131–1132, the abbots and priors of this region made it clear that by their profession they had committed themselves to the Rule as a whole rather than to each of its details[91] or the customs.[92] These latter existed only as an aid to the practice of the Rule, they were to be judged by it and not vice versa.[93] In regard to all of this,

90. The question of St Bernard and the Rule of St Benedict is considered in a special study; see below, pp. 151–167.

91. *Quamvis totam Regulam nequimus implere, quia nec iuravimus nec professi sumus, sicut nec totum Evangelium omnis implet christianus . . .*, ed. U. Berlière, *Documents inédits pour servir à l'histoire ecclésiastique de la Belgique*, vol. 1 (Maredsous, 1894), p. 104.

92. *Legi consuetudinem violenter subigimur . . . si in libertatem spiritus vel ad modicum audemus respicere vel nitimur, iudicamur, damnamur et conspuimur . . . sic sola consuetudine ad onera sua bruta aguntur animalia. . . . Profitemur nos non in consuetudines Cluniacenses iurasse, sed in legem et regulam sancti Benedicti.* —*ibid.*, p. 103.

93. *Cum enim consuetudines a viris Dei religiosis et spiritualibus propter transgressiones, in adiutorium Regulae ordinatae sint et non in destructionem, et non Regula consuetudinibus, sed Regulae militent consuetudines quae bene ordinatae sunt . . . nos non damnandi tam propere . . . si de consuetudinibus illis immutavimus aliqua . . . ut vicinius Regulae propinquaremur.*—*ibid.*, pp. 103f. For his part, an English monk wrote: *Non autem tam in consuetudinibus existit perfectio ordinis monachorum quam in humilitate et munditia mentium et corporum.*—ed. H. Farmer, "Ralph's *Octo Puncta* of Monastic Life," *Studia monastica* 11 (1969): 29.

the Abbot of St Thierry of Rheims, William—the friend and on more than one occasion the instigator of St Bernard—played a role.[94]

At Cluny also, under the influence of the Cistercians, of William of St Thierry and of St Bernard, there was a return to the Rule, but without any servility. Peter the Venerable maintained that those who were the Fathers of an institute had the right to modify certain observances of the Rule.[95] In this he was in complete accord with St Bernard who expressed this by the word *dispensari,* taken in the sense which it has in the writings of St Paul, namely to "administer" the observance of the Rule.[96] But neither Peter nor Bernard would allow that the abbot had the right to legislate or to act according to his own caprice. He too had made profession to obey the Rules, and that limited his authority in administering it.[97]

Where and to what extent could an abbot dispense from or modify the Rule? In spite of the different terminology they employ, Peter the Venerable and Bernard were in agreement in replying that this could be done only in regards to those prescriptions which the former called "changeable,"[98] and the latter "stable."[99] What were the criteria? This time they did not even differ in vocabulary: conformity to the demands of charity said both the Abbot of Cluny[100]

---

94. See J. Déchanet, *William of St Thierry: The Man and his Works,* Cistercian Studies Series 10 (Spencer, Mass.: Cistercian Publications, 1971).

95. *Plenam patres nostri in mutandis pro salute commissorum regulae quibusdam quae pro tempore datae sunt observantiis potestatem habuerunt.*—Epist., 28, 20, ed. G. Constable, *The Letters of Peter the Venerable* (Cambridge, Massachusetts, 1967), 1:95.

96. *Per homines, loco et efficio illis canonica electione succedentes licite . . . dispensantur.*—De praecepto et dispensatione, no. 4, *S. Bernardi opera,* 3:257; trans. C. Greenier in *The Works of Bernard of Clairvaux,* vol. 1, Cistercian Fathers Series 1 (Spencer, Mass.: Cistercian Publications, 1970), p. 108.

97. See "S. Bernard dans l'histoire de l'obéissance," *loc. cit.,* pp. 287ff. And the Introduction to the English translation of *De praecepto, loc. cit.,* pp. 88–91.

98. *Epist.* 28, ed. Constable, 1:89.

99. *De praecepto,* no. 4, *ed. cit.,* p. 256; trans., p. 108.

100. *Quando caritas imperat, absque aliquo transgressionis timore movenda sunt. Nec suspecta esse debet hoc respectu regulae professis regulae praevaricatio, quia regula illa illius sancti patris, ex illa sublimi et generali caritatis regula pendet, ex*

and the Abbot of Clairvaux.[101] It is interesting to note this agreement in regard to the principles between these two great spirits even though they did not agree on the applications, because each defended the tradition which he had received and was seeking to justify it. Later on a Cistercian, going further than his confreres of the time of St Bernard, reproached the Clunisiens with the crime of "perjury" because they did not carry out in practice the entire Rule according to which they had made their profession.[102] Peter the Venerable had already replied to this when he noted that the object of the vow was the "Rule of charity," on which the Rule of St Benedict depended;[103] this applied as much to the Cistercians.

Thus, during the first half of the twelfth century the return to the Rule and the controversy which it occasioned gave to two abbots who were men of God and theologians the opportunity to establish the principles of the evolution which was in progress in the domain of monastic legislation. This evolution ought to be founded on the Rule and not on the customs. It was not to be limited by these latter, keeping in mind that adage which came from the Fathers of the ancient Church along the route of canonical tradition: "The Lord said: 'I am truth,' he did not say 'I am custom.' "[104] The Black

---

qua et in qua iuxta ueritatis uerba universa lex pendet et prophetae. *Epist.* 111, ed, Constable, 1:285.

101. *At si, e contrario, contraria forte aliquando caritati visa fuerint, his dumtaxat quibus hoc posse videre datum est . . ., nonne iustissimum esse liquet, ut quae pro caritate inventa fuerunt, pro caritate quoque ι . . . vel omittantur, vel intermittantur, vel in aliud |forte commodius demutentur? Sicut e regione iniquum . . . foret, si statuta pro sola caritate, contra caritatem tenerentur.—De praecepto,* no. 5, ed. cit., p. 257; trans., pp. 108–109.

102. Dia, col. 1593.   103. Cited above, note 100.

104. In regard to the text of Yvo of Chartres, Gregory VII and their sources, see G. B. Ladner, "Two Gregorian Letters," *Studi Gregoriani* 5 (Rome, 1956): 225ff., with many citations and considerations which give a great deal of light in regard to the notion of *consuetudo*. In regard to the general way in which Scripture was used as a context for the texts of this period, I have given some indications in an article entitled "Bible et réforme grégorienne," *Concilium,* no. 17, p. 67. In the monastic controversies of the twelfth century, it is cited by the anonymous author of "Dialogus de esu volatilium," ed. Pez, *Thesaurus anecdotorum novissimus,* vol. 2, part 2 (1721), p. 565, and by the author of Dia, col. 1592.

Monks, in affirming in different ways, against the Cistercians who
were already tending towards a contrary solution, the supremacy
of truth over custom, made their contribution just as much as the
Cistercians, though in a different way, toward the evolution of a
proper idea of return to the Rule. They orientated it in this way not
to the letter but to truth, that is to say, to the exigencies of real life.
We do have to honestly recognize that the Rule is not sufficient to
itself, that it has need of customs. These ought to remain subordinate
to it, though they cannot go contrary to certain of its prescriptions.[105]

This theoretical solution is confirmed by the practice of the
Roman Curia. In its documents it distinguishes clearly between on
the one hand the canonical orders which live according to the Rule
of St Augustine and such and such institutes—those of Prémontré,
of Arrouaise, of St Rufus, and others[106]—and on the other hand the
monastic orders living according to the Rule of St Benedict and
such and such institutes—those of the Cistercians,[107] of the Carthusians,[108] of the Recluses of Saint Damian.[109] Each order ought to
remain faithful to its ideal, and this ideal ought not to remain
something indeterminate but ought to be defined and specified by
"the Rule and the *institutio* which ought to be the norms of the
religious life."[110] By the fact that the Holy See never speaks only
of the Rule of St Augustine or of the Rule of St Benedict, it gives

---

105. This is said very precisely by a historian who has studied particularly
these institutions: "The Benedictine Rule does not provide a complete code
for monastic life. On the foundation of this Rule alone it is impossible to
insure the good order of a monastery and all the details of its life. Therefore,
one is not surprised to find in the text, and above all, in the lives (and we could
add in regard to this present work's point of view, the customaries) many
practices which do not figure in the Rule of St Benedict or which contradict
it in regard to a particular point."—J. Hourlier OSB, "La Règle de S. Benoît
source de droit canonique," *Etudes d'histoire du droit canonique dédiées à Gabriel
Le Bras*, vol. I (Paris, 1965), p. 165. The author cites in note 16 two series of
examples, the first showing examples that are "outside the Rule" and the
other showing those that are "contrary to the Rule."

106. Texts cited by J. Dubois, "Les orders religieux au XIIᵉ siècle selon la
curie romaine," *Revue Bénédictine* 78 (1968): 302ff. and 287ff.

107. *Ibid.*, p. 293.   108. *Ibid.*, p. 296.

109. *Ibid.*, p. 306.   110. *Ibid.*, p. 310.

recognition to the fact that one ought not to live or make profession according to a rule alone, but according to three elements among which there exists a hierarchy and which complete one another. First of all, the design of God in regard to the one who is called to the religious life—this is what Peter the Venerable had spoken of as the "Rule of Charity." Then there is the venerable rule which as a whole retains a permanent value. And finally, there is the "institution" which represents the changeable element and which can modify the rule on certain points. This is the position of the Church in regard to every religious order. It makes no difference whether or not in the formula of profession they have made mention of the constitutions or of the rule alone. God and the Church know that one cannot commit himself to the religious state without these three elements being present.

FROM THE MIDDLE OF THE TWELFTH CENTURY TO
THE MIDDLE OF THE TWENTIETH CENTURY

BETWEEN LITERALISM AND LIBERALISM

The Point of Departure and the Evolution

How then did this evolution proceed? At its point of departure there was, we might say, a cult of the Rule, such as was unthought of previously. St Bernard had not hesitated to write that one could live "according to the Rule" without observing it right to the finger tips, *ad unguem*.[111] During the second half of the twelfth century a Cistercian less intelligent than he went farther than he and reproached him for this "thoughtless" assertion.[112] It is the

---

111. *Sicut enim non omnes omnia tenent, etiam boni christiani, quae in Evangelio sunt, omnes tamen secundum Evangelium vivunt . . ., sic quoque qui secundum Regulam vivere statuunt, etsi non ad unguem . . . totam custodiunt.—De praecepto,* no. 48, *S. Bernardi opera,* 3:286. The first part of this phrase is in precise agreement with the second part of the phrase of the abbots of the province of Rheims who were cited above in note 91.

112. *Videtur tamen Abbas ille (Bernardus) minus considerate adduxisse similitudinem de Evangelio ad Regulam, quia quae in Evangelio continentur, quaedam sunt consilia, quaedam praecepta; quae vere continentur in Regula . . . monachis omnia sunt praecepta.—*Dia, col. 1612.

period when there began to be written many commentaries on the
Rule; the list is a long one,[113] and their history merits to be studied.
The more ancient of them do not seem to attach importance to the
idea of profession according to the Rule.[114]

During this same period, and in a way that is somewhat para-
doxical, we see the development of the customs. It is normal that
they should have continued to exist, among the Cistercians as among
others, for in no preceding period had anyone lived according to
the Rule alone without adding some customs. What is new is that
in the Cistercian Order, where some wished to return to the Rule
alone, the customs were multiplied more than elsewhere and became
fixed. Whereas the Founders had reacted against the preponderance
accorded to the customs among the monks of the preceding era,
their successors, with discernment and liberty, took from the
Black Monks a good part of their usages.[115] Even more, these
entered upon a long series of efforts which have come to be spoken
of as the "codifications of Cistercian law."[116]

---

113. I have begun a collection which is already vast. The search must be
continued and the results classified.

114. There is nothing concerning Chapter 58 and profession in the parts of
the commentary preserved in the manuscript of Auxerre, No. 50, which has
been published by C. H. Talbot under the title of "A Cistercian Commentary
on the Benedictine Rule," *Analecta monastica* 5, *Studia Anselmiana* 43 (Rome,
1959): 102ff. and "The Commentary on the Rule from Pontigny," *Studia
monastica* 3 (1961): 77ff. There is nothing concerning the profession according
to RB in P. Boherius, *In Reg. S. Benedicti commentarium* (Subiaco, 1908), c.
58, pp. 659ff.

115. See B. Schneider, *Cîteaux und die Benediktinische Tradition. Die Quellenfrage des Liber usuum im Lichte der Consuetudines monasticae* (Rome, 1967);
Analecta SOC 16 (1960): 189ff. and 17 (1961): 73ff. and the review which I
published under the title of "Une Thèse sur Cîteaux dans la tradition monastique," *Collectanea Cisterciensia* 24 (1962): 358ff.

116. Characteristic are the titles of the works of C. Bock, "Les codifications
du droit cistercien" which appeared in *Collectanea OCR* (1947–1956) and of
B. Lucet, *La codification cistercienne de 1202 et son évolution ultérieure* (Rome,
1964). The evolution which is singled out here has been characterized in the
same way by A. Veilleux, "De l'interprétation d'une règle monastique,"
Collectanea Cisterciensia 31 (1969): 204ff. Already J. Lefèvre and B. Lucet, "Les
codifications cisterciennes aux XIIe et XIIIe siècles d'après les traditions
manuscrites," *Analecta SOC* 15 (1959): 8ff. have shown that the initiative of

And, in fact, the evolution proceeded along the lines of literalism. It is true that this was not the case everywhere. St Sylvester Guzzolini, when founding in the thirteenth century a monastery and a congregation, remained Benedictine in regard to the principal orientations of his monasticism but was eclectic in regard to the letter of RB and the customs prevailing among the Black Monks. He adapted himself, or at least he tried to, to the new times. Even if he did lack creative genius, he was nonetheless free.[117] However, in general, literalism took over, especially among the Cistercians. It is among them toward the end of the twelfth century that the idea is expressed for the first time that they wished to observe the Rule "to the letter."[118] How can we explain this? Should we again look to a modification in the general conception of law in the Church? We have come to the time when the canonical collections gave place to the law of the Decretals, which became more and more centralized and was permanently established in pontifical documents on which commentaries were written. From here the evolution led to the time toward the end of the Middle Ages when one could say that all that was done was to "write glosses on the glosses of the glossers"—*glossare glossatorum glossas*. May we not also see here the influence of casuistry, whose progress was assisted by the development of scholastic theology? There are in the *Quodlibetales* questions which could lead us to believe that this was so. It is asked, for example: "If all that is contained in the Rule of St Augustine obliges as a precept?"[119] Or again: "If a professed

---

Arnaud I (1202–1220) consisted of mixing together in one single legislation two types which were up until then quite distinct, namely, the constitutional law, represented by the *Summa cartae caritatis,* and the non-constitutional law, made up of the customs as a whole: *Ecclesiastica officia, Usus conversorum,* etc.

117. This is what I have shown in a paper entitled "Un fondateur monastique au XIIᵉ siècle: Pour un portrait spirituel de S. Silvestre Guzzolini," *Inter fratres* 27 (1967): 21ff.; trans. in *Downside Review* 87 (1969): 1ff.

118. EM, p. 64.

119. Gérard d'Abbeville, according to P. Glorieux, *La litterature quodlibétique de 1260 à 1320,* vol. 1 (Paris, 1925), pp. 113ff.; the same question in Henri de Gand, *ibid.* 1:186, 17; and in Nicolas Trivet, *ibid.* 1:254, 16.

regular is bound to observe all that is in the Rule?"[120] Or "If a
religious goes against what is in his rule does he commit a mortal
sin?"[121] The conflict between the rule and custom in the monastery
is also a question.[122]

An echo of these controversies, at least in so far as they concern
monasticism, and a very wise response is found in the commentary
on the Rule of St Benedict which was written by a contemporary
and friend of St Thomas, Bernard of Monte Cassino, who was a
student at the same time as Thomas in the school of that abbey.
"Some," he wrote, "think that the monk, in virtue of his profession,
is bound to observe as an obligation, because of his vow, every word
of the Rule and the whole of the Rule. . . . For my part, and having
respect for a better judgment, I am not of that rigid opinion
that every word and every prescription of the Rule binds a monk
under pain of mortal sin. It is necessary to understand that promise
in a large sense."[123] And here he refers back to what he had written
in his *Mirror for Monks*. The subject of that work was, as the sub-
title indicated, the question of what a monk obliges himself to by
his profession, and what in the Rule has the force of a precept, of a
commandment, and of a council.[124] We have here the vocabulary
of St Bernard. And in fact, from the beginning, in his interpretation
of the formula "according to the Rule,"[125] Bernard of Monte

120. Gerard of Abbeville, *ibid.*, 1:116, 4.

121. William of Woderford, *ibid.*, vol. 2 (Paris, 1935), p. 127, 16.

122. *Utrum ille qui profitetur regulam secundum consuetudinem non observantium
eam in aliquo monasterio, protestando quod sic profitetur et non aliter, transgrediatur
ea quae sunt in regula.*—Remigius of Florence, *ibid.*, p. 253, 11.

123. *Quod vero ait:* Promiserit se omnia custodire *etc., intelligunt quidam, quod
ex isto verbo monachus quodlibet verbum regule ex debito et ex voto teneatur servare,
et ad totam regulam servandum sit adstrictus, et ex voto maxime. . . . Ego vero salva
meliori sententia non sum huius rigide opinionis quod pro quolibet regule statuto vel
dicto monachus mortale peccatum incurrat large sumatur hoc* promittendi *verbum.*—
In Reg. S. Bened.*, ed. A. Caplet (Monte Cassino, 1894), p. 363. Concerning the
author, *ibid.*, p. ix.

124. "*Speculum monachorum seu quaestio de his, ad quae in professione obligatur
monachus, et quae sint in regula quae habeant vim praecepti, quae mandati et quae
consilii,*" ed. P. H. Walter (Fribourg-en-Brisgau, 1901).

125. *Ibid.*, p. 6.

Cassino depends on the Abbot of Clairvaux, and above all on his treatise, *On Precept and Dispensation.*[126] In the Fourth Chapter, entitled *Concerning the Obligation of the Rule,* he adopts the form of a disputed question, presenting arguments for and against the proposed reply and then finally the verdict of a master.[127] Bernard of Monte Cassino presents the same balanced solution as St Bernard, who was essentially in accord with Peter the Venerable. Nevertheless, there continued to develop a whole literature more or less centered on the problem of the obligation contracted by profession.[128]

Is it necessary to cite some witnesses of this mentality? Nicholas of Fractura, Abbot of Saint-Vincent of Volturno, toward the end of the thirteenth century wrote a commentary on the Rule of St Benedict in which he supported his interpretations "both by canon law and by civil law."[129] A fifteenth-century manuscript preserves a treatise by a certain James the Carthusian on the question of "scruples" in observance of the Rule of St Benedict.[130] Thus we see to what a point of decadence one had arrived in approaching this legislator so full of discretion. In 1646 an abbot of La Oliva, named Bravo, published some *Literal Notes for the Authentic Interpretation of the Rule of St Benedict in Regard to the Obligation of Conscience, with an Appendix against the Opinions of John Caramuel.*[131] To this latter

126. The references of St Bernard are given in the *Index auctorum,* p. 231.

127. *De obligatione regulae,* pp. 97ff.

128. Witness the work of Guillaume Peyraut OP often transcribed under the title of *Tractatus de professione monachorum,* but whose authentic title is *Expositio professionis quae est in Regula S. Benedicti.* See P. Delhaye, DS 6:1232–1233.

129. According to *Bibliothèque générale des écrivains de l'Ordre de S. Benoît,* by a Benedictine Religious [D. Francois] of the Congregation of Saint-Vanne, Member of several Academies, 4 vols. (Bouillon 1777–1778), 1, no. 329. In the MS Paris, B. N., lat. 13804 a typical title is attributed to the author: *Expositio Regulae S. Benedicti secundum Nicolaum abbatem S. Vincentii, decretorum doctorem.*

130. Jacobus Carthusiensis. *De scrupulis in Regulam S. Benedicti, MS* Münster 167 (15th cent.).

131. *Notae litterales pro genuina Regulae S. Benedicti intelligentia de conscientiae obligatione una cum lacinia adversus Joannis Caramuelis placita,* D. François, *op. cit.* no. 148.

Dom Calmet attributed "foolish and lax opinions in regard to morals."[132] Another work of the seventeenth century bore the title of: *Police régulière tirée de la Règle de S. Benoît.*[133] "Police" is used not with the modern significance of this word in French but with the meaning preserved in the English word "policy."[134] It would be interesting, and perhaps amusing, to study the whole history of the interpretation of the Rule since the Middle Ages until the present moment, when in the middle of the twentieth century the science of philology has come to temper the imagination of the commentators.

Where We Stand Today

At the end of the evolution which we have outlined, coming to the close of the nineteenth century and into the first half of the twentieth century, we can see the interpretation of the Rule and of the profession that one makes to observe it moving into two opposite directions. On one side—and this was especially true among the Benedictines—it has moved towards a sort of laxism or liberalism which allows one to justify by recourse to RB every realization of Benedictine life no matter what its nature or at what moment in history it had appeared. The Rule became the pretext for spiritual considerations, sometimes very elevated, by means of which one read into it whatever one wished to see. One found there arguments in favor of living in a parish or arguments in favor of life tenure of the abbots or against the presence of monks at general chapters. Sometimes this "liberalism" went hand in hand with a certain literalism—this was above all true, though it was not a monopoly, of certain Cistercians and above all some Trappists. They attached themselves to certain accessory prescriptions of the Rule while at the same time leaving aside the letter and the spirit of

132. A. Calmet, "Commentaire littéral, historique et moral sur la Règle de S. Benoît," 2, in the *Liste alphabétique des auteurs qui ont écrit sur la Règle de S. Benoît* (Paris, 1734), p. 594.

133. According to D. François, *op. cit.* no. 107.

134. See Littré, *Dictionnaire de la langue française* (Paris, 1873), 3:1198.

the Rule on some important points. In regard to this one can cite many examples.

Today an evolution is taking place under the influence of two factors. The first is the progress of historical studies which have for their objects on the one hand the text and objective interpretation of the Rule, and on the other the complexity of the evolution of monasticism in the West. These studies show the meaning of RB and reduce the importance of certain observances which have appeared through the course of the centuries and have become attached to RB. The other new factor is a desire for what we today call authenticity. Monks and nuns wish either to live more fully in conformity with the text they claim to follow, knowing it better and understanding more what it demands; or, if they are going to leave it aside, to recognize clearly what they are doing and to verify whether they have the right, and if so, why.[135]

Jean Leclercq OSB

Clervaux Abbey,
Luxembourg

DISCUSSION

The discussion following Dom Leclercq's talk first sought to clarify what differentiates the monastic way of life from that of canons regular or members of apostolic orders.

By the fourth century there were already present in the Church most of the forms of religious life which we know today, although without all the structures we now have. After the Council of Chalcedon structures became progressively more defined and rigid until today we have a very complex mass of quite inflexible structures.

Among those who are called monks, there have been men who have lived in very different ways. In choosing the Rule of St Benedict one is making an option for one particular possibility among many. According to this Rule the elements which are definitive in determining the monastic way of life are quite clear: a life ordered exclusively to prayer, a certain distance

135. I thank Dom Jacques Hourlier for his kindness in reading this manuscript and for the useful remarks he made upon it.

from ordinary social life and action, real poverty, a rule of life, etc. Yet, it was quickly affirmed, monastic life is not some abstraction which admits an abstract definition. It is an historical reality alive in individual men and women who choose a way of life.

Monastic life in itself is basically a psycho-socio-human phenomenon which is found in almost all developed religious traditions and societies. The main elements are universally the same: a certain separation from the world, a certain asceticism, common property, organization including a law, a superior and obedience, a certain primacy given to seeking transcendence. Christianity has adopted this human fact and transformed it, giving it a specific orientation. Thus Christian monasticism is and remains something unique, even though it shares common human elements, for it is totally directed to the search for God *in Jesus Christ*.

There was further discussion on enclosure as the most significant differentiating factor in monasticism. This is something in monasticism which seems to go contrary to the basic thrust of the Church. Christ prayed that the Father *not* take his disciples out of the world. The monastic charism which draws men away from society is therefore a scandal to the Church. Yet it is needed in the Church to balance the Church, for the Church is and must be both sacred and profane, both in this world and tending to the Father. If it is true that in some way the monk must situate his contemplative life within the various *diakonias* of the Church (it fulfills a service of prayer and witness) yet one must not consider the monastic witness as the practical purpose for monasticism. Consecrated virginity, celibacy for the Kingdom, is not good merely because it produces spiritual fecundity; it is valuable because it has *no* fruit. Centered upon God himself it emphasizes the inadequacy of all other contemporary values. It is a search openly declared and affirmed, a search for ultimate values.

ST BERNARD AND THE RULE OF ST BENEDICT

THE THEME SUGGESTED BY THIS TITLE is vast and has been surprisingly little studied. It is not possible to exhaust the subject in the space of this paper; all that can be done is to point out the interest that such a study holds for us, and to suggest a line of approach. It is generally known that St Bernard has left a teaching on the Rule of St Benedict (RB). He has given a free but faithful commentary of Chapter Seven in his treatise, *On the Degrees of Humility and Pride.* The use which he makes there of RB and its biblical sources merits careful and attentive study.[1] Likewise, in the treatise, *On Precept and Dispensation,* we find a doctrine concerning the monastic profession, the authority of the Rule and the abbot, which entitles Bernard to be ranked among the commentators of RB.[2] Lastly, his entire interpretation of the "Cistercian Fact" proves to be a demonstration of its correspondence with the basic requirements of the Rule.[3]

But, even more than a *doctrine on the Rule,* Bernard has handed on the pure *doctrine of the Rule,* something he was able to do because he

1. *Recueil d'études sur Saint Bernard et ses écrits,* vol. 3 (Rome: Edizioni di Storia e Letteratura, 1969), pp. 80–84, 113–117. Unless otherwise noted the refs. are to works by the author of this paper.

2. See "S. Bernard dans l'histoire de l'obéissance" in *Etudes sur S. Bernard et le texte de ses écrits, Analecta S O Cist* 9 (1953): 148–150; and also *Recueil,* vol. 2 (1966), pp. 47, 127.

3. See "The Intentions of the Founders of the Cistercian Order," CS3, pp. 101–118.

himself had received a *doctrine from the Rule*. Thus it is that his style, mirror of his mind and memory, of his whole psychological make-up, is largely fashioned by the Rule. We can say that after the Bible it is the Rule to which he most frequently refers, either by direct quotation or, more frequently, by evident, or even faint reminiscences. This is the subject which we propose to examine more closely here. After having examined Bernard's works from this aspect, we shall attempt to draw conclusions as to the value attributed by him to the Rule and the type of authority he acknowledged it to have.

This research implies minute analysis of texts, and may therefore be dry and stuffy. However, that is the price to be paid if we are to avoid the pitfall of useless generalities.

BERNARD TAUGHT BY THE RULE

Close examination of Bernard's writings shows that if the explicit citations of the Rule, accompanied by their references, are relatively rare, there are many and frequent reminiscences. It has already been said that Bernard "talks Bible," in the sense that constantly he uses the words of the Bible and even Biblical literary techniques.[4] In the same way, words and phrases of the Rule come spontaneously to his mind: he "memorized" the texts in the same way that he memorized Scripture. And it would be worth analyzing his work and making note of all the allusions, even those which are so faint that they are scarcely noticeable, which he makes to RB. It would be found that he uses the Rule in exactly the same way as he does Scripture.[5] Once this preliminary spade work had been done we would be in a position to give precise and complete statistical data on the subject; a whole new field of research is waiting to be undertaken.

4. See *Recueil*, vol. 1 (1962), pp. 298–319; vol. 3, pp. 213–365.

5. In *Recueil*, 1:307, I have given some examples from the *Sermons on the Song of Songs;* others could be given from other works of Bernard.

But even now, the incomplete and provisory recension which I have made allows me to make certain remarks. First, we notice that the chapters to which Bernard most frequently refers are the first seven; the next highest frequency is that of the chapter on monastic profession (c. 58); use is made, though less often, of those chapters of the Rule where allusions are made to the abbot (c. 64) and good zeal (c. 72). Bernard makes the most frequent use of passages from the chapters on humility (c. 7), on the instruments of good works (c. 4); another favorite is the Prologue—which is so important for a theology of vocations—and then the chapters mentioning the abbot (c. 2), the different kinds of monks, (c. 1), silence (c. 6), calling of the brothers for counsel (c. 3) and obedience (c. 5). A first fact now becomes evident: the pages of RB which Bernard remembers the most, and therefore those which he had most frequently read, and probably studied the most attentively, are those which contain a spiritual doctrine.

We may wonder what use Bernard makes of the other chapters of RB, those which deal with observances. Either he does not quote them at all, or else he does so only from time to time, and then nearly always in order to describe, not a practical observance, but a spiritual attitude, a disposition of the soul. Here are just a few examples: *sine murmuratione* (RB 40:9; Sent 1:16); *omnia membra erunt in pace* (RB 34:5; Div 10:1); *otiositas inimica est animae* (RB 48:18; Post Epi. 2:7); *honore invicem praevenientes* (RB 63:10; Purif 2:3); *nemo contristetur in domo Dei* (RB 31:19; Ep 301:1). It is to be noted that in all these instances, and in many more which could be cited, what Bernard retains from RB are mostly counsels of kindness, moderation, discretion. The same characteristic is seen again in the use which he makes of the chapters to which he most frequently refers, those which contain some doctrine. We notice that he has a predilection for phrases such as: *misericordiam superexaltet iudicio* (RB 64:10); *magis studeat prodesse quam praeesse* (RB 64:8). Sometimes he applies to non-monks the spiritual principles which RB has taught him. For example, remembering RB 48:18 which says that idleness is the enemy of the soul, he warns the Templars: *nullo tempore aut otiosi sedent aut curiosi vagantur*

M

(Tpl. 7). Again in writing about the election of a bishop by the clergy, he applies what St Benedict says about the election of an unworthy abbot, *clerici elegerunt vitiis suis consentientem personam* (Ep 328:1: RB 64:3). To an archbishop, St Bernard does not hesitate to propose St Benedict's own line of conduct in matters concerning the humble exercise of authority (Ep 42:34: RB 2:13, 7:34; Ep 42:36: RB 7).

These examples already show that Bernard "memorized" the Rule. Another witness to this process of memorization is the use he makes of Scripture. It is noticed that not only does he quote frequently and preferably those verses of the Bible which are found in RB, but that very often he cites them according to the version transmitted by RB. This seems to show that his source for these quotations is not the Vulgate, but the Rule. And since the Rule quotes verses of the Bible which are rich in spiritual density even in connection with observances, it is normal that Bernard should have sought and found in this "Benedictine Bible," this "Bible according to St Benedict," principles of action, ideals, rather than practical details. This point seems to confirm the observation we have already made concerning the use which Bernard makes of the Rule in general.

Mention has been made in another study of the use Bernard makes of the Scriptural texts transmitted by RB.[6] Many other examples might be added to the list already established; we shall give here only a few among the many possible examples. Prov 18:21: *Mors et vita in manibus linguae* is cited in Ep 89:2 and Div 17:7 as it is in RB 6:5; again, Mt 25:40: *quod fecistis his minimis meis* in Ep 119, is closer to RB 36:3 than it is to the Vulgate; *Deus propitius esto mihi peccatori* found in Quad 4:4, is the verse of Lk 18:13 as quoted in RB 7:65; *ambulat in magnis et mirabilibus super se* in the same context, is taken from Ps 130:1 after RB 7:3; the *vinum apostare facit etiam sapientes* of Pent 3:1 comes from Sir 19:2 as quoted in RB 40:7; the *Percute filium tuum virga,* etc., in Bernard's Ep 1:2 is a citation of Prov 23:14 after RB 2:29. Particularly frequent is the

6. See above, note 5.

use of Tob 4:6 after RB 4:9: *Et quod sibi quis fieri non vult, alio ne fecerit* (Div 18:4; 61:1; Ep 265, etc.).

It even happens that in Bernard's mind references from the Bible and from the Rule are confused, so that he attributes the latter to the former. In Ep 335, for example, he writes to a young cardinal: *Non expavit Jeremias, non formidavit Daniel, licet ambo pueri essent, senes impudicos.* It is difficult to see to what exactly Bernard is alluding when he mentions Jeremiah who does not seem ever to have fulminated against the elders in particular; on the contrary at Jerusalem, they supported him (cf. Jer 26:16–17). Possibly it was Samuel whom Bernard had in mind, since RB 63:6 states, after 1 Sam 3:18: *quia Samuel et Daniel pueri presbyteros iudicaverunt.*

Other remarks of the same kind could be made on this subject. But, by way of conclusion, let us just reiterate the two facts which we have illustrated: on the one hand, Bernard is thoroughly acquainted with the Rule; and on the other, what he retains most, on testimony of his own citations, is a spiritual doctrine and not mere observances.

BERNARD TEACHING THE RULE

Having constantly been in contact with the Rule and made it his own by assiduous meditation, Bernard not only came to memorize it, to know it by heart, but he imbibed it so thoroughly as to be formed by it, and it is only natural that he should hand on the teaching of the Rule. It would be rewarding to study his writings from this point of view but, once again, we can do no more here than quote a few examples.

A program

First, let us take a look at Letter 142, written to monks who had adopted the Cistercian observance and where Bernard gives the great and famous definition of the monastic "order" to which he belonged:

Stemus nos in ordine nostro, quicumque elegimus abiecti esse in
domo Dei nostri, magis quam habitare in tabernaculis peccatorum.
Ordo noster abiectio est,
        humilitas est,
        voluntaria paupertas est,
        oboedientia, pax, gaudium in Spiritu Sancto.
Ordo noster est esse sub magistro,
        sub abbate,
        sub regula,
        sub disciplina.
Ordo noster est studere silentio,
        exerceri ieiuniis,
           vigiliis,
           orationibus,
           opere manuum;
        et super omnia, excellentiorem viam tenere,
           quae est caritas
        porro in his omnibus proficere de die in diem,
        et in ipsis perseverare usque ad ultimum diem.

This brief passage is extremely dense. It constitutes a sort of
manifesto, a program of monastic living; and indeed it has been
recognized as such by tradition. When we look closely at the text
we notice that in fact it is nothing else than what might be called
a "Benedictine cento." The ideas found there are contained in RB.
Some are borrowed from the Bible, but they are charged with the
spiritual tonality, the resonance, that is to say, the signification and
we might almost say the sonority which they have in RB. This text
is worth analyzing in detail, idea by idea, word by word.

It opens with a formula found in RB, but to which Bernard
applies one of his favorite methods when using Scriptural texts. The
method consists in reproducing the words of a phrase to express, not
without a touch of humor, the very opposite meaning to the one
they originally conveyed. For Bernard this is a way of causing
surprise to his reader, almost of shocking him, and thus of drawing
his attention to the message.[7] Benedict had written: *Non stet in*

7. See Recueil, 1:302–304; 3:241–245; "Essais sur l'esthétique de S.
Bernard," *Studi Medievali* 9 (1968): 711.

ordine suo (43:4). Bernard says: *Stemus in ordine nostro.* . . . The key
word of the whole of this passage is the word *ordo,* found more
than thirty times in RB. As to the verb *stare,* it is found eleven
times, and in one case in the same grammatical form as in this
passage: *stemus ad psallendum* (19:7). The next part of the sentence
is a citation of Ps 83:11, the verse as such is not found in RB, but
all its elements are: *quicumque elegimus: elegere* is found ten times,
and once at least in a formula very similar to the one here:
quemcumque elegent (65:15). *Abiecti esse,* and a little further on,
abiectis est recalls RB 7:52: *Ego autem sum* . . . *abiectio plebis. In domo
Dei* recalls *domus Dei* which is found three times in RB, one of which
is in the same form as here, *in domo Dei* (31:19). *Magis quam habitare
in tabernaculis peccatorum,* is a continuation of the psalm cited by
Bernard. Twice in the Prologue of RB we read *habitare in tabernaculo
Dei* (Prol. 22, 23), and we have also *habitator tabernaculi* (Prol. 39),
habitandi praeceptum (Prol. 39), *habitationis officium* (Prol. 39).

All this sets the theme of the definition. The key word, *ordo,* is
repeated three times and developed in the form of successive waves,
of which the last, in keeping with another of Bernard's techniques,
is more ample than the preceding ones. We have, as it were, three
variations on the same theme.

The first variation, as is customary with Bernard, is built up
around one of the words of the theme, and whose sources in RB
have already been signaled: *ordo noster abiectio est.* The verb, which
is a concentration of the force and vigor of the statement, recurs
four times. *Humilitas est* has no need of a commentary; the frequency
with which this word is employed in RB is well known, it recurs
even more than *oboedientia.* It is easy to grasp why Bernard mentions
it the first among the terms which he uses to comment on this state
of voluntary *abiectio,* chosen by our own free will, and which he
has just mentioned in connection with Ps 83 and RB. *Voluntaria
paupertas est;* the word *paupertas* is found in RB in a context dealing
with the joyous and willing acceptation of hard and difficult things:
Si . . . *paupertas exegerit* . . . , *non contristentur* (48:7). *Voluntas* is
found twenty-four times in RB. In the chapter which teaches
absolute and radical detachment, it is associated with poverty

quibus . . . nec voluntates licet habere in propria potestate (33:4). The other elements of this first variation of the theme defining the Order are *oboedientia*—which needs no explanation as to its being Benedictine—then *pax* and *gaudium in Spiritu Sancto. Pax* is found nine times in RB, and in more than one instance, it is associated with the idea of the common life in charity. *Cum gaudio Spiritus Sancti* quoted from 1 Thess 1:6 is found in the chapter on Lent, and it is difficult to know whether Bernard is thinking of Paul or Benedict; probably, as often happens, Paul through Benedict.

Then we have the opening of the second variation of the theme: *Ordo noster est. . . .* Each word of this section is preceded by the preposition *sub* which recurs ten times in RB, and twenty-four times it serves as a verbal prefix. This three-letter word is in itself a whole program of spirituality. Bernard goes on to show how it actualizes the spiritual attitude he has described. *Sub magistro* is an echo of *magister* used five times in RB, and in particular: *discipulis convenit oboedire magistro* (3:6). *Sub abbate, sub regula,* suggests the *militans sub regula vel abbate* of RB 1:2. Lastly the *sub disciplina* introduces a term which is found twenty times in RB, that is to say almost as frequently as *regula* (twenty-six times); the word *abbas* recurs even more frequently.

The third and last variation *Ordo noster est . . .*, is the longest. It gives an even more precise definition of this state of abjection which consists in humbling oneself in accepting to obey a rule and an abbot. First *studere silentio*, a formula borrowed from the first phrase of RB 42. Then, *exerceri ieiuniis:* the first of these two words is found three times in RB, the second recalls the *ieiunium amare* of RB 4:13. *Vigiliis*, which follows, is also in RB, as well as *orationibus* —this last word being associated (in RB 49:4,5) with the idea of fasting; *opere manuum* is in the title of c. 48. The conjunction *et* serves as a link between this series of observances and what Bernard says concerning their end. His declaration is introduced by *super omnia,* a Pauline formula (Rom 9:5), as well as a Benedictine one (38:1; 64:22). The *excellentiorem viam tenere* is inspired by 1 Cor 12:31; but St Benedict, too, several times uses the word *via* in this elevated sense, and in the Prologue we even find it in association with one of the words of the beginning of our text: *via tabernaculi* (Prol. 24). *Quae est caritas*: *caritas* recurs sixteen times in RB.[8] *Porro in omnibus*: even the *in omnibus* is a strictly Benedictine echo. RB uses it thirteen times to mark a certain force of insistence: *servata in omnibus puritate* (39:10); *regulam in omnibus conservet* (64:20). *Proficere* is in RB 2:25 and 62:4. *De die in diem*: *dies* is frequent in RB and is used with a spiritual sense of time as something to be used for our salvation. We read, for example: *dies bonos* (Pr 15), *dies huius vitae* (Pr 36). *In ipsis perseverare*: still another Biblical word used by St Benedict (Pr 50; 58:3). *Usque ad ultimum diem*: this closing formula of Bernard's definition suggests the *Qui perseveraverit usque in finem* of Mt 10:22 quoted by St Benedict (7:30). One wonders whether it is mere chance that Bernard in his closing phrase used the word *ultimus* which, strangely enough, in RB is associated—*ultimus omnium stet* (43:5)—with a verb which Bernard used in his opening sentence: *Stemus in ordine nostro*. Those who are familiar with Bernard's writings know that he fancies this sort of discreet, almost imperceptible reminder. Of one thing, however, there can be no doubt: these lines, of profound density and, from a literary point of view, very musical, are a masterpiece of Benedictine centonization resulting from genial memorization. The words and ideas are all Benedictine, but the way they are woven into a free and harmonious pattern is typically Bernardine.

Bernard has even followed a Benedictine plan in this passage. He starts with a general introduction which sets the tone and indicates the theme. The principal inspiration is a Biblical quotation which brings into evidence the words "tabernacle" and "dwelling" found in the Prologue. Then the first variation announces the fundamental spiritual attitudes set out in a cleverly devised ascendant series leading from abjection to joy, passing through humility, poverty, obedience, peace. The second part indicates the major factors of the institutional setting in which this program is to be realized: a master or an abbot, a rule and a discipline. Finally

8. See H. de Sainte Marie, "Le vocabulaire de la charité dans la Règle de S. Benoît," *Mélanges offerts à Mademoiselle Christine Mohrmann* (Utrecht-Anvers, 1963), pp. 112–120.

Bernard mentions particular observances: silence, fasting, watching, prayer, work; all that leads to a progress in charity, urging on to the final reward. This is exactly the pattern of RB, which starts with an analysis of the vocation, in the Prologue, and leads up to a harmonious and final synthesis which is the "summit of perfection," described in the last chapter, which is the epilogue. Between the two are all the hard and rough things—*dura et aspera*—of everyday observance, the cobblestones of the royal way.

Applications

Let us now examine a series of texts where Bernard, on particular points, comments on the Rule or teaches something derived from it. Here again he uses the words and ideas of RB for the purpose of transmitting a message which is both Benedict's and his own. *Quaeramus Spiritum*: this formula amalgamates two expressions used by St Benedict. We have *quaerere*, which applies to God (58:7) and to his kingdom (2:35) and *Spiritus* (Prol. 11) or *Spiritus Sanctus* (7:70; 49:6). This search is the central theme of an entire passage on the Second Sermon for the Feast of St Andrew (4–5). St Bernard comments on it with the words of St Benedict: we have *tota sollicitudine* suggested by the *omnis sollicitudo* of RB (27:5; 31:9; 71:4); the *operam demus* of RB (49:4); *licet mereamur*, this last word being found twice in the Prologue (21, 50).

Really seek God: the *vere Deum quaerit* of RB 58:7 leads Bernard to develop at length the two words *verissime quaerentium* in the sermon *De diversis* 37:9 where we can read the verb *quaerere* ten times; the "truth" we read about in this passage is equivalent to *simplicitas* which recurs five times.

In Letter 385:1f, Bernard takes up the theme of *curritur via* found in the Prologue in RB (Prol. 49).

The *sic stemus ad psallendum* of RB (19:7) is found in a passage of *Super Cantica* (7:4f), concerning prayer in presence of the angels and which begins with these words: *Cum statis ad orandum vel psallendum*, and ends with a citation of Ps 46:8: *Psallite sapienter*, quoted by Benedict in this same Chapter Nineteen.

And again on prayer, we have the finale of Sermon 47:8 on the

Song of Songs which gives a justly famous description of the way to sing Psalms. It is really a humorous travesty in which Bernard sketches the wrong way of going about things. When he wrote these lines, Bernard was amusing himself and intended to amuse his reader too, and also to edify him. It will be noticed that this humorous text is set in a context inspired by St Benedict. It begins with the statement of a principle, with an express reference to the Rule, which is rare for Bernard: *Ex regula namque nostra nihil operi Dei praeponere licet* (RB 43:3). The entire text is built up with words from the Benedictine repertory: *laus* is found seven times in RB; *solemnia* only once, but we have also *sollemnitas, sollemniter*; *oratorium* recurs twice; *quotidie* seven times and on two of these occasions it is used in connection with the divine office; *persolvere* is twice applied by Benedict to psalmody; *intende, pure, reverenter* go to make up the vocabulary of prayer in RB. The phrase *Pure vero, ut nil aliud, dum psallitis, quam quod psallitis cogitetis* unites the Benedictine principles on both private and public prayer: *pura oratio* (RB 20:4) and *Mens nostra concordet voci nostrae* (RB 19:7).

This is a literary sermon, it was not spoken in public, but dictated in private to a secretary; and it has a distinctly artificial ending which Bernard brought in as a conclusion to the doctrinal development which he considered to be complete. He had nothing more to say so he made the excuse of having to break off because time was short. He also wanted to present effectively a teaching on prayer which he built up from reminiscences of St Benedict. In the context we see that he was respecting the signification of the words which state that nothing may be preferred to the work of God. In the Rule itself, however, this statement is not a sort of law of the Medes and Persians concerning the absolute primacy of office, but simply an application of the principles laid down elsewhere in the Rule about obedience. When the order is given to go to another occupation which is enjoined by command or by law, then nothing is to be preferred to it, and we have to go to it without delay (RB 5). This example shows that though Bernard takes his inspiration from St Benedict, he does not accord greater weight to his words than the Founder himself intended.

The sermon *De diversis* 26 begins by an allusion to a Gospel phrase which Bernard's monks had just heard quoted by the Rule: *Audistis nunc ex regula nostra, fratres, de humilitate sententiam Christi.* . . . The verse in question is that where Luke says: *Omnis qui se exaltat humiliabitur, et qui se humiliat exaltabitur* (Lk 14:11) quoted in RB 7:1. Hearing is not enough, we have to think as well: *cui ergo, quoties legitur, toto animo intentos vos esse volo.* In the brief commentary which Bernard gives of this verse, we find a formula of Bernedict: *quod minus habet in nobis nature* (Prol. 41) coming spontaneously to mind: *quidquid in aliis minus habemus,* says St Bernard.

In connection with silence Bernard writes in Ep 385:1f: *addere aliquid ad priorem silentii regulam,* which recalls the *augeamus nobis aliquid solito penso* of RB 49; *alienande vos . . . ob actibus saeculi huius* is inspired from RB 4:20: *Saeculi actibus se facere alienum.*

Speaking of discipline in Sermon 23:6 on the Song of Songs, Bernard says *bonumque in se natura, quod superbiendo amiserat, oboediendo recipiat,* which recalls the beginning of the Prologue (2); the *non metu disciplinae* evokes *non iam timore gehennae* of RB 7:69; and the *socialiter . . . quieteque* make us think of the *in congregatione quietus* of RB 65:21.

The description of the *fidelis oboediens,* in the sermon *De diversis* 41:7, is centered on the words *festinare* and *festinanter; festinare* is found six times in RB where we also read: *summa cum festionatione curratur* (43:1). *Nescit moras* is equivalent to the *sine mora* of the chapter of RB on obedience (5:1), to which may be added *absque mora* (22:6) and two other uses of *sine mora* (31:16, 71:8). *Ignorat tarditatem* is an echo of *non tarde* of the same Chapter Five, where we also find expressed the idea of concomitance of the giving of an order and its execution. Bernard uses in this context the words *voci, manus, pedes,* as St Benedict does when he writes *manibus, pede, vocem.*

Concerning the exercising of authority, in Sermon 76:7 on the Song of Songs St Bernard writes *quasi rationem pro animabus nostris redditui* which is a reminiscence of both Lk 16:1: *Redde rationem villicationis tuae,* and of the seven passages in which St Benedict applies this formula to the account which the abbot will have to render to God; in one of them it is a question of the "souls" confided to his care: *animarum Domino redditur est rationem* (2:34). A little further on, the *commissis dominicis ovibus* recalls *dominicis . . . ovilibus* of RB 1:8; *salutem animarum sibi commissarum* (RB 2:33); *gregis sibi commissi* (RB 2:32); *gregem sibi commissum* (RB 63:2). Again, *multum sollicit* reminds us that Benedict applies to the abbot the words *sollicitudo* (2:33, 27:1, 27:5) and *sollicitus* (2:39).

The *res si quas habet* which begins a sentence concerning the offering which the novice shall make of his goods to the monastery (RB 58:24) gives Bernard an opportunity to play on the word *habere*. The renunciation of everything which one might possess— *quidquid habere poteristis . . . relinquendo*—leads to possession of God: *et eum habere propriam possessionem* (Ded 1:3).

The sermon *De diversis* 53:3 mentions manual labor. St Benedict had said that by *labor manuum*, we imitate the Apostles (RB 48:8). Thus Bernard, having mentioned this *labor*, goes on to quote three passages of St Paul which contain references to work, and of which several are to be found in RB: *operam ditis, quieti, operemini manibus* (1 Thess 4:10); *in labore, operantis, non in quieti* (2 Thess 3:10). In St Bernard's sermon these quotations lead up to the final formula, *opus manuum*, which comes not from St Paul but from St Benedict whose teaching is confirmed by the authority of the Doctor of the Gentiles: *Vides quam sollicite observandum praecepit Doctor gentium opus manuum.*

Let us now go back to the life of the Knights Templars. We have already seen that Bernard applies to them the text of RB 48. A little further on in the same passage (Tpl 7), he uses Rom 12:10 as in RB 62:17 and 72:4: *Honore invicem praevenientes.* Then, in the same sentence, he applies to the Templars words which recall certain "instruments of good works": *opus inutile* suggests the *non pigrum* of RB 4:38, *risus immoderatus* suggests *risum multum aut excussum* (ibid. 55), *murmure vel tenere, non murmuriosum* (ibid. 39).

Lastly, there is a vast field of research which could be done on the abbot as St Bernard thinks of him according to St Benedict. We have already pointed out the frequent use of certain elements taken from the two chapters of RB which deal with the abbot.

There exist many other indications of Bernard's thought on this matter; some are more important than others, but it would be worth listing them all. We shall only give a few here, by way of example. In his letters to abbots, especially when he wants to teach patience, kindness, longanimity, and the humble exercise of authority, Bernard refers to RB. This is the case in the formula which introduces the wonderful ending of Letter Seventy where Bernard acknowledges that he lost his temper with his brother Bartholomew, and that he acted wrongly in expelling him from the monastery, but that he had submitted to the judgment of the community who requested that he should be allowed to come back.[9] This same reference to RB is found in a series of Letters where he pleads in favor of fugitives which the respective abbots are unwilling to take back.[10] Again in the Letter to Rainaud of Foigny, Bernard employs and comments on five Scripture texts mentioning humility and quoted by St Benedict (Ep 72:1). In the following Letter, addressed to the same correspondent, Bernard insists on the same ideas and uses the expressions and passages of RB recommending indulgence and compassion toward the weak (Ep 73:2). Other reminiscences of RB 2:38 on the abbot are found in Letter 58:2. In Letter 325 there is reference to RB 28 and 64, on how to deal with a rebel monk. Letter 7:17 reminds the abbot that he is obliged to keep the Rule just like any other monk, as is written in RB 64:20. In the Sermon *Ad abbates* 6, it is Chapter Two of RB which serves to teach the conformity which should exist between an abbot's teaching and his conduct. There are other allusions to the Rule in this sermon.

In the majority of instances Bernard uses the Rule in the same way that he uses Holy Scripture. Either he starts from a citation of RB, which he then develops, or else he introduces into his own text words of the Rule which have inspired his theme. He makes them his own, assimilates them so much to his own thought that

9. See *Etudes,* pp. 90–91; *S. Bernard et l'esprit cistercien* (Paris, 1966), pp. 49–50. (A trans. of this last work will appear shortly in the CS, no. 16.)

10. See "Documents sur les fugitifs," *Analecta Monastica* 7, *Studia Anselmiana* 54 (1965): 95–99.

they become part and parcel of his personal expression of their content. Thus he teaches the doctrine of St Benedict in the very words of St Benedict.

CONCLUSION

THE RULE: A ROYAL ROAD BETWEEN THE LEFT AND THE RIGHT

As we stated at the beginning of this paper, all that we intended to do was to state the problem and to indicate a method of approach. Everything has yet to be done in this field of research. Indeed it is astonishing that study concerning the influence of the Rule of St Benedict on St Bernard has never been seriously undertaken. It would be possible to select from his works a marvelous collection of texts shedding light on many a passage of RB. Would we find the matter for a complete commentary? No, for, as we have seen, Bernard refers only to the great doctrinal chapters; from the others he selects those spiritual principles which are relevant to particular observances. This fact serves to confirm the conclusion of another line of research, that which sought to verify what it means to make profession and to live according to the Rule. The general conclusion is that the important thing is to adopt the major orientations rather than to observe to the letter every minute ruling.[11]

Bernard certainly meditated on the Rule and studied it throughout. He would not have been able to use the words as spontaneously and frequently as he does if he had not imbibed the entire text.[12] The fact that he retains certain chapters and certain formulas is then even more revealing of his attitude toward the Rule. It proves that he selected certain elements, those which were for him less a set of rules and regulations than a spiritual program. More than a mere rule of life, RB is the expression of an ideal. It is not a collection of

11. In regards to the meaning of "to make profession according to the Rule" see above, pp. 117–149.

12. It seems that Bernard knew and used the Commentary on the Rule written by Hildemar in the 11th c.; see *Recueil*, 3:133–134.

practices to be observed, but a doctrinal work containing a spiritual teaching, laying down the basic foundations of the spiritual life. Bernard recognizes it to have a legislative value only in so far as it transmits a spiritual doctrine.

Bernard saw just how Biblical is the Rule, or better still, how evangelical it is, for all the quotations of Scripture, even those of the Old Testament, are Christocentric. It is understandable then that often he quotes the Bible from the text of RB, and that he always explains RB by means of texts from Scripture. There is nothing abnormal, then, in the fact that Bernard proposed the spiritual program of RB, in so far as it has, like the Gospel, universal Christian value, to bishops, Templars and other non-monks.

Nevertheless, and this is normal, it is in the texts which are more strictly monastic that the citations and the reminiscences of RB are the most abundant. One could show statistically the higher frequency of Benedictine formulas in the monastic treatises, in the Sermons *De diversis* and in the Sentences, in comparison with the number of references in non-monastic writings, and in the great liturgical sermons. In the *Corpus epistolarum* it is in the first series of letters, dealing with things monastic, that we find most references to RB. Bernard's intention was more to record his doctrinal work rather than elaborate a series of historical documents. His first center of interest in teaching was the monastic life.[13] The major letters placed at the beginning of the collection set the tone and constitute, in epistolary style, an interpretation of the Rule not in its details but in its fundamental demands. These letters are also the expression of what were the intentions of the Founders of Cîteaux as Bernard understood them. We find an admirable homogeneity, as well as a surprising preciseness of vocabulary, in all passages of his works where Bernard reveals his thought on the monastic life, whether it be in his letters, his treatises or his sermons.

Two main characteristics stand out in connection with his attitude to the Rule. The first is his insistence on moderation and discretion, on kindness, indulgence, and broad-mindedness. The

13. See *Lettres de S. Bernard: histoire ou littérature?* which will appear soon.

second is Bernard's liberty with regard to the text of the Rule in the rare cases where a particular prescription is in opposition to the line of conduct which he feels obliged to adopt in order to be faithful to the promptings of the Holy Spirit. An example of this is afforded by the interpretation he gives of RB 61:13, which states that an abbot should not receive a monk coming from a known abbey without the permission of the abbot.[14] This might seem embarrassing if we did not recognize there the freedom of the Spirit.

It is to the Rule of St Benedict, taken as a whole, and above all in its spiritual doctrine, that Bernard owes the balance and harmony of his monastic teaching. Nothing is stranger to his mentality than the literalism which grew up in later periods. The true spirit of the Rule—in other words, the Holy Spirit—leads neither to luke-warmness nor to a stricter observance than that of one's own monastery. To give in to either of these temptations is to accept a bad thought (Div 22:3).[15] On the contrary, there is a just measure which must be maintained in every circumstance. The texts of St Benedict are not to be separated from their realization in living tradition, this is a sure way of avoiding all excess. It is also the teaching of St Bernard on the basis of Scriptural texts which speak of the royal way: there are dangers to the right and to the left.[16]

Jean Leclercq OSB

Clervaux Abbey,
Luxembourg

14. Ep 67:1; PL 182:175; trans. B. James, *The Letters of St Bernard of Clairvaux* (London: Burns Oates, 1953), Ep 70, p. 95. See A. Dimer, "S. Bernard et le droit en matière de *transitus*," *Revue Mabillon* 43 (1953): 51ff.

15. *Putasne, aliquis in vobis est, qui dicat in cogitationibus suis: "Cur praecepit vobis Deus, ut istam Regulam teneretis?" Secundum enim impetum spiritum vestorum huic tepido remissionum, illi ferventi vitam artiorem proponit. . . ."*—Div 4.

16. *Prima vigilia est rectitudo operis, ut ad hanc quam iurasti Regulam omnem vitam exaequare coneris, nec transgrediaris terminos quos posuerunt patres tui in omnibus viae et vitae exercitiis, non declinans ad dexteram neque ad sinistram."*—Vig Nat 3:6. See Num. 20:17; on the theme "the royal way" see *The Love of Learning and the Desire of God*, 2nd ed. (New York: Fordham, 1962), pp. 109–113.

DISCUSSION

The discussion which followed developed some of Dom Leclercq's thoughts in regard to St Bernard's use of Scripture and the Rule. Dom Jean pointed out that, in general, the text of Scripture quoted by St Bernard came mainly from the Liturgy—particularly the Breviary. His quotes are not usually according to the Latin Vulgate, but according to the Rule, the Responsories and Antiphons, and also sometimes according to quotations found in the readings from Ambrose, Augustine, etc.

Bernard liked to "play" with the Scriptures. Accordingly, he is quite free in his use of the text. He used it in a "poetic" way (i.e. "*poein*"—to create). He liked to use Scripture with a certain humor, sometimes using a text in a sense exactly opposite to its real meaning. This was done to evoke the interest and response of the reader.

With regard to Bernard's use of the Rule Dom Leclercq remarked that the Rule had become an integral part of Bernard's personality, it had formed his psychological outlook. There is a real theology in the Rule, and this theology also was fully assimilated by Bernard. It is true that sometimes, as was also the case with the Scriptures, he made conscious and creative use of the Rule, but usually he was simply expressing himself as he had been formed by the Rule. The Rule was living for him and he was able to express it as himself.

One questioned whether the Cistercian interpretation of the Rule did not tend to emphasize the eremitical aspect of the life. To exemplify this he quoted William of St Thierry's *Vita prima Bernardi*. Dom Leclercq responded that the *Vita prima* is not an historical book in the strict sense. Rather, it is historical in somewhat the same sense that we say the Gospels are historical. William was not just an historian; he was also a theologian. Hence the *Vita prima* is more a theological interpretation of the life at Clairvaux. Any theological interpretation is always partial. William centers on the fact that the community as such was in solitude. For an understanding of Bernard's notion of community, one would best turn to his *Sermons for the Dedication of the Church*. These are a theological interpretation of the mystery of the Church and of community.

When asked whether the Rule was for Bernard an ideal or a law, Dom Leclercq said that Bernard in his treatise, *De praecepto et dispensatione*, had spoken of the Rule as law. The early Cistercians held to the notion of the Rule as law, and this played an important part in the tradition from which Bernard drew. But Bernard had a true notion of law, one which included great flexibility. He held to the Rule as law but did not feel obliged to hold to all the particular details of the observances.

NOTES OF A SOCIOLOGIST
ON THE ROLE OF THE RULE IN CISTERCIAN LIFE

THE MOST DELICATE ASPECT of this symposium —and its heart—is the question of the "legitimacy" of the Benedictine Rule for Cistercian life today. It is not sufficient to approach the Rule only in terms of Holy Scripture, theology, liturgy, history, pedagogy, anthropology, but we must also approach it in terms of authority, obligation, "oughtness." It has to be understood not only as of moral obligation but also, more precisely, as of juridical obligation. In a nutshell, it is a matter of conscience —and not simply of consciousness—as every Cistercian or Benedictine monk knows who makes profession to live under a rule and an abbot.

Law is something quite complex. It has different levels of reality. Dom Jean Leclercq in his paper comes to almost the same conclusion: "First of all, the design of God in regards to the one who is called to religious life—this is what Peter the Venerable had spoken about as the 'Rule of Charity'." (This was referred to in the discussion as the ideal.) "Then there is the venerable Rule which as a whole retains a permanent value." (This was spoken of as the *institutio* or *ordo*.) "And finally there is the 'institution' which represents the changeable element and which can change and could modify the Rule on certain points."[1]

---

1. See above, p. 143. The terminology is irrelevant. In law and especially in the social sciences we have an extremely complex problem of terminology. It is a sort of jungle. And so it is always important not to give too much importance to words.

N

What seems clear is that we are faced with three levels of reality: the monastic ideal, the Rule, and the customs. The Rule of St Benedict represented the three levels for the community at Monte Cassino. But it was obvious from the beginning that the third level (customs, traditions, observances, and so forth) is by nature flexible. If today we experience a certain tension, I am convinced that it is not on that level. The problem is rather on the second level, on the level of the *institutio*—the legal principles of the Rule. I do not accept the position that holds that the Rule is simply for us today some sort of pious reading. I believe for Benedictines and Cistercians the Rule of St Benedict still has a juridical value: it still commands, it is still something that must be obeyed, not on the level of the customs, traditions or observances, but rather at the level of its permanent principles.

In order, however, to speak about the role of the Rule as *institutio* or *ordo* in Cistercian life, it is necessary to analyze more precisely the relationships between the Rule and "community."

Community

It is impossible to think of a rule without a community, and it is very easy to see why. A hermit does not need a rule; he can decide for himself. He can decide what he will eat and what he will not eat, when he will work, and what he will do, when he will have hours of prayer or whether he will just depend on spontaneous prayer. He can, of course, have some sort of rule, in the sense of a plan. But would there be an obligation to follow it? Where is the legal authority that binds him?

In a monastic rule there is an obligation which binds. There is a "must," an "oughtness." It is not just an ideal, even an ethical ideal. There is something more specific, the kind of obligation implicit in any valid law. A law may be written or unwritten, spontaneous or deliberate, rigid or flexible, but never is it purely a wish or an ideal. Always—at least implicitly—it is enforceable by the authority of a group or its representative or its personification in the charismatic leader.

If we ignore the third term—the community and its well-being

—and we limit our analysis to the two terms: the individual monk and the abstract legal principles, we might create a false problem.

Toward the end of Father Basil Pennington's paper, there is a passage which undoubtedly stands out in his mind as important since he read it to us at the beginning of the Symposium:

Certainly the Rule is for the monk, not the monk for the Rule. The Rule is there to protect the personal charism of the individual. The candidate coming to the monastic life studies the Rule and examines how it is lived in this monastery, to see if he can identify with it, if his way is to be found within. If so, he enters into life under it, and it protects and preserves, in face of the community, his right to live according to his own personal call.[2]

There is little doubt that a true monastic vocation is a very personal choice—for better or for worse until death do us part . . ., the vision of an ideal which evokes a deep personal answer. Nevertheless, the monastic vocation is also a conversion, a process of learning, a progressive change into something else. This individual transformation in the cenobitic tradition is made possible essentially through incorporation into a particular community, not only through the guidance of the spiritual father, the *Abba*, but by living under a rule which at the psycho-sociological level is the constitutive element of the community. Let us replace the word "Rule" by "community." We can say that "certainly the community is for the monk," but in the perspective of the Mystical Body of Christ, can we say that certainly the monk is not for the community?

From a sociological point of view, the most essential and practical aspect of this discussion is the need to emphasize that the immediate subject of the juridical obligation is not the individual monk but the local monastic community. In Dom Cuthbert Butler's critical edition, the title of the Rule is *Sancti Benedicti Regula Monasteriorum* (St Benedict's Rule for Monasteries) and not a "Rule for Monks." It is through participation in the life of a local community that the

2. See above, p. xiii.

monk understands the Rule and accepts the duties implied in its observance. The monastic profession—or consecration—is not expressed in the framework of the traditional vows of chastity, poverty, and obedience, which are individual vows of renunciation of marriage, wealth, and power; it is rather like baptism, an act of incorporation into a local monastic community through stability, observance of the local rule, and acceptance of the local authority, which is the representative of Christ.

The Rule is not only a social instrument which allows every individual monk to do his own thing in peace without being bothered by others, nor on the other hand, a mere instrument of torture which, through asceticism, will lead the individual monk to total self-renunciation. This cenobitic Rule is, first of all, the ordering principle of common life, the realization in act of a shared life in a communion of persons, the guidelines for a creative answer by a community to the challenge of its present situation. The Rule is not first of all control and repression, but rather a channel toward a deeper experience of the life of the Church.

Consensus

The Rule orders the common life, gives it strength and continuity. But it is the community which accepts or creates the Rule, maintains it and transforms it into a living reality capable of adjustments to new conditions or situations. Those familiar with the sociology of law know that the ultimate source of authority is never a text or a book or a constitution or a code, but it is these texts *as received* by a living community. It is a fair level of consensus among members of a group in good standing which is the source of the experience of legal obligation, an essential aspect of the life of any group given to the performance of a task, even if the task is nothing other than living a full life together. Obviously in the formation of this consensus or in its maintenance, leaders, officers, people fulfilling various special functions have normally an important role. The extent to which this consensus is conscious or unconscious is an interesting problem, but what is most relevant is its existence or non-existence.

The actual phase of *aggiornamento*, the important changes in the legal structure of the Church, even some refinement of her moral exigencies affect deeply the moral consensus of various Catholic communities. The main aspect of this phenomenon is that laws are not easily accepted purely on the basis of authority, especially traditional authority. Past consensus does not seem to imply present consensus. There is a need for understanding, for logical consistency in the legal system, and most of all for the right adaptation to the situation in which the Church and monasteries find themselves today. Any legal system is always in a precarious position. It is caught between a moral ideal which tends to be atemporal and an actual situation which is always changing, and sometimes changing drastically. Consequently today the Rule of St Benedict is to be evaluated in terms of a deeper understanding of the monastic ideal in its cenobitic form as well as in terms of the present conditions of our technological culture which affect deeply the psyche of modern man.

The Problem of Individualism

During the last centuries the extreme individualism which appeared in the time of the Renaissance tended to destroy the function of the community in establishing a vital link between the individual and the legal system. The community could even be reduced to a system of ritual observance and an organized chain of command. We could illustrate this kind of alienation of the law from any actual community sharing by reminding ourselves of the well-known differences between Cistercian and Trappist traditions.

When Abbot de Rancé decided to reform the monastic order, he chose a kind of literal observance of the Rule of St Benedict which produced an extremely social form of religious life with very little privacy. This is what was typical in the description of the Trappist life in this earlier period: the monk was never alone. He was always with his brothers, in choir, at work, in the scriptorium. He may have had a sort of alcove in the dormitory, but it was basically a common dormitory. Certainly, objectively, it was a very holy life. But what is most striking for the sociologist is that notwithstanding this external form of common life, there was tremendous individualism at the level of the person. In one of my very first retreats to Cistercians, I tried to develop at length the important element of community. Afterwards, a very holy old brother came to me and said, "Oh, Father, you are so right. Your sermon was very beautiful. You cannot be a good Trappist if you do not love loneliness." I had not spoken about that at all that day. I was saying just the opposite. Why did he react this way? He then went on to tell me that he had been there for thirty years and he was always completely alone with God and that he was, indeed, very happy. There was no doubt about it. Yes, he was absolutely alone with God. The Trappists had an extremely well-organized system of functional relationships, but at the level of being, at the level of personality, it was truly an eremitical life, a life without sharing. It was aloneness with God.

From the little I know of the Cistercian Fathers, I get an entirely different impression of their community life. The Cistercian Order was formed in a unique period in the development of the Church and society. At that time there was emerging an extremely healthy equilibrium between the community and the individual, much healthier even than at the time of St Francis and St Dominic. After a long period of intense community life, the time of St Bernard was the time when the sense of the person was emerging and was able to begin to affirm itself, yet in the context of an extremely strong community life and community experience. All that broke down in the fourteenth century. The *devotio moderna*, the modern piety, was essentially "myself and God," and the Church, God's people, the Mystical Body, had become Canon Law, ritual, authority suffering from a kind of alienation through objectification. In this new social aspect of the Church, each one had his own private business with almighty God. Sanctification was a purely individual matter.

In this climate de Rancé forced the literal observance of the Rule, forced the type of community life that was asking for extreme cenobitism. That the reform succeeded is not due so much to its inner dynamism as to the occurrence of the French Revolution and the ensuing developments of the nineteenth century. A fantastic will power was needed to maintain that strict observance for so many decades.

The Ecclesial Dimension: a Community of Virginal Love

Today there are many discussions about the eremitic and the cenobitic life. Which one came first? But what is important beyond all these discussions, and even beyond the historical fact, is that eremitism is fully expressive of the monastic ideal. The fact that eremitism for so long was considered to be superior to cenobitism establishes this. The hermit is a real monk, a full monk. Nevertheless there has always been a tendency towards something else. Even if one is a very holy hermit, is there not something lacking? It is true, it can be said that the hermit is living in communion with God, with the risen Christ, and even in some sense in actual communion with all the saints. Nevertheless it is a very special kind of community, a special kind of *Koinonia*. It is difficult to read the Gospels without sensing that the fullness of Christian life is the expression of the love of God and the love of the brethren.

Cenobitism came as a real growth in monasticism. The monks, being a part of the Church, felt the need to be living fully the life of the Church. And indeed I like to look upon cenobitism as "the Church of the desert." I do not deny that the hermit can be a perfect monk and be in communion with the rest of the Church. But there is something in monasticism which tends toward the making of the fullness of the Church in the desert. You can leave the world, you can renounce wealth, you can renounce culture, you can renounce art, you can renounce every aspect of humanism, but you cannot renounce the mystery of the Church.

What I would like to bring in here, and I believe that it is extremely important, is the link between cenobitism and virginity. The essence of religious life is virginity. Undoubtedly it is true as St Paul says so beautifully, "We are all one in Christ." Yet still we are men and women; these are two quite different ways to be human beings in the Church. And there are Jews and Gentiles, and these two things are utterly incompatible. And though today there are few Jews in the Church, and though the Mother Church, the Church of the Hebrews, died out, there is something lacking in the fullness of the Church in that we are just the Church of the Gentiles and not at the same time the Church of the Jews. The mystery of the Church is made of Jewishness and Gentility, two incompatible things. In the same way, although there is but one Christ, there is in his Mystical Body two things which are utterly incompatible, virginity and marriage. The essence of religious life is virginity. And I believe monasticism is radical virginity, virginity brought to its logical consequences.

Cenobitism is not simply virginity, but virginity in common life and there is a mysterious relationship between the two. Christian life almost always manifests itself as a certain special way to live human life. Generally grace informs nature, charity informs nature. The typical example is the sacrament of marriage, the family life. You do not need to be a Christian to be validly married. You do not need to be a Christian to have a good family life. But charity informs, transforms, and transfigures the natural activity of married life. The same can be true of professional life, of social life; all the aspects of our human life can be informed by charity. It is only when we celebrate the Eucharist and on other very rare occasions that we see the Church as not involved in a normal human activity.

Here we can see what is the essence of cenobitism, what specifically brings the monks together in a cenobium. It is pure charity. And this is possible only in virginity. The first expression of the Church on Mount Zion, the primitive Church of Jerusalem, shared everything. But it did not work out. Century after century there have been efforts to create communities like this, and they seem never to have succeeded. In these days in California and in Arizona there are communities being born every day—and dying every day. Constant efforts to achieve a true *Koinonia* have never succeeded except in virginity. Only in virginity is it possible to build a community relationship which is not based on family life, professional activity, art, culture, politics or anything else, but solely on Christian love. And thus we immediately see how in cenobitism there is not only a relationship to the transcendence of the living God, an affirmation of the Resurrection, of the Parousia, of the new creation, but also a witness to the essence of the mystery of the Church, to the basic *Koinonia*, which is the essence of the Body of Christ.

A monastery may become a great tradition, a famous school, a center of political power, etc. A monastery can become a super-organization in the terms of big business. But anyone who really knows what religious life is, especially in its pure state, knows that it is not a team working in a school, a team working in a hospital, a team working to accomplish something in the world; but a group of people who live together without any human purpose except to live together. If it were not for the love of God, charity, genuine cenobitic life would be impossible.

What this implies is that as cenobites, not simply as monks or hermits, but as cenobites monks must experience the challenge of ecclesiology. They must see the challenge of the mystery of the Church. They must know that they are called to make visible this mystery in all its purity. The mystery of the Church is not a bunch of bachelors living together under the same roof, a group of hermits each one doing his own private business with the Lord in the secret of his soul. It is a life of sharing, a life of sharing which is not simply a life of interrelations. To use Martin Buber's terminology, it is not simply an "I" and "You"; it is the emergence of the true "we." But what is the "we"?

The "We" of Community

To be a monk is not simply to enter into a monastery which is a certain kind of organization, to be full of charity, always to respect your neighbor, to have this marvelous ideal of service which is so popular today, to give yourself in the service of others. There is something more than all that. You enter into a "we"; you participate in a "we"; you become part of something.

The "we" is possible—the real "we," not the "we" of interpersonal relationships—only if the members are open to each other. If instead of walls, instead of the instinctive fence of self-protection and of affirmation of the self, there is an openness, there is a receptivity, there is a willingness to be hurt. If monks are open and try to enter into a genuine "we," they are going to be hurt. But if they refuse to be hurt, if they refuse to enter into the Passion of our Lord Jesus Christ and to die with him in order to receive the fullness of the spirit of "we," then they do their own business with God alone. The "we" is something that is very difficult to achieve, to live, an openness to each other. It is the mysterious work of sharing.

One of the great insights of the Roman jurists was to insist that in order to have a society it is necessary to have three persons. When there are two, there is a face-to-face encounter, but in order to be fully one, the two have to be turned together toward a third person, object, task—something. Marital life really comes about in a young couple at the birth or the announcement of the coming of the child. The young married couple, of course, had already achieved a genuine kind of unity, but it was simply a unity of inter-personal relationship without the real fusion of the spirit achieved in their common centering on another human person.

In cenobitic monasticism the "we" comes about when together the monks face a common task. It is this common task which is going to bring unity.

On the functional level, the first lesson in sociology is to move a stone. First one tries and he cannot move it, then ten get together and they move it easily. Obviously there had to be some functional organization for them to be able to move this stone together. But this presupposes something else, another level of unity. There has to be a sharing. There has to be something in common at this moment which is the context, the matrix of this common activity, something, for example, as elementary as a common sign language.

In the apostolic orders, Franciscans, Dominicans, etc., where men are giving themselves to the work of the Church in the world, the members can participate as a team in this work. But what about the monk? We have seen how virginity makes possible genuine com-munity, genuine charity. In this context it is contemplative life itself which becomes the principle of sharing, of unity. A mon-astery is not a society when the monks only admire each other in respect and charity. It is the turning toward God which is the essence of monastic life, and the sharing of this experience brings as deep a unity as the endeavors of apostolic life. Therefore it is wrong to speak of the contemplative life as a secret dialogue between a soul and God. How can monks base a community on such a premise? How are they going to celebrate together the Divine Office, pray together, if they are convinced that the whole of the contemplative experience is a secret discourse between the soul and God? We have to learn to be one; we have to share. Very often in the militant Church, team work comes from going forth to convert the world, to bring Christ to the world. But the monks have the much more difficult task of creating a "we" only in terms of God. I do not think that there can be a genuine community spirit in a monastery without genuine contemplative life.

Role of the Rule in Cistercian Life

Such a sense of community is the key to our discussion of the role of the Rule in Cistercian life because a true law is not something written in a book, a text, a constitution, a code. Such law has no strength, no force. A real law is always a certain consensus among the members of a group. What makes people move? What is this real dynamic power which we know is not biological, nor merely psychological? It is precisely that mysterious consensus which is now confronting us. Today many simply do not accept the law; a consensus is not present. It is a very serious problem. We see it in a number of areas in the life of the Church. Things that were formerly accepted without any doubt by everyone are suddenly called into question. No one says no. No one rebels. But the consensus is not present. The power that was there has suddenly evaporated.

Consensus is the ultimate power of law. I have tried to bring this out because it explains what our problem is with the Rule. The Rule of St Benedict is effective to the extent to which it is accepted in the *local* community. As we have seen, communities in the earlier days had no hesitation in taking two or three rules and making, as it were, a cocktail out of them, and that was the rule of the community. The basic rule (and that is the way I understand *conversatio morum* in the Rule) was the consensus of a particular community.

In the case of the Cistercians, however, we must also speak of a community of communities. The dream of Cîteaux was to achieve a real unity of the monastic order through a strict and identical observance of the Rule in all monasteries. But such a common observance needs to be based on a living consensus. Obviously it is much more difficult to attain a consensus among various communities than to obtain it within one community. In periods of rapid social change as today, the difficulty is compounded. The temptation of doing nothing because a consensus cannot be reached —and in the process, becoming rapidly obsolete—is very great indeed. The field of history is covered with institutional corpses.

At this moment when the Cistercians are reducing the legislative power of the General Chapter, when they are accepting plurality and taking the risk of giving all sorts of power to the individual monasteries to organize their daily life with great freedom, they must find the legal authority to impose the new way of life. If it is not to come from the General Chapter, from whence is it to come?

We have learned in the past from our text books that only the Church and the State can make laws. But in actual fact, clubs make laws, universities make laws, any kind of organization can make internal laws. Any active, well-organized community can create valid laws which are applicable only to that particular body. So any monastery which is a real community is capable of creating laws which are valid for this particular community but not for others. At the moment when the General Chapter declares that large areas are to be left free to the decision of the local community, which has to find its own equilibrium, a very real problem arises. This is not a question of spirituality or of theology, of politics or of public relations. It is a question of a genuine community which has to define itself and establish what is going to be its way of life.

A practical differentiation among the various levels of juridical reality we mentioned earlier can lead to a workable solution. The General Chapter will progressively clarify the area of the *ordo*, of the juridical principles which formed the main structure of life in Monte Cassino under St Benedict and in Cîteaux with the Founding Fathers. On the other hand, each monastery will create new customs, traditions and observances in terms of its own concrete situation.

But where, at the local level, is the locus of authority, not executive but legislative? In the abbot or the chapter?

There is no solution to this question to be found in the Rule. To the Western monks, St Benedict gave a strong constitution and to the Benedictine abbot a strong executive power—not unlike our American political system. He foresaw minor adaptations, which he left to the discretion of the abbot. But his Rule is the classical summary of two centuries of creative monastic experience and to it he gave a kind of atemporal quality without providing procedures for orderly change of structures. He emphasizes more than once the abbot is subject to the Rule. It seems logical to expect that no legislative process will be under his jurisdiction.

Still, in his own community the abbot is the teacher, the guardian of the living tradition. In the evolution or creation of a local observance, his function is unique—not unlike the bishop's. And the chapter, the community as a corporate personality, is not outside the abbatial charisma. It is in the harmonious unity of abbot and monks that we ought to find the locus of local legislative power which is now needed as a result of the decisions of the General Chapter.

A true community can provide it. But are there yet true communities? Are we not, rather, pilgrims on our way towards Truth?

In heaven there will be no law; St Paul has sung of the complete freedom of the new creation. But are we yet fully in the new creation? Monks are living members of the militant Church, and as all other Christians they experience the tension between the new man and the old who refuses to die. This is why the militant Church needs laws, regulations, observances, customs, etc. Torn between an ideal high above human resources and the exigencies of unregenerated nature, the Church needs *discretio*, a pragmatic, workable way of life which will allow the Spirit to work freely in men.

Because the ideal of monasticism is evangelical radicalism, it is very difficult to contain it in the framework of law. It was the genius of St Benedict to present it in its communal form to the weak, to those who had not yet reached the full freedom of the sons of God, to present it with *discretio*.

A genuinely charismatic community would have no problem adapting the juridical insight of St Benedict to the new social and cultural happenings. But real communities, ordinary communities, are not in the same position—and sometimes far from achieving a harmonious unity. In their case, the process of change, the creation of new traditions, customs or observances must not be left completely to spontaneity but must be controlled by a proper juridical process. In this way, no monk who is loyal and wants to serve under a rule and an abbot will be troubled or vexed in the house of God![3]

Vincent Martin OSB

St Andrew's Priory,
Valyermo, California

DISCUSSION

The discussion following Dom Vincent Martin's paper strove mainly to clarify the meaning of consensus and to ascertain the ways of attaining to it. Consensus is not majority rule. For a community to arrive at consensus often much time is required. The rhythm of a community decision is quite different from the rhythm of an individual decision. All must be convinced that the "we" is important and that community life is much richer than individual experience. One must not worship community, but one must have a sense of respect for the community. Each member of the community has his role to play, but no one can force the process. If it is carried out with love and trust, it will come about in time.

Fr Raphael Simon pointed out that the community can make use of the social sciences and various techniques as helps, but these will not be *the*

3. RB 31:19. The author would like to stress that what is presented here are merely notes contributive to a symposium and not a finished paper.

answer nor suffice by themselves. Consensus for Cistercians includes a spiritual problem. Nor can it be solved simply at the level of the individual. If one tries to improve the community solely by improving individuals, it will not work. For there are ills which are social as well as ills which are individual.

Consensus for St Benedict was a consensus of the community with the abbot. They accept his decision, but at the same time his mind is formed by listening to the community. Consensus has to flow from values and response to these values rather than merely from authority. If there is real community, the decision of the abbot will be the expression of consensus rather than the cause of consensus. The abbot has too frequently been conceived of as apart from the community. The abbot's real role is now no less necessary than before; rather it is even more necessary: the abbot has to engender consensus.

One asked about the extent to which a community can provide for pluralism and still remain a community. Dom Martin replied that one can have a very complex pluralism within a large community, it depends on the size. In a small community it is possible to have pluralism of persons rather than pluralism of groups. Ten is about the largest group in which one can have real contact with and awareness of each person. Beyond that it is too large to maintain awareness of each one, and this introduces a certain impersonal element. Thus in large communities one can have the serious problem of an impersonal world unless ways are found to foster sub-groups where each one can have definite person-to-person relationships. The example of Subiaco was cited, where St Benedict provided for twelve monasteries of twelve monks each. Later, at Monte Cassino, he provided for the deanery system. In any case, it is necessary to strive for a consensus of the whole community to the existence of pluralism within it. This means that there must be communication within the community. There can be well-defined sub-groups, but there must also be among them a certain exchange and communication.

FORMING MEN TODAY FOR LIFE ACCORDING TO THE RULE

THERE ARE TWO WAYS of dealing with an assigned topic. One is to determine precisely what is desired and then write a paper which addresses itself accurately to that subject. The other is to write whatever one wants to say and then find some device for incorporating it under the title assigned. I have chosen the latter system. What will follow consists, therefore, of some rather random remarks about monastic formation. I have chosen to cover the whole subject broadly and, I fear, superficially, rather than to treat one particular aspect of it in great detail.

The term "monastic formation" designates the entire process which is involved in a man's becoming a monk. The *Apophthegmata Patrum* relate an appropriate story about the great Macarius of Egypt: after many years of effort, he had reached the summit of perfection, but he quite sincerely declared that he had not yet become a monk. He said, in fact, that he knew of only two men who were really monks: they dwelt all alone in the remote recesses of the desert and had accomplished the return to paradise so thoroughly that they wore no clothing at all.[1] On the other hand, the *Verba Seniorum* tell of a young man who put on the monastic habit, took up residence in a cell, and announced, "I am a desert monk." The Fathers forcibly removed him from his cell and made him go around and apologize to all the solitaries for his arrogant

---

1. *Apophthegmata Patrum,* Macarius Aegyptius, 2; PG 65:260.

presumption saying: "Forgive me, for I am no solitary, but have only now begun to become a monk."[2] The point is that the process of becoming a monk lasts as long as life itself; there is no time at which one can say, "I am now a monk; my formation is finished." A man can be more or less a monk; if he stops growing, then his formation is indeed finished, but so is his monastic life.

The first stages in the process of becoming a monk are not all that there is to formation, but they are the most significant part of it, because they involve the difficult transition from another way of life to that of the monastery and because they have, or should have, a decisive influence upon all the rest of the process. Hence discussion of formation usually centers upon what happens during the novitiate and the years immediately following. We ought to have some clear ideas about what should be happening during that time and how we can help it to happen. Obviously, we cannot force such a development in another person. The Holy Spirit is the agent, and the person himself is the one who holds the key of his own freedom to unlock his heart to the flow of grace. The "director of formation" must stand before this mystery in awe and reverence, and try to assist its accomplishment by helping the novice to understand what is happening to him.

There is an obvious parallel between formation for the Christian life in general and formation for the monastic life in particular. Hence our consideration of the latter subject may benefit from some of the insights achieved by the contemporary renewal of catechetics. While the latter is still beset by uncertainty and controversy when it comes down to details, there seems to be general agreement that the process of becoming a Christian (and this too is a process never finished in this life) involves three things: instruction, formation and initiation.

Instruction is concerned with intellectual formation, the imparting of those facts and truths of which every Christian must have some knowledge. This is not all that is involved in becoming a Christian, and one of the principal emphases of the catechetical revival has been

---

2. *Verba Seniorum,* 10:110; PL 73:932.

to point out the limitations of a purely cerebral approach to Christianity. Instruction is nonetheless necessary, for Christianity is rooted in historical events and contains revealed doctrine; and in fact the reaction against instruction has sometimes been excessive and disastrous.

Becoming a Christian, however, also demands *formation,* in the sense of acceptance of a new set of values. This is directed to the will rather than the intellect, and involves the shaping of a man's whole outlook and behavior according to Christian standards. There is nothing proper to Christianity, however, about instruction and formation thus understood; the same might apply equally well to any philosophical or ethical system.

What is decisive is the factor of *initiation:* introducing a human person into the mystery of personal fellowship with God. This is the noblest element in the process, for it touches the heart of the mystery. God does not reveal merely an abstract set of truths or an ethical code, but himself: Vatican II says that through revelation "the invisible God out of the abundance of his love speaks to men as friends and lives among them, so that he may invite and take them into fellowship with himself."[3] Thus a man is led through the obedience of faith, "by which man entrusts his whole self freely to God,"[4] to personal communion with God. Christianity is life with God: "This is eternal life, that they know you the only true God, and Jesus Christ whom you have sent,"[5] says St John, in that Gospel which was written "that believing you may have life in his name."[6]

If we use the term "formation" in the restricted sense explained above, then I do not know what term ought to be applied to the whole process, of which formation is only one part. Perhaps, if we cannot find a comprehensive term, it would be better to call it "initiation," both because this is the most important factor (as well as the most elusive), and because of the traditional use of this term to describe the sacramental beginnings of the Christian life in a man.

3. Dogmatic Constitution *Dei Verbum,* par. 2.
4. *Ibid.,* par. 5.   5. Jn 17:3.   6. Jn 20:31.

In any case, it seems to me that these three elements of the total process must be taken into consideration in the initiation of a man into the monastic life, analogously to general Christian initiation. I would like, therefore, to reflect upon these three factors in the process of becoming a monk.

INSTRUCTION

A certain amount of instruction is necessary to help a candidate for the monastic life to explore and personally to assimilate the Christian message and that monastic doctrine which translates the message into a particular way of life. People come to the monastery with vastly different backgrounds and capabilities; some may already possess a great deal of information and have done considerable reflection upon it, while others may be still in need of even elementary instruction. This considerably complicates the practical problems involved in providing instruction in the monastery. It also underlines at the outset the necessity of attention to the individual needs of each person. A random collection of information, even if extensive, may be more harmful than beneficial if it is not integrated and has not been personally assimilated in such a way as to make it one's own; it only creates another illusion that will have to be demolished.

Some candidates will be capable of reading fruitfully and learning by themselves; with them the principal need is to guide their reading, teach them how to approach it and how to assess its significance. If they cannot read profitably at all and cannot acquire the self-discipline needed for reading, it will be a rather strong counter-indication to a monastic vocation. For those who fall somewhere in between, and to a certain extent for all, some formal instruction will be needed. The manner in which this is done can be marked by a certain informality, which is attractive to young people today, but it must not be allowed to degenerate into aimless discussion which amounts to only a mutual sharing of ignorance and keeps alive the disastrous illusion that they know what they are talking about.

In this regard, the essential disposition which the candidate must have is docility. This is a bad word today, chiefly because it is not understood. It does not mean abdication of one's faculties of judgment, nor obsequious acquiescence to authority. It means, quite simply, willingness to learn. If a candidate is not willing to learn, if he already knows everything and is so fixed in his prejudices that he is unwilling to submit them to critical scrutiny, to test his opinions, to evaluate them, to move beyond them, to abandon them if necessary, to open himself to other minds and other viewpoints and other experiences, then it is all over before it starts. He will eventually leave anyway, and it is better that it be sooner rather than later. He does not want to learn anything, to move beyond the point where he is now, and so he does not really want to be a monk, because being a monk involves changing, and changing radically. This is merely another way of saying that becoming a monk entails conversion—and conversion means changing one's mind as well as one's heart. Neither the monastery nor any other agency can do anything for him until he becomes willing to learn, no matter how many talents or other engaging qualities he may have. On the other hand, no matter how few talents and how many faults he may have, there is *some* hope if he is docile.

At the same time, the formation director should not make the mistake of equating docility with passive acceptance of everything he says—especially if he has a habit of saying things that are absurd. Docility means willingness to learn, not to be indoctrinated. One ought to be grateful for minds which offer a challenge, which are not satisfied with slipshod thinking and vapid repetition of slogans without any real meaning, minds which demand clarification and justification, which want to make every doctrine their own instead of merely putting it on the shelf with all their other baggage. It is beneficial to have one's own favorite assumptions challenged, one's private myths exploded. On the other hand, one ought to be suspicious of people who are too ready to accept anything and everything, because they are too lazy to examine it for themselves, or so indifferent that it does not really make any difference one way or the other, or so obsequious that they do not want to make any waves and thus destroy their self-image of the humble and obedient monk. The chief danger with these people is that they might want to stay.

In regard to the approach to be taken, it seems to me that two general remarks may be made. The first is that the learning which takes place during the novitiate, or even during the whole formation period, is only a beginning, and therefore an introduction to a whole life of continued learning: the initial phase of a lifelong process. Or, to put it the other way around, the rest of life is an extension of the novitiate. Here there is a distinct difference between a monastic novitiate and that of an active religious congregation. In the latter case the novitiate is a phase quite distinct and different from the rest of a man's life, and is intended to furnish him with the instruction and inspiration which he will need to carry him through—though of course he may go back from time to time for tertianship or a period of renewal. The monk, on the other hand, is expected to go on living the same kind of life in a more mature way, and to go on learning. One should not suppose that he will stop reading when he completes his formation period (actually, he never completes it!). Hence the formation director should not try to teach him everything. He should rather try to get him started on the right tracks and prepare him to continue thence on his own.[7]

The other remark concerning the approach is that it should not be the same as seminary or university training in the sacred sciences because its objective is different. This has always been recognized, but the difference was sometimes made to consist in the amount and the quality. It used to be thought that monks did not need to know much, so any sloppy old thing would do. When it came to be realized that they did need to know something, the first reaction was uncritically to adopt the same academic approach used in clerical training—which is itself undergoing considerable revision now. Now we are beginning to see that what we really need is a different *kind* of theology, though it will take us a while to rediscover

7. In practice, of course, many aspects of the life of the active religious are also a continuation of his novitiate. The difference, while real, is not easy to specify in detail and should not be exaggerated.

this and work it out in contemporary terms. Medievalists, particularly Father Jean Leclercq,[8] have for a long time been pointing to the "monastic theology" of the Middle Ages and explaining what distinguished it from the scholasticism of the universities. We need a modern version of this monastic theology; not a theology which spurns discursive reasoning and intellectual values, but one which, while using and respecting them, goes on to develop a capacity for experiencing the truth of theology in the life of prayer. Call it intuitive, or sapiential, or mystical, or what you will; it is an orientation which ought to be given to monastic studies from the very outset.

I do not want to get involved here in drawing up some kind of "ideal novitiate curriculum," but something should be said about the content of studies in a monastery. There are two things, at the very beginning, which are not in any way distinctive of the monastic life but none the less essential to its faithful prosecution: the Bible and the liturgy. The Bible is important because it is the revelation of the mystery of Christ, it forms the basis of the monk's *lectio*, and it provides the substance of his prayer life in the liturgy. He must have the kind of instruction which will enable him to read it fruitfully. Not all of this can be done in the novitiate, but he must receive there that minimum of instruction which will give him a correct approach to it, and which can later be expanded and filled out.

Here I think we have to take a sensible view of modern biblical science. On the one hand, an austere scientific approach which never gets beyond philology and history is hardly calculated to stimulate a sapiential reading of Scripture; on the other hand some kind of vague pneumatic or mystical approach which is in no way rooted in the literal sense and depends upon outmoded methods of exegesis is a blind alley. It should not be supposed that sound scientific methodology is in any way opposed to a spiritually fruitful use of Scripture. Rather the contrary is true; it will be really

---

8. J. Leclercq, "Théologie traditionelle et théologie monastique," *Irénikon* 37 (1964): 50–74.

fruitful to the extent that it is based upon sound methodology. Here is a place where the achievements of theological renewal must be incorporated into the traditional monastic exercise of *lectio divina*. The approach should be sapiential rather than strictly scientific, but it should not ignore or transgress valid scientific findings—this out of a simple concern for truth. The novices do not have to become biblical scholars, but they should not be led to act as if the biblical revival had never taken place or were at best a mixed blessing.

This can be applied particularly to the psalms. With regard to the Psalter, we are faced with a paradox. On the one hand, it seems to me that in a treatment of the Old Testament, the psalms are just about the last thing that should be considered. The prayers of a people are the distillation of their whole religion: the psalms sum up all that Israel was and became through the centuries; hence I do not think that they can be thoroughly understood until all the rest of the Old Testament has been studied. On the other hand, they are the first thing that the young monk has to deal with, as he meets them every day in the liturgy. I do not know the solution to this, except to offer him a first initiation in the novitiate and then come back to them later when he is ready for a fuller treatment.

The psalms are under fire today by people who say they are outmoded, pre-Christian forms of prayer, and that our refined and sophisticated sentiments would be better expressed in a totally new kind of office incorporating the swinging intercessions of Malcolm Boyd and Company. Without getting side-tracked on this controversy here, I would merely say that the relevance of the psalms for our prayer is a problem which should be faced squarely with today's novices who are not at all inclined to take such things for granted. I do believe that the insights of modern biblical science in regard to the form-criticism of the Psalter and the esthetic value of Hebrew poetry have something to do with the answer. Here, as elsewhere in the Bible, I believe that the prayer value of the psalms is increased, not diminished, by a wise use of modern discoveries.

The psalms have already brought us to the subject of the liturgy. Here, too, it is not a question of developing scholars, but of simply teaching people to understand and appreciate what goes on in their life. If the office has too often become more a burden than a joy, perhaps this is not entirely due to its structure and execution, but just as much, if not more, to a failure to understand what is happening. Monks ought to see it as an indispensable source of their prayer life and learn to use it fruitfully, not just endure it as a meritorious penance. It will be helpful for them to have as much knowledge as possible of the history of the liturgy and the methodology of studying it, so that they can be aware of the relativity of liturgical forms and the real value of tradition. This is more than ever necessary in view of the changes taking place today and the contradictory opinions being aired on all sides. But it is more important that they have a theological vision of the liturgy as the life of the Church and know what they are doing when they go to choir or celebrate the Eucharist.

This brings us to the study of the Fathers, and specifically of the monastic literature. Patristics is an enormous field and not much can be done about it in the novitiate except, hopefully, to introduce the young monks to the reading of the Fathers and bring them to an appreciation of the immense values contained there. These values are precisely the ones which have the most to contribute to the kind of sapiential orientation of monastic studies of which we have spoken.

One may profitably begin with the monastic Fathers. If the Rule occupies the center of the teaching imparted in the novitiate, it must nevertheless be placed in its context and seen against the background of the earlier monastic literature. I believe that this can best be done by tracing the development of monastic spirituality and introducing the literature at the appropriate places in the development. The novices should be brought into contact with the desert Fathers, the Pachomian literature, Basil and Cassian, to mention only the most important. They should be helped to see the value of these writings and their continued relevance to our own situation. Very probably they will not see this unless some point is made of it; modern man has to be helped to read the classics fruitfully.

One does not have to try to defend everything in the monastic Fathers, for there are things that are outmoded or simply wrong, or out of conformity with valid viewpoints that have been acquired in the course of further development. But we have to keep people from throwing out the baby with the bath water, for the greater proportion of the traditional teaching remains valid and useful, though it takes a discerning reader to grasp its profundity, and novices are not likely to be discerning readers unless they are taught to be. A real task of translation has to be undertaken here, and not merely translation from one language to another, but from one culture to another. It is a question of preserving the continuity of tradition, which Father Leclercq has defined as "the past living in the present."[9] A few years ago Fr Adalbert de Vogüé suggested that we have a task of "historical ecumenism" to perform in mediating the teaching of the great spiritual masters of the ancient world to the men of today.[10] It is an indispensable process of intercultural communication. In fact, many of the values contained in the Fathers are precisely the values that men of today are looking for, if they can be helped to see through the opaque language in which these works are written.

For us, the Rule of St Benedict must continue to occupy the center of attention; it is the principal channel through which we contact the monastic wisdom of the past. The novice must be led to see it in its historical context, to understand what was the function of a rule, what it set out to do, and to face squarely the problem of its authenticity and literary relationships. In the course of a detailed exegesis of the Rule, he must be shown how it has summed up and distilled the preceding monastic tradition. Above all, the problem of the relevancy of the Rule must be taken up, so that it can be seen how its doctrine is really appropriate to the individual monk today, and in what sense it can be the norm of life for a community of men in the twentieth century.

There needs to be some instruction, too, in the theology of the spiritual life, especially in regard to prayer. Some attention should

9. J. Leclercq, "Tradition: A Door to the Present," *Monastic Studies* 4 (1966): 1–15.

10. A. de Vogüé, "Le procès des moines d'autrefois," *Christus* 12 (1965): 113–128.

be given to the ordinary development of the life of prayer in a way that will be helpful to novices in their own efforts. But here I think it is better to do too little than to do too much. There is no point in giving answers to all kinds of problems that people do not yet have. These solutions do not really mean anything until one has faced the problems in his own experience. When that happens, it will be time enough to deal with them. At the beginning, it may suffice to follow St Benedict's advice, "If anyone wants to pray, let him simply go in and pray;"[11] or, as Abbot Chapman used to say, "Pray as you can." The rest can be taken up later.

There remains the question of other sacred studies, of philosophy, the humanities, and various secular subjects. I believe that the things already mentioned are ordinarily enough for novices to occupy themselves with, but these other subjects cannot be excluded from later stages of the formation process. A monk should be capable of dialogue with the world outside, and this presumes that he must have some knowledge of the great issues which agitate his contemporaries. Nothing human can be foreign to him, even if he cannot be expected to be a specialist in anything except his own profession of being a monk. This raises the much larger question of relationship to the world and, beyond that, the question of the sacred and the profane. Here we cannot go into all of that.[12]

FORMATION

Formation, in this restricted sense of the term, means the process of acquiring a new set of values, of reorienting one's life. It is, obviously, something that a man can only do for himself, by the exercise of his own free will, but he can be helped by being brought face to face with the challenge, by having pointed out to him where the real problems lie and what must be done about them. He has to

11. RB 52:4.
12. See the reflections of T. Merton, "Renewal in Monastic Education," *Cistercian Studies* 3 (1968): 247–52.

be confronted with the need for renunciation, a turning of his back upon his past insofar as it represents a false direction, and a conversion or reorientation of his values.

Just how this is done is a very subtle thing that is hard to get one's hands on. How do parents communicate to their children their sense of moral values? Ordinarily the environment of the first few years seems to be decisive; it is a question of the total environment with all the subtle interacting forces that go on in it. Sometimes something goes wrong and parents produce a black sheep, either because there was something defective about the process (for instance, a credibility gap between teaching and practice), or simply because the free will of the subject refused to accept the training.

This phase of the process of becoming a monk is analogous to such moral training. Here it must be recognized that the role of the novice master, while important, is rarely decisive. What is decisive is the community, the total environment. Whether we like it or not, the new people are formed primarily by what goes on around them. Thomas Merton once put it this way: "Everything depends upon the atmosphere of the community in which you live. If you're living with monks, you become a monk. If you're living with a bunch of clowns, you become a clown."[13] In the latter case, there is really nothing that formation directors can do about it. They can, of course, present ideals, they can honestly acknowledge the deficiencies of the community, they can try to encourage the novices to be prudently and charitably critical of their environment and to stand on their own feet without weakly conforming. In some exceptional cases they may succeed, but the majority will sooner or later adopt as if by osmosis the style of life around them.

It is, indeed, a "life style," a whole new way of life with its particular hierarchy of values, which the candidate has gradually to adopt as he says good-bye to the one he had before. The ancients would have called it a monastic *conversatio*. In the jargon of modern

13. T. Merton, in a discussion following his talk to the Cistercian novice masters during their meeting at Gethsemani in June, 1968; see the mimeographed minutes, p. 8.

psychology it is known as an "existential project." It is the totality
of that form of life which is lived by a particular community. And
here is where a problem often arises. For there ought to be a clearly
defined existential project which squares with the official doctrine
that is given out in the instruction. In other words, the community
needs a sense of identity which is cogently articulated in its whole
style of life in a way that corresponds to its declarations of policy. If
the novice master finds that what really goes on in the life does not
correspond to what he is expected to say is going on, then he has
problems, for young people have a way of zeroing in on credibility
gaps. Things ought to be clear; there has to be a sense of identity
with which new members can in turn identify.

In most American Benedictine monasteries, for example, this
question of identity is the basic problem which influences almost
every other aspect of renewal and makes the problem of formation
particularly difficult. This has been explicitly acknowledged by the
General Chapter of the American Cassinese Congregation in its
1969 statement, *Renew and Create.*[14] The first half of the statement
provides an extremely perceptive analysis of the problems faced by
American monasteries today and shows how the specifically
Benedictine problems are all derived in one way or the other from
the problem of identity. Unfortunately the benefit of this analysis
remains inoperative, since the second part of the statement, in my
opinion, far from offering a forthright solution, has been carefully
emasculated to cover up the problem and thus implicitly deny that it
exists. But the problem of identity, however much it may be
disguised by rhetoric, self-congratulation, or the latest theological
fad, obstinately refuses to go away, and no one is more conscious
of this than the novices and the people who try to train them.

Cistercian identity is, at least on the surface, much more clearly
defined and presents less of a problem. When one gets down to
details, however, I am not so sure that it is as clear as it seems. I

---

14. *Renew and Create: A Statement on the American-Cassinese Benedictine
Monastic Life* (Manchester, N. H.: St Anselm's Abbey, 1969), especially pp.
38–40.

prudently leave this question to your own consideration. I would only remark that one avenue of approach may be explicit acknowledgment of pluralism within a community and tolerance thereof. We have always had some of this, whether we like it or not; it is now a question, I think, of formulating an official policy and practice in its regard, and undertaking the difficult task of determining what are its limits. My purpose here is only to draw attention to the importance of this question for formation.

To come back to the subject of adoption of a new life style, it must be made clear that this is not simply an intellectual process. It is the whole of a man's life that is involved. The heart of the process is situated beyond the limits of intellectual exploration. The right questions should be asked and the right answers given, as far as possible, but there is a point beyond which none of this has any meaning, when a man has to confront himself in all the inner poverty of his spiritual nakedness, and try to find out what his life is all about: what does it mean to be a man and to stand before God as one really is, totally stripped, with all one's carefully constructed facades shattered at one's feet, and make the choices that alone can give real meaning to life? What does it mean to turn completely from what one has been and become someone else, to put off the old man and put on the new, to rebuild the shattered image of God that is hidden within the soul?

It means death and resurrection. It is not by any amount of preaching and teaching, but by one's own bitter experience, that one learns what it means to have the sufferings of Christ reproduced in oneself. "Was it not necessary that the Christ should suffer these things and so enter upon his glory?"[15] Nothing rises that has not died. It is the law of nature itself: "Unless a grain of wheat falls into the earth and dies, it remains alone; but if it dies, it bears much fruit."[16] It is the law that Israel had to learn by experience in the death of the exile, the law to which Christ submitted in exemplary fashion, to which the Church, the new Israel, is constantly subject, the law which brings the mystery of death and life into the

15. Lk 24:26.   16. Jn 12:24.

experience of every Christian. The woman in travail has sorrow because her hour has come, but her suffering is productive of life.[17] And now the whole universe groans in travail, waiting for our adoption as sons.[18] Joy does not come as a reward for faithfully enduring suffering; it is right in the suffering itself that one finds the joy. It is in being buried with Christ that one rises to life.

These insights can be personalized and interiorly assimilated only by living through the experience of dying to self. The monk has to learn to find the meaning of his life not in facile explanations, but in the realm of mystery, in the paradox of the cross. This is the real crisis of the novitiate; the instruction will not help much if this is evaded or missed. The novice has to be led gently into this crisis, forced to face himself in the loneliness of personal decision. He has to be helped to destroy the illusions about himself that keep him from this confrontation with his own nothingness; he has to be brought to the brink and given a push forward. In the solitude of the desert one is cut off from all the familiar deceptions which keep him from seeing himself as he is. Therefore the master must make him face up to solitude and not allow him to evade it by taking refuge in a comfortable conformism. When he has been through the desert, then he can once more take up residence among men— and only then begin to see his community in a new light.

INITIATION

At this point we have already begun to cross the boundaries into the realm of initiation. Perhaps that is because I have not followed my logical outline, or perhaps the outline was too logical and should not be followed because it does not conform to reality. Or perhaps it merely means that the three phases I have suggested are not adequately distinct and merge one into another. What is certain is that they are at best only logically distinct and not separable in reality. They all have to be going on simultaneously, reinforcing

17. Jn 16:21.   18. Rom 8:22–23.

one another and interacting. If any of them is chronologically first, it ought rather to be initiation, for here we encounter the mysterious action of grace that leads a man to the monastery and draws him gradually into the mystery of monastic life.

By design I say the *mystery* of monastic life. All life is a mystery; every man's life is to some degree inexplicable. It is not something that can be solved by calculation and reasoning; it can only be lived. This is all the more true of the mysterious life which the Spirit stirs up in us. Indeed, we ought to be able to explain to ourselves and to others why we want to be a monk, and to justify our life to those who question it. But we must also be conscious of the limits of these explanations. They do not touch the heart of the mystery. We must be suspicious of answers that are too pat, too sure, as if we could fully explain the mystery of our own vocation. Our life is hidden with Christ in God.[19] When it comes to probing the depths of his own life, every monk must remain *scienter nescius et sapienter indoctus.*

The task of the theologian is to explain revelation and to situate where the mystery lies, but not to explain away the mystery. His work must be complemented by the mystic, whose knowledge of God is derived not from reason but from the inner personal experience of encountering God in prayer. We need monastic theologians, but we need still more men who have real experience of the life and who by experience know that in its profoundest dimension we come up against a mystery that can only be contemplated in awe and wonder. A master who would initiate another man into this life must have both knowledge and experience. For the problem of doing this is not simply an intellectual one; it is a total existential problem. He must be aware that he is dealing with a profound mystery, the mystery of another man's life, the mystery of God who loves him and calls him to union with himself, who invites him into personal communion.

How can one initiate another into this experience? Father Alfonso Nebreda tells the story of a Zen master whom he met in Japan, and

19. Col 3:3.

to whom he put the question, "How do you communicate your teaching to your disciples?" The old Buddhist monk answered, "It cannot be done in words, but only by rubbing two people together." Nebreda comments that for him this provided a deep insight into the biblical meaning of the term "knowledge."[20] The knowledge we have of persons is different from the knowledge we have of objects. It cannot be adequately conceptualized or expressed in words. It is a personal, intuitive insight. (This is what is so absurd about hiring a computer to choose your marriage partner.) A man knows his wife because of a profound interpenetration not merely of bodies, but of personalities. A person reveals himself to us not only by his words, but by all that he does and is.

Christ did not reveal himself to mankind merely by his teaching, but by the witness of his life. The Church, too, which is his Body, reveals herself—and thus reveals Christ to men—by the totality of her life. God is revealed in Christ, and Christ is revealed in men who are his members. Now the mystery into which the monk must be initiated is not an abstraction, but is the living God himself. And hence the revelation of the mystery, in that cloud of unknowing in which God is known by being perceived as unknown, can take place only on a personal level. The master is the mediator who deals with these profundities.

The master does not transmit merely a doctrine to his disciples, but a life. This is the reason why the disciple's needs cannot be satisfied from books alone, but require a living teacher who has himself had experience of what he is to communicate. The disciple comes to him seeking the life-giving word which will unlock for him the meaning of his own life and introduce him to divine life and salvation. The "word" which he gives is not merely the teaching contained in his instructions, but the witness of his whole being. He has a charism: that is to say, he is a man who already possesses the Spirit and is able, in a subtle and mysterious manner, to communicate the Spirit to others.

20. A. Nebreda, "Role of Witness in Transmitting the Message," *Theology Digest* 12 (1964): 67–73.

The relationship between the master and the disciple must therefore be an intensely personal and individual one. The master must respect the freedom of his novice, respect his vocation, and together with him explore the design which God has upon his life. He must help him to see his own problems, confront his own weaknesses, and gently but firmly administer the cross to him. If he does not have a genuine love for him, he will not be able to understand him and have a sympathetic view of his situation: "it is only with the heart that one sees clearly." And this love expresses itself in concern for the welfare of the young man and compassion for the suffering which he must endure in order to discover his real self.

There are many examples of such loving compassion in the *Sayings of the Fathers*. For example:

The Abbot Pastor said: "If a man has sinned and does not deny it, but says: 'I have sinned,' don't scold him, or you will break the purpose of his heart. But rather say to him: 'Don't be sad, my brother, but just watch yourself from now on,' and you will rouse his heart to repentance."[21]

With this we may compare the following reflections of a modern master of the spiritual life:

When I was being tonsured this morning I watched the novices milling around getting ready for work—standing in their patched coveralls, with their white woolen hoods, some taking pains to be recollected, some being very businesslike, most of them quite happy. . . . I was moved by the sight of them and at the thought that we get so much in our own way and try to carry so much useless baggage in the spiritual life. And how difficult it is to help them without unconsciously adding much more useless baggage to the load they already carry, instead of relieving them of it (which is what I try to do). I can at least love them in simplicity and thus preserve the climate in which the Holy Spirit unbinds the impossible and futile burdens. . . .[22]

21. *Verba Seniorum,* 10:48; PL 73: 921.

22. T. Merton, *Conjectures of a Guilty Bystander* (Garden City: Doubleday, 1966), pp. 45–46.

Also relevant is this other passage, inspired by a visit to the novices' scriptorium during the night watch:

> Looking at the dark empty room, with everyone gone, it seemed that, because all that they loved was there, "they" in a spiritual way were most truly there, though in fact they were all upstairs in the dormitory, asleep. . . . I felt . . . that though they themselves might not understand what they are going through, and though many of them may fail, may leave, or may have to look elsewhere to get the real meaning of their lives, yet the sign of love is on these novices and they are precious forever in God's eyes. . . . It is very good to have loved these people and been loved by them with such simplicity and sincerity, within our ordinary limitation, without nonsense, without flattery, without sentimentality, and without getting too involved in one another's business.[23]

These texts scarcely need any commentary. They make the point well that the relationship of master to novice must be conditioned by love if it is to bear fruit, for love is precisely the atmosphere required for the work of the Holy Spirit.

Parenthetically, I would add that this atmosphere of love, of human understanding and sympathy, seems to me to be the key to the solution of the generation gap about which we hear so much today. I do not think that we ought to panic at the supposed difficulties of relating to and communicating with the younger generation. They are not some new, three-legged species from outer space—they are human beings like ourselves. What we have in common is much more basic and more important than the cultural differences which separate us. Is it so impossible for us to understand an African, or a Japanese, or an Indian? Their basic human drives and responses are the same as our own. *A fortiori,* the gap between sub-cultures in our own country should not be unbridgeable. The hypothesis of a novice's leaving, even though he has a real vocation, simply because we cannot communicate with him, is, or should be, a false dilemma. If this happens, something is wrong which could be

23. *Ibid.,* pp. 193–194.

corrected. If we have an open mind and an open heart, and genuine love conditions us to listen with sympathy—and if he manifests the same willingness towards us—we can learn from each other.

Love turns to compassion in the presence of another person's distress. Now distress will quite regularly be the lot of the young monk struggling to enter into the mystery of a new way of life. His inner turmoil and suffering must be approached as themselves a mystery, that mysterious share in Christ's sufferings which the Lord always inflicts upon those whom he would draw closer to himself. The ancient monastic literature shows a delicate psychological insight into the sufferings through which a monk is purified and made to see the wasteland of his own inner self, and it defines *consolation* as an essential function of the spiritual father.[24]

Indeed, the monk cannot himself understand what he is going through at the time of his suffering. He has to seek help. According to the ancients, the cause of affliction was "thoughts" (*logismoi*). "What shall I do, Father, for I am troubled by my thoughts?" They disturb him, wage war against him, leave him without peace and without fruit. While the thoughts may take on various forms, they are essentially challenges to perseverance. The monk may have begun with great energy and enthusiasm, but in the desert nothing ever happens, and in the long and oppressive silence he begins to wonder whether this is not all a waste of time, whether such inactivity can really be of any value, can be pleasing to God, whether it is not rather a way of "copping out." This is the ultimate temptation, to leave the desert and give up the monastic way of life entirely.

The authentic master can have compassion upon the weakness and suffering of the disciple because he has had experience of the same kind himself and is humble enough to be aware of his own fragility. In illustration of this, one can scarcely refrain from referring to the delightful story which Cassian tells about the Abbot

24. See the excellent study of M. Matthei, "Aflicción y consuelo en los Padres del Desierto," *Studia Monastica* 5 (1963): 7–25; also I. Hausherr, *Direction spirituelle en Orient autrefois*, Orientalia Christiana Analecta 144 (Rome: Pont. Institutum Orientalium Studiorum, 1955).

Apollos. When a young monk, seeking consolation from an elder, confessed to him that he was violently tempted to fornication, the old man heaped reproaches upon him and told him that he was unworthy to be a monk. Sunk in despair, the youth was about to return to the world and look for a wife, when the Abbot Apollos met him and persuaded him to reveal the reason for his sadness. Treating him with kindness and compassion, the wise old man encouraged him and was able to persuade him to postpone his departure for at least one day. Then he prayed fervently that the temptation might leave him and attach itself instead to the elder who had been so insensitive to his weakness. Immediately he saw a hideous Ethiopian shooting fiery darts into the elder's cell. A moment later the old monk came running out like a madman and made a beeline for the nearest town. The Abbot Apollos confronted him, revealed what had happened, and gave him a well-deserved lecture, so that in future he would know how to treat the sufferings of others with compassion.[25]

The young monk alone is not capable of dealing with his thoughts, of discerning the spirit which inspires them. He does not yet see clearly the workings of his own soul and the struggle that goes on there between the angel of darkness and the angel of light. The spiritual father must produce for him the word of life which will unmask the illusions, must manifest to him in the concrete the will of the Spirit.

> A brother said to the Abbot Arsenius, "What shall I do, Father, for I am troubled by my thoughts that say to me, 'You cannot fast, or work, or visit the sick, and these are the things that are profitable.'" The old man, seeing that the devil had been sowing in him, said, "Go, eat, drink and sleep, so long as you don't go out of your cell," for he knew that perseverance in the cell brings the monk to his goal.[26]

Perseverance in the cell: this means inexorably facing oneself. The

---

25. Conf. 2:13: E. Pichery, *Jean Cassien: Conférences* SC 42 (Paris: Cerf, 1955), pp. 125–130.
26. *Verba Seniorum,* 7:27; PL 73:900.

monk has to learn that his real problems are not situated in any of the places he thought they were—such are the illusions that rule our lives—but they are within ourselves and accordingly can be solved only by surrendering ourselves to the grace of the Holy Spirit.

The Fathers used to say, "If temptation befalls you in the place where you live, do not desert this place in the time of temptation; for if you do, no matter where you go, you will find in front of you the thing you are fleeing from."[27]

The novice has to learn patience, and primarily patience with himself, the most difficult kind.

A certain brother who lived as a solitary was disturbed, and making his way to the Abbot Theodore of Pherme he told him that he was troubled. The old man said to him, "Go, humble your spirit and submit yourself, and live with other men." So he went away to the mountain, and dwelt with others. Afterwards he came back to the old man and said to him, "Neither do I find peace in living with other men." And the old man said, "If you cannot be at peace in solitude or with other men, why did you want to become a monk? Was it not to endure tribulation? Tell me now, how many years have you been in this habit?" And the brother said, "Eight." The old man replied, "Believe me, I have been in this habit seventy years, and not for one day have I found peace—and you want to have peace in eight years?"[28]

On another occasion a brother came to the same Abbot Theodore and again the reply came out of the depths of his experience:

He began to discuss and inquire into things which he had not yet performed. And the old man said to him, "You have not yet found your ship, nor loaded the cargo into it, nor begun to sail, and have you already arrived in the city to which you planned to go? When you have first labored in the matter of which you speak, then speak from the experience of it."[29]

27. *Ibid.*, 7:32; PL 73:901.   28. *Ibid.*, 7:5; PL 73:893.
29. *Ibid.*, 8:8; PL 73:906.

Thus the young monk is initiated—by advice, by rebuke, by consolation, by loving but firm imposition of obediences and trials —into a whole way of life. He does not know what he is entering. The monk who thinks he can explain his life, who has it all figured out, deceives himself and is due for a rude awakening. The authentic master is the one who knows that it is a mystery, which can only be approached dialectically and by the open-hearted acceptance of paradox, and who can share his wisdom and insight to bring a disciple to an unreserved submission to grace. Initiation into a mystery is itself a mystery, I think. It is a dim reflection in man of that wisdom and love in God who summons us, for reasons that we cannot understand, to a life to which we are unequal and of which we are not worthy—the creative love which incomprehensibly makes something out of the nothing which we are.

Claude J. Peifer OSB

Holy Mother of God Monastery,
Oxford, North Carolina

DISCUSSION

The discussion following Fr Peifer's paper centered on the problems relating to formation within a monastic community.

Formation can no longer be as uniform as it was in the past, due to the development of pluralism. Thus arises the question as to the limits of pluralism. How much difference of thought and activity can be allowed within a single monastery? A certain common minimum must be accepted by all. And for this there must be a basic common training and instruction given to all the candidates.

There then arose the question of the role of the community in deciding this and also its role in the formation of the young monk. If the community itself does not have a true monastic formation, it must first face this issue and decide what position it wishes to take in regard to the future. That the community by its manner of life be decisive in the formation of candidates is actually an ideal to be striven for if true *Koinonia* is to be attained. The novice master, like the abbot, should be seen as a part of the community, the exegete of the community to the novice. At the same time, a novice seeking a true monastic life should not be allowed to conform to false currents in the community. The community must accept its responsibility.

The formative power of the community stems basically from the values that it accepts. This idea is closely related to Dom Vincent Martin's assertion, the only real law is the law accepted by the community. If the community does not come to a consensus, values will not be passed on. Each community has a tradition of its own which will shape and color the formation given. Hopefully the positive elements of this tradition will counterbalance the negative elements which are inevitably present in a community in a period of transition. At the same time the novices must learn to be tolerant of those in the community who fail.

At the end Dom Leclercq pointed out that there can be a third person dealing with the novice, besides the novice master and the community: this can be "the friend." He urged that all be reeducated to a proper esteem for friendship and that the role that it can play in bridging the gap between the novice and the community be not overlooked.

SUMMATION

THE FIRST CISTERCIAN STUDIES SYMPOSIUM brought out how the Cistercian Fathers strove to live the Gospel according to the Rule of St Benedict. This second Symposium aimed precisely at determining the role of the Rule in Cistercian life, both yesterday and today. This question is all the more actual since the last General Chapter of the Cistercian Order determined that the Rule of St Benedict, along with the Charter of Charity, would be considered the primary legislation of the Order (see *Ecclesiae Sanctae*, 12ff.). Moreover, if the Cistercians are to continue to make profession according to the Rule of St Benedict, it is quite important for them to know how and to what extent the Rule is normative for them.

This Symposium was an interdisciplinary approach to the problem. In the papers that were presented the role of the Rule was analyzed from different points of view: that of the exegete of monastic sources, that of the historian of the Order, that of the Biblical scholar, and that of the sociologist. Each paper was followed by a discussion in which the conclusions—at times apparently contradictory—of the experts were gradually brought to a certain synthesis which was accepted by general consensus. Although the

NOTE.—This Summation is largely the work of Fr Armand Veilleux OCSO. It was discussed, emended and approved by the participants at the final general session of the Symposium.

analytical exposition and the process toward synthesis were simultaneous this summation presents them here under two different headings for the sake of greater clarity.

Analytical Approach to the Problem

From the point of view of the exegete of the Rule of St Benedict, who seeks to situate the Rule in its broad historical context, it appears that the fundamental rule under which monks live is the living monastic tradition which flows from the Scriptures, the teachings of the Apostles, and the example of the Fathers of the Desert. This is the common possession of all Christian monasticism. Any written rule, such as the Rule of St Benedict, is a partial and transitory crystalization of this universal rule, specifying and concretizing it in service of a particular time and place. The Rule of St Benedict therefore may be considered from two points of view. As a remarkable expression of the ancient monastic tradition, it remains for us a privileged monument of tradition around which the present-day efforts of renewal ought to be centered. As the crystalization of the tradition for a particular situation in time and place, it has long ceased to strictly be the Cistercians' rule of life.

Other historical studies concerning the manner in which monks through the course of history have understood their profession and their life according to the Rule show that the Rule has always been considered as a fundamental document, a guideline which was complemented and adapted to the various situations by customaries. Monks never made their profession simply according to the Rule, but—explicitly or implicitly—according to the Rule as interpreted and lived in a particular monastery. Since the customs are rooted in the Rule but modify it as far as it is a code of observances we may say, according to Dom Jean Leclercq, that the Cistercians follow the Rule, but they do not practice it.

The study of the early reforms of the Cistercian liturgy, as Father Chrysogonus Waddell brought out, throws light upon the attitude toward the Rule proper to the Cistercian Fathers. They loved the Rule of St Benedict and they considered it as a privileged way to lead them to the fulfillment of their monastic vocation. They were intransigent in their fidelity to the observances of the Rule and would not do anything contrary to it. However, they were gradually led to reform their initial determination, which could be justified at the level of abstract principles, since it could not be wholly justified at the level of living experience.

As it was brought out in a study of St Bernard's use of the Rule, although the Cistercian Fathers were intransigent in their fidelity to the observance of the Rule, their main concern was for the fundamental spiritual options of the Rule. St Bernard, for example, quotes mostly from the first seven chapters of the Rule. The Fathers were so deeply formed by the Rule that they were in no way enslaved by it and could go beyond it.

Scripture scholars showed that the Rule is deeply rooted in Scripture and that therefore the monk should be above all a man of the Bible. From this necessarily follows the importance of Biblical orientation and study in the process of monastic formation. Mother Kathryn Sullivan, in showing how a fundamentalist approach which makes too much of the letter has been in the past so fatal to proper understanding of the Scriptures, warned against a similar mistake in approaching a document such as the Rule.

A sociological study brought out the importance of law as a basic structure of human society. The thematic paper of the Symposium had drawn a distinction between principles and values on the one hand and provisions and observances on the other. The sociologist went a step further and distinguished among the principles and values between the monastic ideals themselves and their juridical expression at the level of the legal principles which form the basic structure of the monastic life as it is presented in the Rule of St Benedict. Thus there are three levels: (1) the monastic ideal; (2) the basic legal principles which are the juridical expression of this ideal; (3) the provisions, observances or customs which give immediate practical expression to these principles. The monastic ideal is that to which we have committed ourselves. The concrete provisions are the element which has to be constantly adapted to the concrete situation. As for the basic legal principles of the Rule, it is their logical consistency and their equilibrium which constitute the specificity of the Benedictine Rule; any substantial change in this equilibrium would result in a new form of monastic life. For the sociologist, at this level the Rule of St Benedict is still the proper Rule of the Cistercians.

Synthesis

All these different points of view helped the Symposium to clarify its position and to come to a certain consensus. They affirmed the conviction that after the Gospel the Cistercians of today should embrace the Rule as being an expression of monastic spirituality and also as the expression of their own monastic tradition. At the same time it is obvious that they do not and ought not actually follow many of the observances of the Rule and that even their spiritual teaching differs in some respects from the spiritual doctrine of the Rule. These variations in details of observance and in points of spiritual emphasis should serve to strengthen them in their fundamental orientation and in the vitality of the tradition they receive, live, and pass on to those who come after them.

In regard to the intermediary area constituted by the basic legal principles of the Benedictine way of life, these principles are seen as providing concrete means by which today's Cistercians receive, enter into, and grow in the rich heritage of monastic tradition transmitted to them by the Rule. There was considerable discussion on this point; this discussion, however, manifested more differences of stress than differences of doctrine. Some of the participants of the Symposium insisted more on the fact that the Cistercians are obliged to these options because they have made profession to live according to the Rule of St Benedict. Others insisted on the fact that these fundamental options are inner exigencies of the form of monastic life to which they have committed themselves and that the Rule is to keep them mindful of these inner exigencies. All agreed that these two points of view are complementary and each one is valid inasmuch as it integrates the other.

The new situation created in the Cistercian communities by the Statute on Unity and Pluralism gives to all a much greater responsibility towards the Holy Rule. To a greater extent than ever before each community under the leadership of its abbot has to interpret the Rule and to incarnate its spirituality and its fundamental options in observances that are proper and adapted to the particular community. This involves "dynamic interpretation" by means of which the monk of each succeeding age is able to enter, through living contact with the text of the Rule of St Benedict, into a dialogue which should lead to an experience of the charismatic reality which the text itself cannot circumscribe nor sufficiently express. Here the sociologist noted the fact that many of the details of the life which were formerly the object of particular laws are no longer provided for by law on the level of the Order. Consequently new laws— written or unwritten—must be established at the local level and the communities must be aware of this fact. He suggested a line of reflection and of research that could perhaps be profitably explored: that is, the application in the government of our communities of the distinction between the legislative and executive powers in suchwise that an abbot would function legislatively when, with the community, he was establishing new laws and executively when he was implementing already established legislation.

The work of adaptation and renewal must always be accomplished in a spirit of fidelity both to the monastic ideal to which the Cistercian has committed himself and to the Spirit who speaks daily to him and in him. If his spirit of fidelity is true, there will arise no conflict between charism and institution. The institution will continue to convey to today's monk the charism of the Founders, and he will be able to revitalize the institution by a deep creative response. Moreover, the Spirit himself will bring the communities to that consensus which is the fundamental basis for the efficacy of all law.

The final conclusion might be that it is only a truly deep love for the Rule of St Benedict that will lead the Cistercian of today to the truth that will make him truly free.

APPENDIX I

DECLARATION OF THE GENERAL CHAPTER OF 1969 ON THE CISTERCIAN LIFE

We Cistercian monks feel a deep desire to interpret for our own times the traditions which our Fathers have handed down to us. Yet we must admit that we are faced with a variety of different trends in our Order which reflect its present situation. We may feel at times that certain of these trends could well obstruct the renewal and healthy evolution of the Order.

And yet, when these difficulties came to light at the opening of this Chapter for renewal, we all felt a profound sense of communion in the lived experience of our common spiritual values. We are convinced that the work of this Chapter will become constructive to the degree that we foster this communion and the mutual confidence which it inspires.

We shall do this by recognizing all that really unites us in the Holy Spirit rather than by trying to impose unity through a legislation that would determine observances down to the last detail. Individual communities can, in fact, look after such details according to local needs and in conformity with the directives of the General Chapter—so long as our wholly contemplative orientation is maintained. We are convinced that the best laws are those which follow and interpret life and it is in the concrete experience of our Cistercian vocation that we would first of all recognize this life.

Our wish is to clarify the content of this experience which we all share and by so doing to further as best we can the values which inspire it. That is why we feel moved to make the following declaration on our own particular way of life:

Following the first Fathers of our Order, we find in the Holy Rule of St Benedict the practical interpretation of the Gospel for us. A sense of the Divine Transcendence and of the Lordship of Christ not only pervades the whole of this Rule but also permeates our life, totally orientated towards an experience of the Living God. God calls and we respond by truly seeking him as we follow Christ in humility and obedience. With hearts cleansed by the Word of God, by vigils, by fasting and by an unceasing conversion of life, we aim to become ever more disposed to receive from the Holy Spirit the gift of pure and continual prayer.

This search for God is the soul of our monastic day, a day composed of the Opus Dei, lectio divina and manual work. Our Cistercian life is basically simple and austere. It is truly poor and penitential "in the joy of the Holy Spirit." Through the warmth of their welcome and hospitality our communities share the fruit of their contemplation and work with others.

We carry out this search for God under a Rule and an abbot in a community of love where all are responsible. It is through stability that we commit ourselves to this community. It lives in an atmosphere of silence and separation from the world which fosters and expresses its openness to God in contemplation—treasuring, as Mary did, all these things and pondering them in her heart.

The Church has entrusted a mission to us which we wish to fulfill by the response of our whole life: "to give clear witness to the heavenly home for which every man longs and to keep alive in the heart of the human family the desire for this home . . . as we bear witness to the majesty and love of God and to the brotherhood of all men in Christ." (See Gaudium et Spes, *no. 38;* Ad Gentes, *no. 40;* Letter of Pope Paul VI to the Abbot General of the Order of Citeaux, *December 8, 1968).*

APPENDIX II

UNITY AND PLURALISM

A STATUTE OF THE GENERAL CHAPTER OF 1969

This present General Chapter is convinced that "the unity which is based on charity and which has been the strength and beauty of the Cistercian Order ever since its origins" (Letter of Paul VI to the Abbot General), will best be served today by a deep sense of communion in the lived experience of our common spiritual values. That is why the present Chapter, in its Declaration on the Cistercian Life, has already insisted on the contemplative orientation and fundamental observances of our Order.

In the present statute those observances which demand special attention in our times are presented in a more concrete fashion. Thus the fundamental values of our life are guaranteed without imposing a detailed uniformity where in fact a legitimate diversity should exist. Conditions are laid down so that each community, in union with the other monasteries of the Order and following these guidelines, may deepen its own living experience of the Cistercian life.

Guidelines

1. Faithful to the thought of their Founders, Cistercian monks live under a Rule and an abbot. They live, united in the love of

Christ, in a community which is stable and effectively separated from the world.

2. The abbot, as spiritual father of his community, should try to discover the will of God. One important way of doing this is by listening to his brethren in the spirit of Chapter Three of the Rule.

3. In our daily horarium we keep the balance between the *Opus Dei, lectio divina* and manual work as required by the Rule of St Benedict.

4. The hour of rising is to be regulated so that vigils, which follows it, should keep its traditional character of nocturnal prayer—as we watch for the coming of the Lord.

5. The monk, who is tending to a life of continual prayer, needs a fixed amount of prayer each day. The abbot will see to this for the community as a whole or for each individual in particular.

6. This search for a life of prayer should be lived in an atmosphere of recollection and silence for which all are responsible. In particular, the great silence at night and the silence in the regular places will be maintained.

7. Separation from the world demands that journeys out of the monastery should be infrequent and only for serious reasons. The use of radio and television will be exceptional. Discretion is needed in the use of other media of communication.

8. Our monasteries should practice generous hospitality, but this should not be allowed to interfere with the contemplative nature of our way of life.

9. Our diet should be simple and frugal. The monastic practice of fasting and abstinence should be retained.

10. The habit is to be retained as the distinctive sign of the Order. Its use can differ from house to house.

11. The life of the community, as of each monk, should be marked by simplicity and poverty. Fraternal correction in the spirit of the Gospel is a help in this direction.

Conditions

12. Within the limits of the above guidelines the monasteries of our Order are free to arrange the details of their observance. An effective consultation of the community should accompany these experiments—though the manner of it may vary.

13. Anything in the second or third parts of the Constitutions or in the Usages which does not fall under common law retains only a directive force.

14. The results of these experiments will be reviewed by the visitor, who will make a statement on them in his report to the General Chapter.

15. The experiments should be discussed at the Regional Conferences so that communities may be helped in their work of renewal.

LIST OF ABBREVIATIONS

NOTE: For references to Sacred Scripture the abbreviations found in the Revised Standard Version are employed. Abbreviated references for the Works of St Bernard are listed separately below.

CC   Charter of Charity, ed. J. B. van Damme, *Documenta pro Cisterciensis Ordinis Historiae ac Juris Studio* (Westmalle: Typis Ordinis Cisterciensis, 1959, pp. 15–21; trans. D. Murphy in L. Lekai, *The White Monks* (Okauchee, Wis.: Cistercian Fathers, 1953), pp. 267–273.

CF   Cistercian Fathers Series (Spencer, Mass.: Cistercian Publications, 1970–).

Cist S   *Cistercian Studies.*

Conf.   J. Cassian, *Conférences*, ed. I. E. Pichery, 3 vols., SC 42, 54, 64 (Paris: Cerf, 1955–1959).

CS   Cistercian Studies Series (Spencer, Mass.: Cistercian Publications, 1969–).

CS3   M. Basil Pennington, ed., *The Cistercian Spirit: A Symposium*, CS3 (Spencer, Mass.: Cistercian Publications, 1969).

CSCO   Corpus Scriptorum Christianorum Orientalium (Louvain-Washington).

CSEL   Corpus Scriptorum Ecclesiasticorum Latinorum (Vienna).

DACL   *Dictionnaire d'Archéologie chrétienne et de Liturgie* (Paris).

Dia   *Dialogus inter Cluniacensem Monachum et Cisterciensem de*

Diversis utrisque Ordinis Observantiis, ed. Durandus-Martène, *Thesaurus Novorum Anecdotorum*, vol. 5 (Paris, 1717), col. 1569ff.

Dial   *Dialogus* or *Dialogues.*

DS   *Dictionnaire de Spiritualité* (Paris).

DTC   *Dictionnaire de Théologie catholique* (Paris).

Ep   Epistle or Letter.

EP   *Exordium Parvum* or the Little Exordium, ed. van Damme; trans. R. Larkin in *White Monks*, pp. 251–266.

EM   *Exordium Magnum Cisterciense sive Narratio de Initio Cisterciensis Ordinis auctore Conrado*, ed. B. Griesser, Series Scriptorum S. Ordinis Cisterciensis, no. 2 (Rome, 1961); trans. Benedicta Ward, *Cistercian Origins*, CF 30.

Hom.   *Homilia* or Homily.

Insti.   J. Cassian, *Institutions Cénobitiques*, ed. J. C. Guy, SC 109 (Paris: Cerf, 1965).

MGH   *Monumenta Germaniae Historica.* The abbreviations for the several series are usually readily comprehensible.

PG   *Patrologiae cursus completus, series Graeca*, ed. J. P. Migne (Paris).

PL   *Patrologiae cursus completus, series Latina*, ed. J. P. Migne (Paris).

PLS   *Patrologiae cursus completus, series Latina, Supplementum*, ed. A. Hamman (Paris).

R   *Regula* or Rule.

RB   *Benedicti Regula*, ed. R. Hanslik, CSEL 75 (Vienna, 1960); trans. L. Doyle, *St. Benedict's Rule for Monasteries* (Collegeville, Minn.: Liturgical Press, 1948).

RHE   *Revue d'Histoire ecclésiastique.*

RM   *Regula Magistri*, ed. A. de Vogüé, *La Règle du Maître*, 3 vols., SC 105–107 (Paris: Cerf, 1964); trans. L. Eberle, *The Rule of the Master*, CS 6.

SC   Sources Chrétiennes (Paris: Cerf, 1943–).

SM   M. B. Pennington, "Towards Discerning the Spirit and Aims of the Founders of the Order of Cîteaux," *Studia Monastica* 11 (1969): 405–420.

ABBREVIATIONS FOR THE WORKS OF ST BERNARD

NOTE: With the publication of the critical edition, *S. Bernardi Opera*, 8 vols. (Rome: Editiones Cistercienses, 1957–) a standard set of abbreviations has been established for references to the works of St Bernard. We give here only the ones employed in this volume. We also indicate where these works will be found in the Cistercian Fathers Series.

Ded   *Sermones in Dedicatione Ecclesiae, Opera* 5; *Sermons for the Dedication of the Church*, CF 34.

Div   *Sermones de diversis, Opera* 6; *Occasional Sermons*, CF 46–49.

Ep   *Epistolae, Opera* 7–8; *Letters*, CF 28, 37.

Pent   *Sermones in Die Pentecostes, Opera* 5; *Sermons for the Feast of Pentecost*, CF 25.

Post Epi   *Sermo Dominica prima post octavam Epiphaniae, Opera* 4; *Sermon for the First Sunday after the Octave of Epiphany*, CF 10.

Pre   *De praecepto et dispensatione, Opera* 3; *Monastic Obligations and Abbatial Authority: St Bernard's Book on Precept and Dispensation*, CF 1.

Purif   *Sermones in Purificatione Sanctae Mariae, Opera* 4; *Sermons for the Feast of the Purification of the Blessed Virgin Mary*, CF 22.

Quad   *Sermones in Quadragesima, Opera* 4; *Sermons for Lent*, CF 22.

Sent   *Sententiae, Opera* 6; *Sentences*, CF 50.

Tpl   *Liber ad Milites Templi de Laude Novae Militiae, Opera* 3; *In Praise of the New Knighthood*, CF 19.

Vig Nat   *Sermones in vigilia Nativitatis Domini, Opera* 4; *Sermons for the Vigil of Christmas*, CF 10.

ANALYTIC INDEX

The following abbreviations are used: abb=abbey; abt=abbot; bp=bishop; e=emperor; k=king; n=note; p=pope; st=saint.

laus tibi Christi

CISTERCIAN FATHERS SERIES

Under the direction of the same Board of Editors as the CISTERCIAN STUDIES SERIES, the CISTERCIAN FATHERS SERIES seeks to make available the works of the Cistercian Fathers in good English translations based on the recently established critical editions. The texts are accompanied by introductions, notes and indexes prepared by qualified scholars.